3000 Jokes and One-Liners

Edited by Dave Phillips

Magpie Books, London

Constable & Robinson Ltd
3 The Lanchesters
162 Fulham Palace Road
London W6 9ER

This edition published by Magpie Books,
an imprint of Constable & Robinson Ltd 2005

A copy of the British Library Cataloguing in Publication Data
is available from the British Library

ISBN 1 84529 028 3

Printed and bound in the European Union

3 5 7 9 10 8 6 4 2

Contents

Animals

A farmer needed to buy a bull to service his cows but, in order to afford it, he had to borrow money from the bank. The banker who lent him the money stopped by a week later to see how his investment was shaping up. The farmer complained that the bull just ate grass and wouldn't even look at the cows, so the banker suggested calling in a vet to take a look at the animal.

The following week the banker returned to see if the vet had been of any use. The farmer looked very pleased. 'The bull serviced all my cows twice,' he said, 'then broke through the fence and serviced all my neighbour's cows three times.'

'Wow!' exclaimed the banker. 'What did the vet do to that bull?'

'Just gave me some pills to give him,' replied the farmer.

'What kind of pills?'

'I don't know,' said the farmer, 'but they sort of taste like chocolate.'

What kind of monkey can fly? – A hot air baboon.

One afternoon in the Arctic, a father polar bear and his polar bear son were sitting in the snow. The cub turned to his father and said: 'Dad, am I 100 per cent polar bear?'

The father replied: 'Of course, son, you're 100 per cent polar bear.'

A few minutes later, the cub turned to his father again and said: 'Dad, tell me the truth. I can take it. Am I 100 per cent polar bear? No brown bear or black bear or grizzly bear?'

The father answered: 'Son, I'm 100 per cent polar bear, your mother is 100 per cent polar bear, so you are definitely 100 per cent polar bear.'

The cub seemed satisfied, but a few minutes later he turned to his father once more and said: 'Dad, don't think you're sparing my feelings. I've got to know. Am I 100 per cent polar bear?'

The father was becoming distressed by the continual questioning and said: 'Why do you keep asking if you're 100 per cent polar bear?'

The cub said: 'Because I'm freezing!'

Did you hear about the hyena that swallowed an Oxo cube? – He made a laughing stock of himself.

In the early hours of the morning, two bats were hanging upside down in their cave. The first bat turned to the other and said: 'How about getting some nice tasty blood for a late-night snack?'

'Where are we going to find blood at this time of night?' asked the other.

'I'll show you,' said the first. 'I'll go myself.'

An hour later, the first bat returned to the cave with blood dripping from his mouth.

1

'What happened to you?' said the second bat. 'How did you get all that blood on you?'

'See that tree over there?'

'Yeah.'

'Well, I didn't!'

What happened when the lion ate the clown? – He felt funny.

A zookeeper needed some extra animals for his zoo, so he decided to write a letter. But unfortunately he didn't know the plural of 'mongoose'.

He started the letter: 'To whom it may concern, I need two mongeese.' But that didn't sound right, so he tried again. 'To whom it may concern, I need two mongooses.' But that didn't sound right either. Then he had an idea. 'To whom it may concern, I need a mongoose, and while you're at it, send me another one.'

A six-year-old boy was standing with his father in front of the polar bear enclosure at the zoo. The father was telling the boy how dangerous polar bears were and that, of all the animals in the zoo, they were the ones that the keepers feared most.

Eventually the boy said: 'Dad, if the polar bear escapes and eats you up . . . ?'

'Yes, son?'

'Which bus do I catch home?'

Did you hear about the shepherd who drove his flock through town, and got a traffic ticket for making a ewe turn?

Two cows were talking in a field one day.

The first cow said: 'Have you heard about the Mad Cow Disease that's going around?'

The second cow said: 'Yeah, makes you glad you're a penguin, doesn't it?'

How do you stop a pig from smelling? – Put a clothes peg on its nose.

If rhino horn is an aphrodisiac, why are rhinos nearly extinct?

A lion woke up one morning with an overbearing desire to remind his fellow creatures that he was king of the jungle. So he marched over to a monkey and roared: 'Who is the mightiest animal in the jungle?'

'You are, Master,' said the monkey, quivering.

Then the lion came across a wildebeest.

'Who is the mightiest animal in the jungle?' roared the lion.

'You are, Master,' answered the wildebeest, shaking with fear.

Next the lion met an elephant.

'Who is the mightiest animal in the jungle?' roared the lion.

The elephant grabbed the lion with his trunk, slammed him repeatedly against a tree, dropped him like a stone and ambled off.

'All right,' shouted the lion. 'There's no need to turn nasty just because you don't know the answer.'

What do you call a camel with a flat back? – Humphrey.

A tourist guide was talking with a group of schoolchildren at America's Yellowstone Park when one boy asked him whether he had ever come face to face with a wolf.

'Yes,' said the guide, 'I did come face to face with a wolf once. What made it worse was that I was alone and unarmed.'

'What did you do?'

'What could I do? First, I tried looking him straight in the eyes but he slowly advanced towards me. I crept back, but he kept on coming, nearer and nearer. I had to think fast.'

'Wow! How did you get away?'

'As a last resort, I just turned around and walked quickly to the next cage.'

Why do gorillas have big nostrils? – Because they have big fingers.

A zookeeper spotted a visitor throwing ten-dollar bills into the elephant enclosure.

'Why are you doing that?' asked the keeper.

'The sign says it's OK,' replied the visitor.

'No, it doesn't.'

'Yes it does. It says: "Do not feed. $10 fine."'

How do you fit five donkeys in a fire engine? – Two in the front, two in the back, and one on top going eyore, eyore, eyore!

The elephants were playing the ants at soccer. With time running out, there was still no score but then the ants' star player began dribbling towards goal until an elephant defender lumbered over towards him, trod on him and killed him.

'What did you do that for?' demanded the referee.

'I didn't mean to kill him,' protested the elephant. 'I was just trying to trip him up.'

If milk is high in fat and cholesterol, why don't cows die of heart attacks?

A man was driving down a country lane when he spotted the most beautiful horse he'd ever seen, standing in the middle of a field. He slammed on his brakes and stopped to have a quick look. 'I must buy that horse,' he said to himself and immediately went in search of the owner. Arriving at a nearby farmhouse, he knocked on the door.

'Are you the owner of that magnificent animal in the field back there?' he asked.

'Yes,' replied the farmer.

'Then I simply must buy him from you.'

'I can't sell him,' said the farmer. 'He doesn't look so good.'

'What do you mean? He's the most beautiful horse I've seen in my life.'

'Well, OK,' conceded the farmer, 'if you insist. Does a thousand dollars sound reasonable to you?'

'Absolutely,' said the man, and he took the horse home on a trailer.

A few days later, the farmer heard another knock on his door. It was the man with the horse. 'You ripped me off!' yelled the man. 'That horse is as blind as a bat!'

'I tried to warn you,' answered the farmer. 'I told you he doesn't look so good.'

What do sheep count when they can't get to sleep?

A hungry lion was scouring the jungle looking for food. In a clearing he spotted two men. One was sitting on a rock, reading a book; the other was scribbling a letter. Without a moment's hesitation, the lion pounced on the man reading the book and ate him . . . because even lions know that readers digest and writers cramp.

A farmer kept a donkey in a stable, but the donkey's ears were so long that they repeatedly hit the top of the door, causing the animal to kick out dangerously. So the farmer decided to raise the height of the door frame.

He spent all day toiling away with his hacksaw. Seeing that he was struggling to complete the task, his neighbour suggested: 'Instead of lifting the door frame, wouldn't it be easier if you simply dug out the ground in the doorway and made it deeper?'

'Don't be an idiot,' said the farmer. 'It's the donkey's ears that are too long, not his legs!'

What was going through the mind of the first person ever to pull on a cow's udder?

One frozen winter, Jim and John built a skating rink in the middle of a field. A shepherd leading his flock decided to take a shortcut across the rink, but the sheep were afraid of the ice and refused to cross it. So in desperation the shepherd began tugging them to the other side.

'Look at that,' said Jim to John. 'That guy is trying to pull the wool over our ice.'

Do cows have to watch where they step in fields?

A naturalist found evidence of a hitherto unknown breed of giant elephant living in the rainforests of South America. Eventually he raised sufficient funds to launch an expedition to bring back this direct descendant of the mammoth.

After weeks battling their way through the jungle, the party stumbled upon a three-foot tall pygmy standing next to the dead elephant. The naturalist approached the pygmy and exclaimed: 'My God! Did you kill this elephant?'

'Yes,' replied the pygmy.

'But it's so big and you're so small!'

'Yes,' said the pygmy.

'How on earth did you kill it?' asked the naturalist.

'With my club,' said the pygmy.

'How big is your club?' inquired the naturalist.

'Well, there are about a hundred of us.'

A mother kangaroo jumped in the air with a squeal before glaring down into her pouch. 'How many times do I have to tell you? No smoking in bed!'

What's light, white, and sweet and hangs from trees? – A meringue-utan.

Three mischievous boys went to the zoo one day on a school outing. They decided to visit the elephant enclosure but within an hour, they were picked up by a police officer for causing a commotion. The officer hauled them off to security for questioning and the teacher in charge told them to give the police their names and say what they were doing at the elephant house.

The first boy said: 'My name is Gary, and I was just throwing peanuts into the elephant enclosure.'

The second said: 'My name is Kevin, and all I was doing was throwing peanuts into the elephant enclosure.'

The third boy was a bit shaken up by the ordeal and said: 'My name is Peter, but my friends call me Peanuts . . .'

What did the farmer say to the infertile goat? – You must be kidding.

One day a gorilla escaped from the zoo, prompting a huge search of the district and appeals on radio, television and in the newspapers. He was finally discovered a few days later in the city library where zoo officials found him sitting at a desk in the reading room with two books spread out in front of him. The gorilla was deep in concentration. One book was the Bible; the other was written by Charles Darwin.

The zoo keepers asked the gorilla what he was doing. The gorilla replied: 'I'm trying to figure out whether I am my brother's keeper or my keeper's brother.'

What did the zoo keeper say when he was charged by a baby aardvark? – 'A little aardvark never hurt anyone.'

Two sheep were standing in a field.
One went: 'Baaaa.'
'Huh,' said the second, 'I was going to say that.'

A farmer was helping one of his cows to give birth when he noticed his young son watching wide-eyed from behind the fence. 'Oh dear,' thought the farmer, 'I'm going to have to explain the birds and bees to him.'

So when he had finished, he asked the boy: 'Well, have you got any questions about what you've just seen?'

'Just one,' gasped the boy. 'How fast was that calf going when it hit the cow?'

What did the doe say as she came out of the thicket? – That's the last time I do that for two bucks!

Armed Forces

A navy psychiatrist was interviewing a sailor for a job. To ascertain how the young man might react to danger, the psychiatrist asked: 'What would you do if you looked out of that window right now and saw a battleship coming down the street?'

The young man replied confidently: 'I'd grab a torpedo and sink it.'
'And where would you get the torpedo?'
'The same place you got your battleship!'

A soldier cradled the dying General Custer in his arms at the Little Big Horn. Custer gasped: 'I'll never understand Indians. A few minutes ago they were singing and dancing . . .'

An army sergeant was passing barracks after lights out when he heard some voices from inside. He threw the door open and barked: 'A few minutes ago you all heard me say "goodnight". What you don't seem to have grasped is that when I say "goodnight", what I really mean is "shut the hell up"!'

The room instantly fell silent. But after a few seconds, a small voice could be heard from somewhere at the back of the darkened room: 'Goodnight, sergeant.'

When a famous admiral died, the navy wanted to lay on a grand ceremony in his honour. After two hours of speeches and hymns, it was suggested that the event should end with a cannon salute.

That was when the organisation of the ceremony threatened to run into trouble for nobody on the four-man planning committee could seem to agree on the number of shots that should be fired in the salute.

'I think one shot would be perfect,' said the first captain. 'It would be moving and deeply symbolic.'

'I think there should be two,' suggested the second captain, 'in honour of the two great battles he won.'

'Well, I think we should have three shots,' said the third captain, 'as a mark of respect to the number of ships he commanded.'

The fourth captain puffed quietly on his pipe until asked for his opinion.

'There's no argument,' he said. 'We must fire four shots at the end of the ceremony to commemorate the late admiral's four decorations for gallantry. In fact, I have already discussed the matter with the Queen, and it has all been approved.'

With that, the other three captains stormed out of the room. One turned at the door and said: 'We wouldn't have bothered coming if we had known it was a four-gun conclusion!'

How can there be such things as peace-keeping missiles?

A new ensign assigned to submarines was eager to impress his commanding officer with all the knowledge he had picked up at submarine school. After listening patiently for five minutes, the senior officer said: 'Listen, it's simple. Add the number of times we dive to the number of times we surface. Divide that number by two. If the result doesn't come out even, don't open the hatch.'

An army major called his wife to tell her that he would be late home because dirty magazines had been found in the barracks, and the soldiers responsible were facing serious disciplinary action.

'The punishment sounds a little harsh,' she said. 'After all, most of the soldiers have pictures of women on the walls of their quarters.'

'No, honey,' he explained patiently. 'Dirty magazines means the clips from their rifles had not been cleaned properly!'

A knight walked into a blacksmith's shop. The blacksmith said: 'You've got mail.'

Through the pitch black of night, a navy captain saw a light dead ahead on collision course with his ship. He immediately sent a signal.

'Change your course ten degrees west.'

The light signalled back: 'Change yours ten degrees east.'

The captain was furious and sent another signal: 'I'm a navy captain. Change your course, sir!'

The signal came back: 'I'm a seaman, second class. Change your course, sir!'

The captain was livid at such insubordination and sent another signal: 'I'm a battleship – I'm not changing course.'

The reply came back: 'And I'm a lighthouse.'

When a knight in armour was killed in battle, what sign did they put on his grave? – Rust in peace.

Trying out a new army computer, an officer typed in a question: 'How far is it from the mess room to the sentry box?'

The computer replied: 'Six hundred.'

The officer typed: 'Six hundred what?'

The computer replied: 'Six hundred, sir!'

What soldiers smell of salt and pepper? – Seasoned troopers.

A drill sergeant at training camp told his recruits: 'Today, I have good news and bad news. First the good news: Private Morgan will be setting the pace on the morning run.'

The men were overjoyed because Morgan was fat and slow. Then the drill sergeant added: 'Now the bad news: Private Morgan will be riding a motorcycle.'

An old British Navy sailor and a retired US marine were chatting about who had experienced the tougher career.

The marine declared proudly: 'I did thirty years in the corps and fought in three of my country's wars. Fresh out of boot camp, I hit the beach at Okinawa, clawed my way up the blood-soaked sand, and eventually took out an entire enemy machine gun nest with a single grenade.

'As a sergeant, I fought in Korea. We pushed back the enemy inch by bloody inch all the way up to the Chinese border, always under a barrage of artillery and small arms fire.

'Finally, I did three consecutive combat tours in Vietnam. We ploughed through the mud and razorgrass for fourteen hours a day, plagued by rain and mosquitoes, ducking under sniper fire all day and mortar fire all night. In a firefight, we'd fire until our arms ached and our guns were empty, then we'd charge the enemy with bayonets!'

'Oh,' said the sailor with a dismissive wave of his hand, 'all shore duty, huh?'

An American tourist went to Portsmouth to see Nelson's flagship HMS *Victory*. On the tour of the ship, the guide pointed out a raised brass plaque on the deck.

'That's where Nelson fell,' said the guide.

The tourist was unimpressed. 'I nearly tripped on the damn thing myself.'

During the Second World War, the SS picked up a number of Irishmen in Berlin and threw them in jail on suspicion of being spies. Determined to escape, the prisoners started using their combs to file through the metal bars on their cell window, disguising the noise with a cheerful Irish refrain. Alas, the German guards were not fooled. As one guard remarked to another with a little song of his own: 'I can always tell . . . when Irish spies are filing . . .'

Airman Jones was assigned to the induction centre where he was to advise new recruits about their government benefits, especially their GI insurance.

After a couple of months his captain noticed that Jones had almost a 100 per cent record for insurance sales – something that had never been achieved before.

Rather than ask him the secret of his success, the captain decided to stand at the back of the room and listen to Jones's sales pitch. First, Jones explained the basics of the GI insurance to the new recruits, and then said: 'If you have GI insurance and go into battle and are killed, the government has to pay $200,000 to your beneficiaries. If you don't have GI insurance, and you go into battle and get killed, the government has to pay only a maximum of $6,000.

'Now,' he concluded, 'which bunch do you think they are going to send into battle first?'

A young ensign had nearly completed his first overseas tour of duty when he was given an opportunity to display his ability at getting the ship under way. With a stream of crisp commands, he had the decks buzzing with men. The ship steamed out of the channel and soon the port was far behind. The ensign's efficiency was remarkable. In fact, word was going around that he had set a new record for getting a destroyer under way. The ensign basked in the glory and was not at all surprised when another seaman approached him with a message from the captain.

He was, however, rather surprised to find that it was a radio message, and he was even more alarmed to read: 'My personal congratulations upon completing your underway preparation exercise according to the book and with amazing speed. In your haste, however, you have overlooked one of the unwritten rules – Make Sure The Captain Is Aboard Before Getting Under Way.'

Sir Geraint and his men returned to the king's castle bearing bags of gold and half a dozen slave women, the fruits of plundering the land for a week.

'Where have you been all this time, Sir Geraint?' asked the king.

'I have been robbing and pillaging on your behalf all week, sire, burning the villages of your enemies in the north.'

'But I don't have any enemies in the north,' protested the king.

'You have now, sire.'

The top brass from the Army, Navy and Marine Corps were arguing about who had the bravest troops. They decided to settle the dispute using an enlisted man from each branch.

The army general called a private over and ordered him to climb to the top of the base flagpole, then let go with both hands and salute. The private quickly complied.

Next, the admiral ordered a sailor to climb the pole, polish the brass knob at the top, salute smartly and jump off. The sailor did as he was told and landed on the concrete below.

Finally, the marine was told to do exactly the same as the army and navy men but in full battle gear, pack filled with bricks and loaded weapon carried high. He took one look at the major general and said: 'You're out of your mind, sir.'

The marine commander turned to the others and said: 'Now *that's* guts!'

Thrown from his horse while fleeing the enemy troops, a cavalryman lay helpless on the ground, his leg broken. With the enemy approaching, the terrified soldier called out: 'All you saints in heaven, help me get up on my horse!'

Then with a superhuman effort, he leaped onto the horse's back, only to go straight over the other side. Once again lying on the ground, he called to the heavens: 'OK, just half of you this time!'

10

You Might Be In The Army If:
You won't let your wife go to the cinema because the laundry room failed inspection.
You have a fence set up around your house that even Rambo wouldn't want to mess with.
Lights out is at 2200hrs every night.
Your kids must perform ten push-ups before entering the dining room.
Your wife's favourite lipstick colour is khaki.
Your kids wear a beret when they go out to play.
You cut the lawn in a pair of jungle boots.
Your dog's name is Ranger.
Your nicest set of clothes is your uniform.
You think waking up at 7a.m. is sleeping in.
You've ever worn camouflage gear to a wedding.
You refer to sex with your wife as being 'on manoeuvres'.
You spend your spare time polishing your boots.
Your family thinks there's nothing wrong when you disappear for a month.
All your friends are in the army, too.

As everyone sat around the table for a big family dinner, the youngest son announced that he had just signed up at an army recruitment office. There were audible gasps from the gathering, followed by laughter as his older brothers expressed their disbelief that he could handle army life.

'Oh, come on, quit joking,' snickered one. 'You haven't really signed up, have you?'

'You'd never get through basic training,' scoffed another.

Finally his father spoke up. 'It's going to take a lot of discipline. Are you ready for that?'

Coming under fire on all sides, the new recruit looked to his mother for help. But she said simply: 'Are you really going to make your own bed every morning?'

A group of young army parachutists went up in the plane for a jump, but the flight was rough and in the end it became so windy that the officer in charge called it off. The plane headed back to base but as it made a remarkably smooth landing, five of the young parachutists were violently sick.

The officer didn't understand it. 'How come you could put up with that rough flight, but you couldn't handle a smooth landing?'

One of the parachutists replied: 'Well, sir, we've always jumped out of planes, but we've never actually landed in one before!'

A cargo plane was preparing for departure from Thule Air Base in Greenland, and they were waiting for the truck to arrive to pump out

11

the aircraft's sewage tank. The aircraft commander was becoming impatient. Not only was the truck late, but also the airman performing the job was extremely slow in getting the tank pumped out. Finally the commander snapped and promised to punish the airman for his slowness.

The airman replied: 'Sir, I have no stripes, it is twenty below zero, I'm stationed in Greenland, and I am pumping sewage out of airplanes. Just what are you going to do to punish me?'

A group of soldiers on a first-aid course were tested by the instructor. He asked the recruits: 'If the sergeant major sustained a head injury during an exercise, what would you do about it?'

One soldier piped up: 'I'd wrap a tourniquet around his neck and tighten it until the bleeding stopped.'

In the year 2000, a Belgian man went to his local priest and confessed: 'Forgive me, Father, for I have sinned. During the Second World War, I hid a Jewish man in my attic.'

'That's not a sin,' said the priest. 'It was an act of great kindness.'

'But I made him agree to pay thirty-five francs for every week he stayed.'

'I admit that wasn't particularly charitable,' said the priest, 'but you did it for a good cause.'

'Thank you, Father,' said the man. 'That is a great relief to me. I have just one more question.'

'What's that?'

'Do I have to tell him the war is over?'

At the recording of a television game show, an army major was in the hot seat for the last big question. The host read the question slowly and carefully but, to his dismay, the major didn't know the answer. However the major was not prepared to miss out on the chance of winning a fortune, so he put his contingency plan into operation. He let out a sudden cough, and from the back of the stage four mounted knights-in-armour appeared, waving their lances threateningly at the host.

The host looked momentarily terrified, but then a steely determination set in as he refused to allow the major to cheat his way to the big cash prize. Suddenly the host leapt into the air and karate kicked the first knight onto the floor. He picked up the lance from the stricken knight and fought off the second, who also fell sprawling to the floor. The second knight's horse shied and bolted, colliding with the third knight in the process.

The game show host was just beginning to enjoy himself now. He waved the spear he was still carrying at the fourth knight, looked back at the contestant and said: 'Is that your final lancer?'

Babies and Birth

Three men were waiting expectantly outside the labour ward of the city hospital. After a few minutes, a nurse came out to tell the first man: 'Congratulations. You are the father of twins.'

'Twins!' he exclaimed. 'How about that? I work for the Doublemint Chewing Gum Company!'

Five minutes later, a nurse came out to tell the second man: 'Congratulations. You are the father of triplets.'

'Triplets!' he said. 'What an amazing coincidence! I work for the 3M Organisation!'

The third man stood up ashen-faced and muttered: 'I need some air. I work for 7-Up!'

Two women sitting in the doctor's waiting room began discussing babies.

'I want a baby more than anything else in the world,' said one. 'But I guess it's impossible.'

'I used to think that,' said the other. 'But then everything changed. That's why I am here. I'm going to have a baby in three months.'

'You must tell me what you did.'

'I went to a faith healer.'

'But I've tried that. My husband and I went to one for nearly a year and it didn't help a bit.'

The other woman smiled and whispered: 'Try going alone, next time.'

Should women have children after 35? – No, 35 children are more than enough.

When a woman discovered that she was pregnant, her four-year-old son overheard his parents' conversation. But he didn't say anything until a week later when a family friend asked him if he was excited about the prospect of a new brother or sister.

'Yes,' said the boy, 'and I know what we're going to name it. If it's a girl, we're going to call her Emily, and if it's another boy we're going to call it Quits.'

A man was about to become a father for the first time, with the baby due to arrive at some point during the World Cup.

His friend said: 'What will you do if your wife is having the baby on the same day that your team plays?'

'Don't worry, I just bought a VCR. I can watch the birth after the game.'

Parents' Dictionary:
AMNESIA: Condition that enables a woman who has given birth to have sex again.

BOTTLE FEEDING: An opportunity for Dad to get up at 2 a.m. too.

CARPET: Expensive floor covering used to catch spills and clean mud off shoes.

DATE: Infrequent outings with Dad where Mum can enjoy worrying about the kids in a different setting.

DRINKING GLASS: Any carton or bottle left open in the fridge.

EAR: A place where kids store dirt.

EAT: What kids do between meals, but not at them.

FAMILY PLANNING: The art of spacing your children the proper distance apart to stop you falling into financial disaster.

FEEDBACK: The inevitable result when a baby doesn't appreciate strained carrots.

GRANDPARENTS: People who think your children are wonderful even though they're sure you're not raising them right.

HEARSAY: What toddlers do when anyone mutters a rude word.

IMPREGNABLE: A woman whose memory of labour is still vivid.

INDEPENDENT: How we want our children to be as long as they do everything we say.

PRENATAL: When your life was still somewhat your own.

PREPARED CHILDBIRTH: A contradiction in terms.

PUDDLE: A small body of water that draws other small bodies wearing dry shoes.

SHOW OFF: A child who is more talented than yours.

STERILISE: What you do to your first baby's dummy by boiling it and to your last baby's dummy by blowing on it.

TEMPER TANTRUMS: What you should keep to a minimum so as not to upset the children.

THUNDERSTORM: A chance to see how many family members can fit into one bed.

TWO-MINUTE WARNING: When a baby's face turns red and he or she begins to make those familiar grunting noises.

WEAKER SEX: The kind you have after the kids have exhausted you.

WHOOPS: Get a sponge!

Thanks to the miracle of fertility treatment, a woman was able to have a baby at 70. When she was discharged from hospital, her relatives came to visit.

'Can we see the baby?' they asked.

'Not yet,' said the 70-year-old mother.

Fifteen minutes later, they asked again. 'Can we see the baby?'

'Not yet,' said the mother.

Another quarter of an hour later, they asked again: 'Can we see the baby?'

'Not yet,' answered the mother.

The relatives were growing impatient. 'Well, when can we see the baby?'

'When it cries.'

'Why do we have to wait until the baby cries?'

'Because I forgot where I put it.'

A man staggered home from the pub pushing a baby carriage.

His wife went mad. 'You drunken idiot!' she screamed. 'That's not our baby!'

'I know,' he said, 'but it's a nicer pram.'

A woman was lying in hospital, giving birth. After half an hour of pushing, panting and sweating, the baby's head suddenly popped out. The baby took one look at the doctor and asked: 'Are you my daddy?'

'No, I'm not,' replied the doctor, startled. And the baby popped back into the womb.

The obstetrician was called to look into this unusual occurrence. No sooner had he arrived than the baby's head popped out again.

'Are you my daddy?' asked the baby.

'No, I'm not,' answered the obstetrician.

The obstetrician decided to fetch the boy's father. 'The baby seems reluctant to come out,' said the worried medic. 'He keeps asking for his father, so would you mind coming to the delivery room?'

The father entered the delivery room and the baby's head popped out again.

'Are you my daddy?' asked the baby.

The father knelt down and said proudly: 'Yes, son, I'm your father.'

Hearing this, the baby started tapping his index finger violently and repeatedly on his father's forehead and said: 'This is pretty damned annoying, isn't it?'

A couple were at their first pre-natal class. So that the husband could get an idea of what it felt like to be pregnant, the instructor strapped a bag of sand to his stomach.

As he walked around with his new bulge, the husband said: 'This doesn't feel too bad.'

Then the instructor deliberately dropped a pen and said to the husband: 'Now I want you to pick up that pen as if you were pregnant.'

'You want me to do it the way my wife would?' confirmed the husband.

'Exactly the same,' said the instructor.

The husband turned to his wife and said: 'Honey, pick up that pen for me.'

Anyone who says it's as easy as taking candy from a baby has never tried it.

For weeks, a six-year-old boy had been telling his teacher about the baby brother or sister that was expected at his house. One day his mother allowed him to feel the movements of the unborn child. Although obviously impressed, he didn't say anything and from then on, he stopped telling his teacher about the impending event.

The teacher finally sat the boy on her lap and said: 'Timmy, whatever became of that baby brother or sister you were expecting at home?'

Timmy burst into tears and confessed: 'I think Mummy ate it!'

One night a woman found her husband standing over their newborn baby's crib. Silently she watched him. As he stood looking down at the sleeping infant, she saw on his face a mixture of emotions: disbelief, doubt, delight, amazement, enchantment, scepticism.

Touched by his unusual display of deep emotions, she felt her eyes grow moist. She slipped her arms around her husband. 'A penny for your thoughts,' she whispered in his ear lovingly.

'It's amazing,' he replied. 'I just can't see how anybody can make a crib like that for only $39.95!'

In the backwoods of Canada in a shack with no electricity, a man's wife went into labour in the middle of the night. The local doctor was summoned to help with the delivery. The doctor gave the nervous father-to-be a lantern to hold, partly to keep him occupied and partly so that he could see what he was doing.

After a few minutes, a baby boy was born and the husband put down the lantern to hold him.

'Don't put that lantern down just yet,' said the doctor. 'I think there's another one on the way.'

Shortly afterwards, a baby daughter was born and the husband put down the lantern to hold her.

'Don't put the lantern down yet,' said the doctor. 'I think there may be another one still to come.'

Sure enough, a few minutes later, another baby girl was born. The father scratched his head and said to the doctor: 'Do you think it's the light that's attracting them?'

Two babies were sitting in their cribs when one called over to the other: 'Are you a little girl or a little boy?'

'I don't know,' replied the other baby giggling.

'What do you mean, you don't know?' asked the first.

'I mean I don't know how to tell the difference.'

'Well, I do,' said the first baby chuckling. 'I'll climb into your crib and find out.'

So he carefully manoeuvred himself into the other baby's crib, then quickly disappeared beneath the blanket. After a couple of minutes, he resurfaced with a big grin on his face. 'You're a little girl and I'm a little boy,' he said proudly.

'You're ever so clever,' cooed the baby girl, 'but how can you tell?'

'It's easy,' replied the baby boy. 'You've got pink booties and I've got blue ones.'

A woman went to her doctor who informed her that she was pregnant. It was her first pregnancy and she admitted that she was a bit worried about the pain of childbirth.

'How much will it hurt?' she asked.

The doctor answered: 'Well, it varies from woman to woman and pregnancy to pregnancy, and anyway it's difficult to describe pain.'

'I know, but can you give me some idea?'

'OK,' he said. 'Grab your upper lip and pull it out a little.'

'Like this?'

'A little more.'

'Like this?'

'No. A little more.'

'Like this?'

'Yes. Does that hurt?'

'A little bit.'

'Now stretch it over your head!'

Bar Jokes

A man came into a bar and ordered a martini. Before drinking it, he removed the olive and carefully put it into a jar. Then he ordered another martini and did the same thing. After an hour, by which time he was full of martinis and the jar was full of olives, he staggered out.

'Well,' remarked a customer, 'I never saw anything as strange as that!'

'What was strange about it?' asked the barman. 'His wife had sent him out for a jar of olives.'

A man went into a bar with a banana on his head. As he served him, the bartender said: 'Look, I don't know if you realise this, but you've got a banana on your head.'

'That's OK,' said the man. 'I always wear a banana on my head on Tuesdays.'

'But today's Wednesday,' said the bartender.

not, is it?' said the man. 'Oh God! I must look a right idiot!'

A guy walked into a bar with a giraffe. They both drank so much that the giraffe passed out on the floor. There was no way the guy could get the giraffe back on its feet so he decided to go home and collect it in the morning. But as he headed for the door, the bartender called out: 'Hey, you can't leave that lyin' there.'

The guy said: 'That's not a lion – it's a giraffe.'

A drunk reeled into a funeral parlour and ordered a scotch. The mortician tried to explain where he was, but the befuddled drunk simply repeated the order.

'Look,' said the mortician, 'we do not serve scotch here. Do you understand?'

'OK,' said the drunk. 'Give me a beer.'

A little pig walked into a bar, ordered a drink and asked where the toilet was.

'Just along the corridor,' said the bartender.

Then a second little pig walked into the bar, ordered a drink and asked where the toilet was.

'Just along the corridor,' said the bartender.

Then a third little pig walked into the bar and ordered a drink. The bartender said: 'I suppose you want to use the toilet too?'

'No, I'm the little pig that goes wee wee wee wee all the way home.'

Two fonts walked into a bar. The bartender said: 'Sorry, we don't want your type in here.'

A man was sitting quietly at the bar when the bartender presented him with a riddle. 'My mother had a child. It wasn't my brother, and it wasn't my sister. Who was it?'

The man thought for a minute before giving up.

'It was me, you fool!' exclaimed the bartender triumphantly.

The man thought it was a good trick and decided to play it on his wife when he got home. He announced: 'My mother had a child. It wasn't my brother, and it wasn't my sister. Who was it?'

His wife looked at him blankly and gave up.

'It was Jim at the Red Lion, you fool!'

A termite walked into a pub and asked: 'Is the bar tender here?'

After a heavy day's drinking in a bar, a tramp fell asleep on a park bench as night closed in. But no sooner had he dozed off than a passer-by, spotting the watch on his wrist, tapped him on the shoulder and asked him for the time.

Roused from his slumbers, the tramp grumpily replied, '11.30' and went back to sleep.

A few minutes later, another passer-by prodded the tramp and asked him the time. '11.34,' said the tramp irritably and settled back down to sleep.

He had barely shut his eyes before another pedestrian woke him to ask the time. '11.39,' muttered the tramp wearily.

When another three people stopped to ask him the time in the space of ten minutes, the tramp could take no more. So he took a piece of card, wrote on it 'I cannot tell the time', and placed it where everyone passing the bench could read it. Then he dozed off to sleep. Two minutes later, a man tapped him on the arm.

'What do you want?' snapped the tramp.

The man said: 'It's a minute to twelve.'

Did you hear about the bailiff who moonlighted as a bartender? – He served subpoena coladas.

A drunk phoned Alcoholics Anonymous.

'Is that AA?' asked the drunk.

'Yes,' said the switchboard girl. 'Would you like to join?'

'No,' said the drunk. 'I'd like to resign.'

A drunk was floundering down an alleyway carrying a box with holes in the side when he bumped into an old friend.

'What have you got there?' asked the friend, nodding towards the box.

'A mongoose,' replied the drunk.

'What have you got a mongoose for?'

'Well, you know how drunk I can get. When I get drunk, I see snakes and I'm scared to death of snakes. That's why I got this mongoose, for protection.'

'But those snakes are imaginary.'

'That's OK. So is this mongoose.'

A guy went into a bar and ordered five pints of beer. The bartender was baffled by the request since the customer was alone, but nevertheless he poured him five pints and lined them up along the bar. The guy proceeded to down all five in quick fashion before wiping his mouth and saying: 'That was good.'

As soon as he had finished, he ordered four more pints. Again they were lined up on the bar and the guy knocked them back quickly. By the last pint, he was definitely beginning to feel a little groggy.

19

Undaunted, he ordered another three pints. These took a bit longer to sink and by the end he was slurring his words.

Even so, he ordered another two pints. After drinking these, he could hardly manage to sit on his stool.

Nevertheless he ordered one more pint.

'I think you've had enough,' said the bartender.

As the guy struggled to focus on him, he said: 'Yeah, you know, it's funny. The less I drink, the drunker I get.'

Two drunks were sitting at a bar. One said: 'What's this thing they call a Breathalyser?'

The other said: 'It's a bag that can tell how much you drink.'

'Oh,' said the first. 'I married one of those things years ago!'

A pork pie walked into a bar. The barman said: 'Sorry, we don't serve food in here.'

A vicar, a priest and a rabbi walked into a pub. The bartender said: 'Is this some kind of joke?'

After a night on the town, a husband lurched home at three o'clock in the morning. Just as he got through the door, the cuckoo clock started and cuckooed three times. Thinking on his feet because he knew that the clock would almost certainly wake his wife, he cuckooed another nine times.

The next morning his wife asked him what time he had arrived home last night.

'Twelve o'clock,' he answered.

When she didn't dispute it, he was convinced that he had got away with it. He was really pleased with himself.

Then she added: 'We really must get a new cuckoo clock. Last night it cuckooed three times, said 'damn', cuckooed another four times, belched, cuckooed another three times, cleared its throat, cuckooed twice more and giggled.'

A man walked into a bar and ordered a glass of white wine. After taking a sip of the wine, he hurled the remainder into the bartender's face. Before the bartender could recover from the shock, the man began weeping.

'I'm sorry,' he sobbed. 'I'm really sorry. I keep doing that to bartenders. I can't tell you how embarrassing it is to have a compulsion like this.'

Far from being angry, the bartender was sympathetic and suggested that the man see an analyst about his problem. 'I happen to have the name of a good psychiatrist,' said the bartender. 'My brother and my wife both go to him, and they say he's the best there is.'

Six months later, the man was back. The bartender remembered him. 'Did you do what I suggested?' he asked, pouring the man a glass of white wine.

'I certainly did,' said the man. 'I've been seeing that psychiatrist twice a week.' Then he took a sip of the wine and threw the rest into the bartender's face.

The flustered bartender wiped his face with a towel. 'The doctor doesn't seem to be doing you any good,' he spluttered.

'On the contrary,' claimed the man. 'He's done me the world of good.'

'But you threw the wine in my face again!'

'Yes, but it doesn't embarrass me anymore.'

Two pieces of tarmac were having a drinking contest to see which was the harder. After a dozen shots of vodka, both were still stone cold sober when suddenly the bar door opened and a piece of red tarmac walked in. Immediately one piece of tarmac abandoned his drink and ran out of the bar.

The other piece of tarmac caught up with him the following day. 'Why did you run off like that when that piece of red tarmac came into the bar?'

'Haven't you heard about him? He's a cycle-path!'

Count Dracula had thoroughly enjoyed his night on the town, drinking Bloody Marys in clubs and biting the necks of unsuspecting women. Shortly before sunrise he was making his way home when he was suddenly hit on the back of the head. Looking round, he saw nothing, but on the ground was a small sausage roll.

A mystified Dracula carried on his way until a few yards further along the road he felt another blow to the back of the head. Again he turned around quickly but could see nothing except, lying on the pavement, a small triangular sandwich. More puzzled than ever, he resumed his journey, only to feel another bang to the back of his head. He whirled round instantly but there was no sign of the culprit. Furious, he looked down and saw a cocktail sausage lying on the pavement. He stood motionless for a few seconds, peering into the darkness of the night. Nothing.

He had walked only a short distance further along the road when he felt a tap on the shoulder. With a swirl of his cape, he turned as fast as he could. Just then he felt a sharp pain in his heart. He fell to the ground clutching his chest, which was punctured by a small cocktail stick laden with a chunk of cheese and a pickle. As he lay dying on the pavement, Dracula looked up and saw a young woman. 'Who the hell are you?' he gasped.

She replied: 'I'm Buffet the Vampire Slayer.'

A man was staggering home drunk in the early hours of the morning when he was stopped by a police officer.

'What are you doing out at this time of night?' asked the officer.

'I'm going to a lecture,' slurred the drunk.

'And who's going to give a lecture at this hour?'

'My wife.'

A husband went out for a few drinks with his pals one Friday evening but ended up getting so drunk at their flat that by the time he came round, it was Sunday lunchtime. Realising that his wife would give him hell over the missing day and a half, he knew he had to come up with a plausible explanation. He was really struggling to think of a good excuse until he had a sudden brainwave. Calling home, he yelled down the phone: 'Don't pay the ransom, darling! I've managed to escape!'

A customer in a bar ordered a beer but as he drank it, he couldn't help noticing that it didn't taste as good as it should.

'Excuse me, bartender,' he said, 'but this beer's a bit warm.'

The bartender glared at him. 'Just shut up and drink your beer!' he snapped.

Upset by the bartender's attitude, the customer decided to take a small measure of revenge when it was time to pay for his drink. Instead of giving the bartender three $1 bills, he threw thirty dimes behind the counter and watched amused while the rude bartender had to get down on his hands and knees to pick them up.

In the hope that things had improved, the customer returned to the same bar the following day, waving a $5 bill. Still seething from yesterday, the bartender thought about kicking him out before remembering that he couldn't really afford to turn away custom. Once again, the beer was rather warm, but the man refrained from complaining. When it was time to pay, he duly handed over the $5 bill. The bartender went to the till to get the change, but, instead of taking out two $1 bills, he took out twenty dimes and threw them all over the pub. 'There!' he said triumphantly. 'There's your bloody change!'

The customer surveyed the scene but remained perfectly calm. Then he took out ten dimes, threw them behind the counter and said: 'Gimme another beer!'

A man walked into a pub and saw a gorilla serving behind the bar.

'What's the matter?' said the gorilla, realising he was being stared at. 'Have you never seen a gorilla serving drinks before?'

'It's not that,' said the man. 'I just never thought the giraffe would sell this place.'

A drunk fell into one of the fountains in Trafalgar Square. As he splashed around aimlessly, he looked up and saw Nelson standing on his column.

'Don't jump!' yelled the drunk. 'This is the shallow end!'

Following a beer festival in London, all the brewery presidents decided to go out for a beer.

Corona's president said: 'I would like the world's best beer, a Corona.'

The barman handed him a bottle of Corona.

Next Budweiser's president said: 'I'd like the best beer in the world, a Budweiser, the King of Beers.'

The barman reached up to the shelf and handed him a bottle of Budweiser.

Then the president of Coors said: 'I'd like the best beer in the world, a Coors, the only one made with Rocky Mountain spring water.'

The barman served him a bottle of Coors.

The three men were then joined by the president of Guinness who said: 'Give me a Coke.'

The other brewery presidents looked across and said: 'Why aren't you drinking a Guinness?'

The Guinness president replied: 'Well, if you guys aren't drinking beer, neither will I.'

A woman was in bed with her lover when she suddenly heard a noise downstairs.

'My God! Your husband is home,' said the lover. 'What am I going to do?'

'Don't worry,' said the wife. 'Just stay in bed with me. He's probably so drunk, he won't even notice you here with me.'

The lover took her advice and sure enough, the husband didn't notice anything untoward when he blundered his way into the bedroom. He crawled into bed and it wasn't until he pulled the covers over himself and exposed six feet at the end of the bed that he became suspicious.

'Honey!' he yelled. 'What the hell is going on? I see six feet at the end of the bed.'

The wife replied calmly: 'Dear, you're so drunk, you can't count. If you don't believe me, count them again.'

The husband got out of bed and counted: 'One, two, three, four . . . Dammit, you're right, honey.' And he climbed back into bed and went to sleep.

A man had been drinking at a bar for eight hours when he happened to mention that his girlfriend was in the car. The bartender, concerned because it was such a cold night, thought he had better go out to check on her but when he peered inside the car he saw the drunk's buddy Mick and the girlfriend going at it on the back seat. The bartender shook his head, came back in and told the drunk it might be a good idea to check on his girlfriend.

The drunk staggered outside, saw Mick and the girl entwined, then walked back into the bar laughing.

'What's so funny?' asked the bartender.

'That fool Mick, he's so drunk, he thinks he's me!'

As a fire engine sped down the road with bells and sirens wailing, a drunk was desperately running behind it. After chasing it for 200 yards, he realised he could no longer keep up and slumped to the ground exhausted. Shaking his fist at the engine as it disappeared into the distance, he yelled: 'Fine! You can keep your bloody ice-cream!'

A horse walked into a bar and ordered a drink. The bartender said: 'Why the long face?'

The bartender asked the guy sitting at the bar: 'What'll you have?'

The guy answered: 'A scotch, please.'

The bartender handed him the drink and said: 'That'll be five dollars.'

The guy said: 'What are you talking about? I don't owe you anything for this.'

A lawyer, sitting nearby and overhearing the conversation, said to the bartender: 'You know, he's got you there. In the original offer, which constitutes a binding contract upon acceptance, there was no stipulation of remuneration.'

The bartender was not happy, but said to the guy: 'OK, you beat me for a drink. But don't ever let me catch you in here again.'

The next day, the same guy walked into the bar. The bartender said: 'What the heck are you doing in here? I thought I told you to steer clear of this joint. I can't believe you've got the nerve to come back!'

The guy said innocently: 'What are you talking about? I've never been in this place in my life.'

Fearing that he had made a mistake, the bartender backed down. 'I'm very sorry, but the likeness is uncanny. You must have a double.'

The guy replied: 'Thanks. Make it a scotch.'

A skeleton walked into a bar and said: 'I'd like a beer and a mop . . .'

A drunk staggered to the men's toilet in a large restaurant. Meandering back, he suddenly stopped and put his hand on a woman's shoulder. The woman recoiled in horror.

'Excuse me,' he said. 'Did I step on your foot about five minutes ago?'

'Yes,' she snapped. 'You certainly did!'

'That's good,' he said. 'I knew my table was around here somewhere.'

Vincent Van Gogh walked into a bar.

The bartender asked: 'Would you like a drink?'

Van Gogh said: 'No thanks, I've got one 'ere.'

Shakespeare walked into a bar and asked for a beer. 'I can't serve you,' said the bartender. 'You're bard.'

A man walked into a bar with an ostrich behind him. He ordered a beer and said to the ostrich: 'What will you have?'

The ostrich said: 'I'll have the same.'

'That's $4.90,' said the bartender.

The man reached into his pocket and without looking or counting, handed the bartender exactly $4.90.

The following day the man and the ostrich called in again. 'I'll have a whiskey,' said the man. 'And what do you want?' he asked the ostrich.

The ostrich said: 'I'll have a rum and coke.'

'That's $6.33,' said the bartender.

The man reached into his pocket and immediately produced exactly $6.33.

The next day the man and the ostrich were back again. The man ordered a gin and tonic and the ostrich asked for a glass of Chardonnay and a packet of nuts.

'That's $6.98,' said the bartender.

The man reached into his pocket and handed over exactly $6.98.

The bartender said: 'There's something I have to ask you. How do you manage to bring out the precise amount of change from your pocket without ever counting it?'

The man explained: 'Last year I was clearing out the attic when I came across an old lamp. For fun, I thought I'd rub it to see whether a genie appeared and, to my amazement, one did. Not only that, but he granted me two wishes. My first wish was that if I ever had to pay for anything, I could just put my hand in my pocket and the right amount of money would always be there.'

'That's great,' said the bartender. 'So many people wish for untold wealth, expensive holidays or fast cars. One other thing though: what's with the ostrich?'

The man said: 'My second wish was for a chick with long legs.'

A man walked into a bar with a strip of tarmac under his arm.
'What'll you have?' asked the bartender.
The man said: 'I'll have a beer, and one for the road.'

Chat-up Lines

* Can I borrow a quarter? I want to call your mother and thank her.
* Do you believe in love at first sight or should I walk by again?
* I'm new in town. Can I have directions to your house?
* Do you have a map, because I keep getting lost in your eyes?
* Hi, I suffer from amnesia. Do I come here often?
* There must be something wrong with my eyes. I can't take them off you.
* Do you know CPR, because you take my breath away?
* You're so hot you would make the devil sweat.
* Do you mind if I stare at you up close instead of from across the room?
* You know what would look good on you? Me.
* If I could rearrange the alphabet I'd put U and I together.
* Was your father an alien, because there's nothing like you on earth?
* Inheriting 90 million dollars doesn't mean much when you have a weak heart.
* I seem to have lost my way. Would you mind taking me with you?
* You know, you might be asked to leave soon. You're making the other women look really bad.
* If I had 11 roses and you, I'd have a dozen.
* Hi, are you here to meet a nice man or will I do?
* If this bar is a meat market, you must be the prime rib.
* Is that a ladder in your stockings or the stairway to heaven?
* I like your dress. Can I talk you out of it?
* I know milk is good for your body, but, baby, how much have you been drinking?
* Are we near the airport, or is that just my heart taking off?
* I don't know what you think of me, but I hope it's X-rated.
* Are you a parking ticket, because you have 'fine' written all over you?
* Are you from Tennessee, because you're the only ten I see?
* Let's have breakfast together tomorrow. Shall I call you or nudge you?
* I've been undressing you with my eyes all night long, and I think it's time to see if I'm right.

- Is it hot in here or is it just you?
- Hi, I'm Adam. You might want to remember it now, because you'll be screaming it later.

Children

A small boy turned to his Aunt Edna and said: 'My God, you're ugly!'

His mother overheard the remark and was appalled. She took him to one side and gave him a real telling-off before ordering him to go back and say sorry to Aunt Edna.

Suitably chastened, the boy went over and said quietly: 'Aunt Edna, I'm sorry you're ugly.'

A little girl made a cup of tea for her mother.

'I didn't know you could make tea,' said mom taking a sip.

'Yes, I boiled some water, added the tea leaves like you do, and then strained it into a cup. But I couldn't find the strainer, so I used the fly swatter.'

'What!' exclaimed mom, choking on her tea.

'Oh, don't worry. I didn't use the new fly swatter. I used the old one.'

A small boy came home from school with a sofa slung across his back and armchairs under his arms. His father said angrily: 'I told you not to accept suites from strangers.'

A mother was putting her young son to bed at the height of a violent thunderstorm.

'Mommy,' he asked nervously, 'can I sleep with you tonight?'

'I'm sorry, darling,' she said. 'But I have to sleep with Daddy tonight.'

'It's not fair,' said the boy. 'Tell the big coward not to be such a baby.'

Why is it that we spend the first two years of a child's life actively encouraging him to speak, only to tell him to be quiet for the next fifteen?

Arriving home, a boy confessed to his mother that he had accidentally broken a lamp at his friend's house while playing football in the living room. 'But, mom,' he added, 'you don't have to worry about buying another one because Craig's mother said it was irreplaceable.'

A little girl was attending a church service with her mother when she started to complain that she was feeling unwell.

'I think I need to throw up,' said the girl.

'Well, go outside,' said the mother, 'and use the bushes by the front door of the church.'

The little girl went off but was back less than a minute later.

'That was quick,' said the mother. 'Did you throw up?'

'Yes, but I didn't need to go outside. I used a box near the door that says "For the sick".'

The boy stood on the burning deck. But he was just trying to stop his pack of cards from going up in smoke.

Children in backseats cause accidents. Accidents in backseats cause children.

Little Johnny came running into the house and asked: 'Mom, can little girls have babies?'

'No,' said his mother, 'of course not.'

Johnny then ran back outside and yelled to his friends: 'It's OK, we can play that game again!'

Why is it that a child will guard a friend's secret with their life but will rat on a sibling in a heartbeat?

A group of Boy Scouts from the city were on a camping trip. The mosquitoes were so persistent that the youngsters had to hide under the blankets at night to avoid being bitten. Then, on seeing some lightning bugs, one boy said to his friend: 'We might as well give up. They're coming after us with flashlights.'

Father: Son, what do you want for your birthday?

Son: Not much, Dad. Just a radio with a sports car around it.

Little Johnny was called over by the lifeguard at the swimming pool.

'You're not allowed to pee in the pool,' said the lifeguard. 'You're going to have to leave.'

'But everyone pees in the pool,' protested Johnny.

'Maybe,' said the lifeguard. 'But not from the diving board.'

Two young boys were staying the night at their grandparents' house. At bedtime they knelt beside their beds to say their prayers. The younger brother said in a really loud voice: 'I pray for a new bike, a portable TV and a Nintendo!'

The other brother said: 'Why are you shouting your prayers? God isn't deaf.'

'No, but grandma is!'

Cleaning while children are around is like clearing the driveway before it stops snowing.

Much to the concern of his parents, an eight-year-old boy had never spoken a word in his life. Then one day after lunch, he turned to his mother and said: 'Soup's cold.'

His mother hugged him and exclaimed: 'Son, I've waited so long to hear you speak! Your father and I have been worried sick. So why have you never said a single word in all these years?'

The boy said: 'Up until now, everything's been OK.'

The Differences Between Boys And Girls:
- You throw a little girl a ball, and it will hit her in the nose. You throw a little boy a ball, and he will try to catch it. Then it will hit him in the nose.
- You dress your little girl in her Sunday best, and she'll look just as pretty when you make it to church an hour later. You dress a boy in his Sunday best, and he'll somehow find every muddy puddle from your home to the church, even if you're driving there.
- If a girl accidentally burps, she will be embarrassed. If a boy accidentally burps, he will follow it with a dozen fake belches.
- Boys grow their fingernails long because they're too lazy to cut them. Girls grow their fingernails long so that they can dig them into a boy's arm.
- By the age of six, boys will stop giving their dad kisses. By the age of six, girls will stop giving their dad kisses unless he bribes them with sweets.
- A little girl will pick up a stick and look in wonderment at what nature has made. A little boy will pick up a stick and turn it into a gun.
- When girls play with Barbie and Ken dolls, they like to dress them up and play house with them. When boys play with Barbie and Ken dolls, they like to tear off their clothes.
- Girls are attracted to boys from an early age. At the same age, boys are attracted to dirt.
- Girls will cry if someone dies in a movie. Boys will cry if you turn off the VCR after they've watched the *Teenage Mutant Ninja Turtles* movie three times in a row.
- Girls turn into women. Boys turn into bigger boys.

A little boy was excited when his father finally agreed to take him to the zoo. When they got home, his mother asked whether he had a good time.

'It was great,' said the boy, 'and Dad really enjoyed himself too – especially when one of the animals came in at 20-1.'

A man called his children together, held up a chocolate bar and asked them who should get it.

'Me . . . me . . . me,' they chorused.

'I'll tell you who will get it,' continued the father. 'Who never talks back to mother and does everything she says?'

Three small voices answered in unison: 'OK, Dad, you can have it.'

While watching a vicar perform a baptism, a little girl turned to her father and said: 'Why is he brainwashing that baby?'

When she got home from school, a seven-year-old girl told her mother that Tommy had kissed her after class.

'How did that happen?' asked the mother, shocked.

'It wasn't easy. Three other girls had to hold him down for me!'

Children rarely misquote you. In fact they usually repeat word for word what you shouldn't have said.

A young girl and a young boy were at nursery. She said: 'Hey, Paul, do you want to play house?'

'Sure. What do you want me to do?'

'I want you to communicate.'

'That word is too big. I have no idea what it means.'

'Perfect,' she said. 'You can be the husband.'

Two children were talking. One said: 'I'm really worried. My dad works twelve hours a day to give my family a nice home and plenty of food. My mum spends the whole day cleaning and cooking for me. I'm worried sick!'

'What are you worried for?' asked his friend. 'It sounds as if you've got it made.'

'Yeah,' said the first, 'but what if they try to escape?'

Little Johnny said: 'Mom, you know that lovely vase in the dining room that's been handed down from generation to generation?'

'Yes. What about it?'

'Well, the last generation just dropped it.'

After losing another tooth, seven-year-old James became even more curious about the elusive tooth fairy. Finally putting two and two together, he came right out and asked his mother: 'Mom, are you the tooth fairy?'

Thinking that he was now old enough to hear the truth, she confessed: 'Yes, I am.'

James thought about this revelation for a moment and then said: 'So how do you get into the other kids' houses?'

Rather than drag his tired three-year-old daughter around the shopping mall, a kindly father gave her a ride on his shoulders. But after a few minutes, she started tugging at his hair.

'Stop that, honey,' he said. 'It hurts.'

'But daddy,' she replied, 'I'm only trying to get my gum back.'

A little boy was performing in the school play when he suddenly fell through a large crack in the floorboards.

The audience gasped, but the boy's mother calmly turned to her friend and said: 'Don't worry, it's just a stage he's going through.'

A mother took her five-year-old son with her to the bank on a busy Friday. They got into line behind an overweight woman wearing a business suit, complete with pager. As the mother waited patiently, the boy looked at the woman in front and observed loudly: 'She's fat.'

The big woman turned around immediately and glared at the child, causing the embarrassed mother to reprimand him quietly.

However, a minute later, the unrepentant boy spread his hands as far as they would go and said loudly: 'I bet her butt is that wide!' Again, the woman turned and gave him a withering look, forcing the mother to give him a stricter telling off.

But a couple of minutes later the boy stated loudly: 'Look how the fat hangs over her belt!' The woman turned and told the mother in no uncertain terms that she ought to teach her son some manners. The mother responded by issuing threats if he did not behave himself. The boy promised to keep quiet.

Three minutes later, the large woman got to the front of the queue but just as she did so, her pager began to emit its distinctive tone. The boy could not help himself. 'Run for your life, mom!' he yelled in panic. 'She's backing up!'

One evening a teenage boy volunteered to babysit so that his mother could enjoy a rare night out. At bedtime he sent the youngsters upstairs and settled down to watch the football on the TV. One child repeatedly crept downstairs, but the teenager kept waving him back up so that he could concentrate on the match.

Then at about nine o'clock the doorbell rang. It was the woman from next door asking whether her son was there.

'No,' said the teenager brusquely.

Just then a little head appeared over the banister and a voice said: 'I'm here, mom, but he won't let me go home!'

A mother asked her young son: 'Why on earth did you swallow the money I gave you?'

'You said it was my lunch money.'

Timmy's father was a rector in a small church, and when the bishop came to visit, Timmy was very excited. The bishop arrived late in the evening, well past Timmy's bedtime, but the next morning the boy asked his father if he would be allowed to meet the important guest.

His father thought about this and decided to let Timmy take the bishop his tea and wake him up. The following instructions were issued: 'First, knock on the door of the bishop's room and then say to him: "It's the boy, my Lord, it's time to get up."'

Timmy rehearsed his lines, repeating them over and over. Finally the tea was ready and he picked up the tray and headed for the bishop's room. A few minutes later, the bishop, still in his pyjamas, was seen running out the door and down the lane.

The father turned to his son and said: 'What happened?'

'I'm sorry,' said Timmy. 'I was so nervous I messed up my lines. I knocked on the door and said: "It's the Lord, my boy, your time is up!"'

On a visit to his impoverished sister, a man was obliged to share a room with his young nephew. Entering the bedroom, he saw the little boy crouched down at the far side of the bed with his head bowed. Thinking the child had been brought up to say his prayers, the man decided to follow his example and kneeled at the near side of the bed with his head bowed.

The boy said: 'What are you doing?'

'The same as you.'

'You'll be in trouble with my mom. The pot's on this side!'

Little Johnny was going to spend the weekend with his friend Timmy and had loaded all his favourite toys into a cart, which he then began pulling the mile or so to Timmy's house. He was doing fine until he reached a steep hill.

As he struggled with the cart up the hill, Johnny began swearing. 'This God damn thing is so heavy!' he moaned.

A passing priest ticked him off. 'You shouldn't be swearing, Johnny,' said the priest. 'God hears you. He is everywhere. He is in the church. He is on the sidewalk. He is everywhere.'

Johnny thought for a moment. 'Is he in my wagon?'

'Yes, Johnny, God is in your wagon.'

'Then tell him to get the hell out and start pulling!'

While staying with his grandma in the country, Little Johnny was asked to go down to the water hole to fetch some water for cooking dinner. As he waded in a few feet and lowered the bucket, he saw two big eyes looking back at him from across the pool. He immediately dropped the bucket and dashed back to grandma's kitchen.

'Where's my bucket and where's my water?' asked grandma.

'I can't get any water from that water hole, grandma,' blurted Johnny. 'There's a big old alligator down there!'

'Now don't you worry about that old alligator, boy. He's been there for a few years now, and he's never hurt no one. Why, he's probably as scared of you as you are of him!'

'Well, Grandma,' replied Johnny, 'if he's as scared as I am, then that water ain't fit to drink!'

Little Johnny's dog Benji was sick and the boy was afraid that his dad would come back from the vet with bad news.

As his dad stepped through the door with Benji in his carrier, Johnny rushed to find out what the vet had said.

'I'm afraid it's not good news, son,' said his father. 'The vet reckons Benji's only got another three weeks or so to live.'

Hearing this, Johnny burst into tears.

'But Benji wouldn't want you to be sad,' said the father, putting a comforting arm around Johnny's shoulder. 'He'd want you to remember all the good times you had together.'

Johnny rubbed his eyes. 'Can we give Benji a funeral?'

'Sure we can,' said his father.

'Can I invite all my friends?'

'Of course you can.'

'And can we have cake and ice-cream?'

'Sure, you can have whatever you want.'

'Dad,' said Johnny. 'Can we kill Benji today?'

'Hey, Mom,' asked Little Johnny, 'can you give me ten dollars?'

'Certainly not!' answered his mother.

'If you do,' persisted Johnny, 'I'll tell you what Dad said to the maid while you were at the hairdresser's.'

His mother was intrigued and, grabbing her purse, handed over the money. 'Well? What did he say?'

'He said, "Carla, make sure you wash my socks tomorrow."'

Cowboys

Two cowboys staggered out of a zoo with their clothes in shreds and their faces covered in cuts and bruises. One turned to the other and said: 'That lion dancing sure ain't as restful as they made out.'

A slow-witted country boy desperately wanted to be a cowboy. For months he pleaded with a local rancher to take him on until eventually the rancher agreed to give him a chance.

On his first day, the rancher showed him a rope. 'This,' he said, 'is a lariat. We use it to catch cows.'

'I see,' said the new recruit, apparently taking everything in. 'And what do you use as bait?'

A tough old cowboy told his grandson that if he wanted to live a long life, the secret was to sprinkle a little gunpowder on his oatmeal every morning. The grandson did this religiously and lived to the age of ninety-eight. When he died, he left sixteen children, twenty-nine grandchildren, thirty-seven great grandchildren, and a fifteen-foot hole in the wall of the crematorium.

The Lone Ranger and Tonto were sitting drinking in a bar when a cowboy came in and asked: 'Whose white horse is that outside?'

The Lone Ranger replied: 'That's my horse – Silver.'

'Well,' said the cowboy, 'he doesn't look too good left out there in the blazing midday sun.'

So the Lone Ranger and Tonto went outside to take a look at Silver who was indeed suffering in the heat. The Lone Ranger gave him a bowl of water to drink and splashed some water over the horse's back. The problem was, there was no breeze, so the Lone Ranger asked Tonto to run around Silver to get some air flowing and to cool the horse down. While Tonto was doing this, the Lone Ranger returned to the bar to finish his drink.

A few moments later, another cowboy walked in and asked: 'Whose white horse is that outside?'

The Lone Ranger turned to face him. 'That's my horse,' he replied. 'What's wrong with him now?'

'Nothing,' said the cowboy. 'I just wanted to let you know that you left your Injun running.'

A cowboy was trying to buy health insurance.

'Ever had an accident?' asked the man from the insurance company.

'Nope.'

'Not any kind of accident, ever?'

'Nope, never.'

'But it says on the application form that you filled in that you were bitten by a snake once. Wouldn't you consider that an accident?'

'Hell no. That dang varmint bit me on purpose!'

Why did the cowboy buy a dachshund? – He wanted to get along little doggie . . .

Cross-Breeds

What do you get when you cross:

A dinosaur and a pig? Jurassic Pork.

A cocker spaniel, a poodle and a rooster? Cockerpoodledoo.

A banana with a red silk dress? A pink slip.

A cat with a lemon? A sourpuss.

An elephant and a skin doctor? A pachydermatologist.

A dog with a cantaloupe? A melon-collie baby.

A hedgehog and a snake? Two yards of barbed wire.

A blue cat and a red parrot? A purple carrot.

A hummingbird with a doorbell? A humdinger.

A strawberry and a road? A traffic jam.

An octopus and a cow? A farm animal that can milk itself.

A parrot with a centipede? A walkie-talkie.

Bambi with a ghost? Bamboo.

A spider with a rabbit? A hare net.

A chicken with a cement mixer? – A brick layer.

A bank and a skunk? Dollars and scents.

A snowflake and a shark? Frostbite.

A parrot with a shark? A bird that will talk your ear off.

A parrot with a woodpecker? A bird that talks in Morse code.

A grizzly bear and a harp? A bear-faced lyre.

The galaxy and a toad? Star Warts.

An evangelist with a hockey puck? A puck that saves itself.

An owl with a goat? A hootenanny.

Poison ivy with a four-leaf clover? A rash of good luck.

A duck with a firework? A firequacker.

The moon with a monk? A nocturnal habit.

A cheetah and a hamburger? Fast food.

A woodpecker with a carrier pigeon? A bird that knocks before delivering its message.

A policeman with a telegram? Copper wire.

A hula dancer and a boxer? A Hawaiian Punch.

A dog with a chicken? A hen that lays pooched eggs.

A dove with a high chair? A stool pigeon.

Batman and Robin with a steamroller? Flatman and Ribbon

Some ants and some ticks? All sorts of antics.

A philosopher with a Mafia hitman? Someone who'll make you an offer you can't understand.

A baby with soldiers? – Infantry.

A dog and a phone? – A golden receiver.

A potato with an onion? A potato with watery eyes.

A duck with a steamroller? A flat duck.

A clown and a goat? A silly billy.

35

A gorilla and a sheep? A nice wool coat, except the sleeves are too long.
An elephant with a Volkswagen? A little car with a big trunk.
An elephant with a kangaroo? – Big holes all over Australia.
An elephant with a skunk? Very few friends.

Dating

A girl brought home her fiancé, a theology student, to meet her parents
for the first time. Her father was keen to learn what prospects the boy
had.

'How do you plan to make a living?' asked the father.
'I don't know,' said the student, 'but God will provide.'
The father raised his eyebrows. 'Do you own a car?'
'No,' said the student, 'but God will provide.'
'I see. And where are you thinking of living once you're married?'
'No idea, but I'm sure God will provide.'
Later the mother asked the father what he thought of their prospective
son-in-law.
'Not a lot, really,' sighed the father. 'He's got no money and seems to
have given precious little thought to the future. But on the other hand, he
thinks I'm God!'

On his first visit to a girl's house, a guy waited in the living room while
she prepared a snack in the kitchen. Left alone, he noticed a small, attrac-
tive vase on the mantelpiece. He picked it up and was looking at it when
the girl walked back in.
'What's this?' he asked.
'Oh, my father's ashes are in there,' she said.
'Oh my God! I'm so sorry . . .'
'Yeah, he's too lazy to go to the kitchen and get an ashtray.'

Two actresses were sitting in a bar when one noticed that the other was
no longer wearing her huge diamond engagement ring.
'What happened?' she asked. 'Is the wedding off?'
'Yes,' replied her friend. 'I saw him in his swimming trunks last week,
and he looked so different without his wallet.'

A young couple parked in a lovers' lane. 'It's lovely out here tonight,'
she sighed romantically. 'It's so quiet and peaceful. Just listen to the
crickets.'
'They're not crickets,' replied her boyfriend. 'They're zippers.'

An 18-year-old boy came home excitedly one night and announced:
'Kelly and me are getting married.'

His father's face fell. He took the boy to one side and said: 'I'm sorry, son, you can't marry Kelly. When I was first married to your mother, I'm afraid I fooled around a lot. You see, Kelly is your half-sister.'

The boy was devastated and it took him six months to start dating again. But a year on, he came home with more good news. 'Ellie and me are getting married.'

His father's face dropped. Once again he took the boy to one side and explained: 'I'm sorry, son, you can't marry Ellie. She's your half-sister too.'

The boy ran up to his room in floods of tears. Later his mother came up to comfort him.

'Dad's done a lot of bad things,' sobbed the boy. 'He keeps saying I can't marry the girl I love.'

'Pay no attention to him,' she said. 'He's not your real father.'

The year was 1959 and college boy Ken went to pick up Laura, his date for the evening. While Laura was getting ready, her father was asking Ken about his plans for the evening.

'We'll probably go to a soda shop or a movie,' said Ken.

The father calmly replied: 'Why don't the pair of you go out and screw?'

Ken was taken aback by the suggestion. 'You think we should go out and screw?' he queried.

'Sure,' said the father. 'After all, you're only young once. And I know how Laura loves to screw. She'd screw all night if we let her.'

Ken was lost for words, but reckoned it was going to be a date to remember. Shortly afterwards, Laura appeared and off they went. Her father sat back to watch the TV but 20 minutes later, the door burst open and Laura ran in, sobbing.

'Dammit, Daddy!' she screamed. 'It's called the twist!'

A girl rushed home to tell her mother: 'I've found a man just like Dad!'

The mother replied: 'What do you want from me? Sympathy?'

A jealous guy caught his girlfriend talking quietly on the phone and immediately confronted her.

'Who was that you were talking to?' he demanded. 'Is there somebody else?'

'Of course not,' she groaned. 'Do you honestly think I'd be going out with a loser like you if there was somebody else?'

Jill: Whatever happened to that couple who met in the revolving door?

Jane: I think they're still going around together.

A protective father took his daughter's first boyfriend to one side for a little chat. 'I hope you're going to treat my daughter properly,' he said. 'I want her to know the difference between right and wrong.'

The boy said: 'I imagine you've brought her up to know what's right, haven't you?'

'Yes, I have.'

'That's good. Well, now I'm taking care of the other side.'

'How was your blind date?' a college student asked her twenty-one-year-old roommate.

'Terrible!' she moaned. 'He showed up in his 1932 Rolls-Royce.'

'Wow! That's a very expensive car. What's so bad about that?'

'He was the original owner.'

Death

Three nuns were killed in a car crash and went to heaven, only to find a sign at the gates saying, 'Closed for Building Work.' Nevertheless they knocked on the gates and St. Peter eventually emerged.

'What do you want?' he said. 'There are no new arrivals this weekend. We're closed for building work. Didn't you read the sign?'

'I'm sorry,' said one nun, 'but we're dead, so we can't really go back, much as we would like to.'

'Now that's where you're wrong,' said St. Peter. 'For this weekend only we're operating a special scheme whereby we will send you back to Earth for two days as whoever you want to be and then, when the rebuilding is complete, we'll accept you back into heaven.'

'That sounds interesting,' the nuns chorused.

'So who would you like to be?' he asked the first nun.

'Tonight, Peter, I would like to be Joan of Arc, because she gave her life to God and died so tragically young.'

'Fine. We can do that,' said St. Peter.

The second nun suggested: 'I would like to be Mother Theresa because she lived such a fulfilling life, selflessly devoting herself to others.'

'OK,' said St. Peter. 'That's no problem.'

The third nun said: 'I want to be Alice Kapipelean.'

St. Peter looked perplexed. 'Who?'

'Alice Kapipelean,' repeated the nun.

'Sorry,' said St. Peter, flicking through his notes, 'but we have no record of any Alice Kapipelean being on Earth.'

'Well, your records are incomplete,' stormed the nun. 'Look, I have proof right here.' And she handed a newspaper article to St. Peter.

St. Peter glanced at the cutting. 'No, sister, you have misread the article. It says that the *Alaska Pipeline* was laid by 500 men in six months!'

An American, an Englishman and an Irishman were due to face a firing squad. The American was first to be lined up against the wall. As the soldiers raised their rifles and took aim, he suddenly shouted 'Avalanche!' The soldiers instinctively turned round to look and by the time they realised it was a hoax, the American had escaped.

The Englishman then prepared to meet his doom. Just as the soldiers raised their rifles and took aim, he shouted 'Flood!' Again they turned round to see what the problem was, and by the time it dawned on them that they had been duped, the Englishman had escaped.

Finally it was the turn of the Irishman who had been greatly impressed by his colleagues' cunning ruses and was determined to come up with a similar diversion. So just as the soldiers raised their rifles and took aim, he shouted 'Fire!'

Did you hear about the man who looked up synonyms for 'death' in a thesaurus? – He found himself at words for a loss.

While sunning himself in the Bahamas, a wealthy English businessman received a telegram from his butler, which read simply: 'Cat dead.' Distraught at the loss of his beloved pet, the businessman cut short his holiday and returned home. After giving the cat a decent burial in the garden, he remonstrated with his butler for the cold-hearted nature of the telegram.

'You should break bad news gently,' he said. 'If I had been telling you that your cat had died, I would have sent a telegram saying: "The cat's on the roof and can't get down." Then a few hours later I would have sent another telegram, saying: "The cat's fallen off the roof and is badly hurt." Finally, a couple of hours after that, I would have sent a third telegram, saying: "The cat has sadly passed away." That way, you would have been gradually prepared for the bad news and would have been able to deal with it better.'

'I understand, sir,' said the butler. 'I will bear that in mind in future.'

With that, the businessman booked another ticket to the Bahamas and resumed his holiday.

Two days later, he received another telegram from his butler. It read: 'Your mother's on the roof and can't get down.'

An elderly couple died in a car crash. They had been in excellent health for years through exercising regularly and also because the wife was obsessed with health foods, keeping a strict watch on both their diets. So when St. Peter welcomed them to heaven, they were keen to take advantage of the first-rate relaxation facilities. The husband was particularly impressed by the eighteen-hole golf course and the Olympic-sized swimming pool.

'This really is a fantastic place you've got,' he told St. Peter.

'And there's more,' said St. Peter. 'Let me show you the restaurant.'

As they observed the sumptuous buffet serving every food imaginable, the husband asked: 'Where's the low fat table?'

'Oh, you don't have to worry about things like that,' said St. Peter. 'You can eat whatever you want, no matter how fatty it is, and it's all free. After all, this is heaven!'

With that, the husband threw his hat to the ground in a fit of temper.

'What's the matter?' asked St. Peter.

Turning to his wife, the husband snapped: 'This is all your fault, Mildred. If it weren't for your blasted bran muffins, I could have been here ten years ago!'

How can a cemetery raise its burial charges and blame it on the cost of living?

An eccentric bachelor passed away and left a nephew nothing but a collection of 433 clocks. The nephew is now busy winding up the estate.

A dead British aristocrat and his dead butler bumped into each other in hell.

'I did not expect to see you here, sir,' said the butler.

The aristocrat sighed: 'I'm here because I lied, cheated and stole to pay the debts run up by that wastrel son of mine. But what about you? You were a faithful, loyal servant to my family for forty years. What are you doing here?'

The butler replied: 'For fathering your wastrel son.'

Unable to attend his father's funeral, a son who lived far away called his brother and said: 'Do something nice for Dad and send me the bill.'

A few weeks later, he received a bill for $200, which he duly paid. Then the next month he got another bill for $200, which he again paid, thinking it was some unforeseen expense. But when the bills for $200 kept on arriving each month, he phoned his brother to find out what was going on.

'Well,' said the other brother, 'you said to do something nice for Dad. So I rented him a tuxedo.'

Taking flowers to a cemetery, a woman noticed an old Chinese man placing a bowl of rice on a nearby grave.

Thinking it a strange form of memorial, she said: 'When exactly do you expect your friend to come up and eat the rice?'

The Chinese man smiled: 'The same time your friend comes up to smell the flowers.'

A woman went to a psychic in an attempt to make contact with her recently deceased husband. After a few false alarms, he finally came through loud and clear.

'How are you, George?' she asked. 'Are you keeping well?'

'I'm fine,' said George. 'I'm standing in this field looking at beautiful cows.'

'Can you see any angels?' asked the wife.

'No, but who needs angels when you're surrounded by cows? There's a real looker standing right in front of me. Lovely long eyelashes . . .'

'What about God?' interrupted the wife. 'Have you met him yet?'

'No, I haven't seen God either. Wow! That cow's a real cracker!'

The wife was becoming irritated. 'Why do you keep going on about cows all the time?'

'Oh, sorry, I should have told you,' said George. 'I've come back as a bull.'

A man was telling his friend: 'My grandfather predicted in advance the very year in which he was going to die. What's more, he knew the exact month he was going to die, the precise day he was going to die, and even the time of day he was going to die. And he was right on every count.

'That's amazing,' said the friend. 'How did he know all that?'

'The judge told him.'

While driving home from a restaurant with his wife, a man was involved in a terrible car crash and died instantly. After a short journey through a dark tunnel with a light at the end, he found himself at the gates of heaven. St. Peter was awaiting his arrival and beckoned him towards the Pearly Gates.

'Sir,' began St. Peter, 'you have proved yourself to be a kind and generous soul. You are worthy of passing through these gates. In order for you to enter heaven, I ask only one thing: that you spell one simple word, a word that epitomises the philosophy of heaven. The word is "love".'

'That's easy,' said the man. 'L-O-V-E.'

And St. Peter opened the Pearly Gates, enabling the man to enter.

Just as the man stepped into the kingdom of heaven, St. Peter's pager went off. God needed him for an emergency meeting. 'Excuse me,' said St. Peter to the man he had just admitted, 'could you watch the gates for me while I'm in this meeting? I shouldn't be more than ten minutes. All I ask of you is that you let nobody in unless they spell the word correctly.'

The man agreed, and St. Peter vanished, leaving him with a bright silver key to the gates.

A few minutes later, the man's wife appeared in front of the gates.

41

'Hello, dear,' she said.

'What are you doing here?' he asked.

'Well, they rushed me to hospital and for a while it seemed as though I might pull through, but I didn't make it. I died of internal haemorrhaging.'

Obeying the instructions of St. Peter, the husband said: 'My beloved, in order for you to pass through the gates of heaven, you only need to spell one simple word. And the word is . . . "onomatopoeia."'

Moments before her husband's funeral, a widow took one final look at his body. To her horror, she saw that he was wearing a brown suit whereas she had issued strict instructions to the undertaker that she wanted him buried in a blue suit. She sought out the undertaker and demanded that the suit be changed. At first he tried to tell her that it was too late but when he could see that she wasn't going to back down, he ordered the mortician to wheel the coffin away. A few minutes later, just as the funeral was about to start, the coffin was wheeled back in and, amazingly, the corpse was now wearing a blue suit.

The widow was overjoyed and, at the end of the service, thanked the undertaker for his swift work. 'Oh, it was nothing,' he said. 'It so happened there was another body in the back room and he was already dressed in a blue suit. All we had to do was switch heads.'

A lawyer was reading out the will of a rich man to the various people mentioned in the will. 'To you, my loving wife Mary, who stood by me throughout our marriage, I leave the house and two million. To my daughter, Jodie, who kept the business going, I leave the yacht, the business, and one million. And to my brother Dan who hated me, argued with me constantly, and thought that I would never mention him in my will, well you are wrong. Hi, Dan!'

While an old man lay dying in his bedroom, his family sat in the living room discussing his funeral arrangements.

Son Arthur said: 'We'll make a real big thing out of it. We'll have five hundred people, and we'll order fifty limos.'

Daughter Emily disagreed. 'Why do you want to waste money like that? We'll have the family and just a few friends. One limo for us will be plenty.'

Grandson Jim proposed: 'We'll have lots of flowers. We'll surround him with dozens of roses and lilies.'

Granddaughter Kylie said: 'That's a complete waste! We'll have one little bouquet – that will be enough.'

Eventually the rest of the family agreed that it would be foolish to spend lots of money on the funeral. They would keep costs down to the bare minimum.

'No use throwing money away,' said son Edward.

Suddenly the voice of the old man could be heard, wafting weakly from the bedroom: 'Why don't you get me my trousers? I'll walk to the cemetery!'

The day after losing his wife in a boating accident, a man answered the door to two grim-faced police officers. They announced in unison: 'We have some bad news, some good news, and some great news. Which would you like to hear first?'

'Give me the bad news first,' said the man.

'Sir, I'm afraid we found your wife's body off Long Island.'

'Oh no,' wailed the man. 'My poor wife. My poor darling wife. What on earth can be the good news?'

'When we pulled her up, she had two five-pound lobsters and a dozen large edible crabs on her.'

'That's terrible,' said the man. 'So what's the great news?'

'We're going to pull her up again tomorrow.'

A woman went to a local psychic in the hope of contacting her dearly departed grandmother. Soon the psychic's eyelids began fluttering, her voice started to quiver, her hands floated up above the table, and she began moaning. Eventually a coherent voice emanated, saying: 'Granddaughter? Are you there?'

The woman, wide-eyed and on the edge of her seat, responded: 'Grandma, is that you?'

'Yes, granddaughter, it's me.'

'It's really, really you, grandma?'

'Yes, it's really me, granddaughter.'

The woman looked puzzled. 'You're sure it's you, grandma?'

'Yes, granddaughter, I'm sure it's me.'

The woman paused for a moment. 'Grandma, I have just one question for you.'

'Anything, my child.'

'When did you learn to speak English?'

Once upon a time there was a very rich businessman who was near death. Having worked hard all his life, he desperately wanted to be able to take some of his wealth with him to heaven and was eventually given special permission by God to bring one suitcase. Overjoyed, the businessman gathered his largest suitcase, filled it with pure gold bars and placed it beside his bed.

Shortly afterwards the man died and showed up at the Pearly Gates where he was greeted by St. Peter. Seeing the suitcase, St. Peter said: 'Wait, you can't bring that in here.'

The businessman explained that he had been granted permission by God. St. Peter checked out the story and confirmed: 'Yes, you have permission to bring in one case, but I must check its contents before letting it through.'

So St. Peter opened the suitcase to inspect the worldly items that the businessman found too precious to leave behind. As the lid sprang back to reveal the gold, St. Peter exclaimed: 'You brought pavement?'

A young preacher new to the area was asked by the local funeral director to conduct a graveside service at a small country cemetery. There was to be no funeral, just the graveside ceremony, because the deceased had outlived all his family and friends.

The new preacher set off early for the cemetery, but soon became lost. After a number of wrong turns, he finally arrived half an hour late. There was no sign of the hearse, and the workmen were relaxing under a nearby tree, eating their lunch. The preacher went over to the open grave and found that the vault lid was already in place. He took out his book and read the service.

As he returned to his car, he overheard one of the workmen say: 'Do you think we should tell him that's a septic tank?'

Two guys were driving down the road on a motorcycle. The driver was wearing a leather jacket that didn't have a zip and finally he stopped the bike to tell his pillion passenger: 'I can't drive anymore with the wind hitting me in my chest.' So he decided to put the jacket on backwards to block the air from hitting him.

They set off again but a mile down the road they took a corner too fast and smashed into a tree. A farmer that lived nearby was first on the scene.

Shortly afterwards a police car pulled up. Surveying the wreckage, the officer asked the farmer: 'Are either of them showing any signs of life?'

The farmer said: 'Well, that first one was until I turned his head around the right way.'

A smartly dressed woman marched into the cemetery and confronted the funeral director. 'I've looked all over the cemetery,' she raged, 'and I can't find my husband's grave anywhere.'

'What name is it, please?' asked the director.

'Alec Wildenstein.'

The director searched through the files. 'Hmm,' he said. 'There must be some mistake. All we have here is a Gloria Wildenstein.'

'No mistake,' said the woman. 'That's my husband, all right. Everything is in my name.'

Two guys walking home after a Halloween party decided to take a short cut through the cemetery for a laugh. As they picked their way through the graves, they were startled by a tapping noise coming from somewhere in the misty gloom. They looked at each other nervously, unsure whether to flee the scene or try and trace the source of the mysterious sound. Choosing the latter option but trembling with fear, they found an old man with a hammer and chisel, chipping away at one of the headstones.

'You scared us half to death,' they said, breathing a huge sigh of relief. 'For a moment we thought you were a ghost! Anyway what are you doing working here so late at night?'

The old man replied: 'They misspelled my name.'

Definitions

Abundance – a baker's ball
Accord – thick piece of string
Accrue – people who work on a ship
Acoustic – thing you use to hit the balls in snooker or pool
Affray – occurs on end of a piece of string when not looked after properly
Alibi – to purchase a back street
Annex – a former partner
Aroma – one who's done a lot of touring
Bigamist – a fog
Canopies – metal tin containing vegetables from a pod
Catastrophe – award for the feline with the nicest backside
Climate – what one does with a ladder
Coffee – person who is coughed upon
Congest – prison joke
Denial – long river in Egypt
Depend – where one can find the best swimmers
Dogma – a puppy's mother
Doldrums – Barbie's bongos
Endorse – last finisher in the Derby
Exchequer – one who counts the eggs
Extractor – farm vehicle that's been demolished
Falsehood – a wig
Flabbergasted – appalled by how much weight someone has gained
Flattery – large apartment block
Handicraft – boat ready to jump into
Hatred – dislike for the colour scarlet

45

Heroes – what a guy in a boat does
Hogwash – garage for cleaning pigs
Illegal – sick bird of prey
Indenture – contents of false teeth
Information – how geese fly
Inkling – a small penned drawing
Intent – preferred accommodation of a camper
Mandate – girl meeting older guy
Minimum – very small mother
Outlying – where politicians are when campaigning
Outmode – cut the grass faster
Parable – two male oxen
Parasites – what you see from the top of the Eiffel Tower
Postage – length of time between sending a letter and its delivery
Probate – in favour of fishing with maggots
Propaganda – elegant male goose
Relief – what trees do in spring
Satire – positioned in a chair above everyone else
Selfish – what owner of a seafood store does
Subdued – lower rank of gangster
Syntax – money collected in confession box
Syrup – stop slouching in your seat
Tandem – what the sun did to sunbathers
Timekeeper – someone who didn't return your watch
Underfoot – eleven inches
Varicose – nearby
Violin – lousy pub

Education

An inflatable boy at an inflatable school was sent to the inflatable headmaster for bringing a drawing pin to school. The headmaster told him: 'You've let me down, you've let the school down, but worst of all you've let yourself down.'

A teenage boy went off to university, but about a third of the way through the semester, he had foolishly squandered the money his parents had given him. Desperate to get more money out of his father, he came up with a cunning plan.

Phoning home one weekend, he said: 'Dad, you won't believe the educational opportunities that are available at this university! Why, they've even got a course here that will teach Fido how to talk!'

'That's incredible!' said the gullible father. 'How do I enrol him on the course?'

'Just send him down here with $1,000, and I'll make sure he gets on the course.'

So the father sent the dog and $1,000, but about two-thirds of the way through the semester, that money had also run out. The boy called his father again.

'How's Fido doing?' asked the father.

'Awesome, Dad, he's talking brilliantly. But you just won't believe this, they've had such great results with the talking dogs course that they're starting up a new one to teach the animals how to read!'

'Read?' echoed his father. 'No kidding! What do I have to do to get him on that course?'

'Just send $2,500. I'll get him on the course.'

His father duly sent the money, but at the end of the semester, the boy was faced with a problem: how to conceal from his father the fact that the dog could neither talk nor read. So the boy decided to take drastic action and shot the dog. When he arrived home, his father was waiting expectantly.

'Where's Fido?' asked the father. 'I just can't wait to hear him talk or listen to him reading something.'

'Dad,' said the boy solemnly, 'I've got some bad news. This morning, when I got out of the shower, Fido was in the living room reading the morning paper, like he usually does. Then suddenly he turned to me and asked: 'So, is your Dad still messing around with that little blonde at number 44?'

The father's face turned red with rage and he shouted: 'I hope you shot that lying dog!'

'I sure did, Dad.'

'That's my boy!'

Why do schools suspend pupils as a punishment for truancy?

The teacher called Little Johnny to her desk. She said: 'This essay you've written about your pet dog is word for word exactly the same essay as your brother has written.'

'Of course it is,' said Johnny. 'It's the same dog!'

Little Johnny's class were having an English lesson, and the teacher asked him to recite a sentence with a direct object. Johnny thought for a second and said: 'Teacher, everybody thinks you are very beautiful.'

'Why, thank you, Johnny,' she said, blushing. 'But what is the direct object?'

Johnny said: 'A good report card next month.'

Teacher: Johnny, why weren't you at school yesterday?

Johnny: Our cow was on heat, so I had to take her to the bull.
Teacher: I'm sure your father could have done that.
Johnny: No, it has to be the bull.

Teacher: Johnny, I told you to write this poem out ten times to improve your handwriting, but you've only done it seven times.
Johnny: Looks like my counting isn't too good either!

Teacher: Who invented fractions?
Johnny: Henry the Eighth.

Teacher: Where's the English Channel?
Johnny: I don't know. My TV doesn't pick it up!

Teacher: I told you to stand at the end of the line!
Johnny: I tried, but somebody was already there.

Teacher: If there are four birds on a fence and you shot one, how many would be left?
Johnny: None.
Teacher: No, Johnny. The correct answer is three.
Johnny: But, miss, if you shot one, the other three would fly away.

Two young men who had just graduated from university climbed into a taxi wearing their graduation gowns.
  'Are you graduates from the city university?' asked the cab driver.
  'Yes, sir,' they announced proudly. 'Class of '99.'
  The cabbie extended his hand. 'Class of '67.'

Genuine Student Exam Answers:
- Monotony means being married to the same person for all your life.
- What is Britain's highest award for valour in war? – Nelson's Column.
- What's a Hindu? – It lays eggs.
- Name the four seasons – Salt, mustard, pepper, vinegar.
- What changes happen to your body as you age? – When you get old, so do your bowels and you get inter-continental.
- Edward VI was a miner.
- What guarantees may a mortgage company insist on? – They'll insist you're well endowed if you're buying a house.
- What is a co-operative? It's a kind of shop that is not as dear as places like Marks and Spencer.
- To prevent contraception, wear a condominium.
- How do you keep milk from turning sour? – Keep it in the cow.
- The pistol of a flower is its only protection against insects.

- A fossil is an extinct animal. The older it is, the more extinct it is.
- Flirtation makes water safe to drink because it removes large pollutants like grit, sand, dead sheep and canoeists.
- I've said goodbye to my boyhood, now I'm looking forward to my adultery.
- Artificial insemination is when the farmer does it to the cow instead of the bull.
- Why was George Washington buried at Mount Vernon? – Because he was dead.
- When did Julius Caesar die? – A few days before his funeral.
- The moon is a planet just like the earth, only it is even deader.
- What is a turbine? – Something an Arab wears on his head.
- Dew is formed on leaves when the sun shines down on them and makes them perspire.
- What is a terminal illness? – When you are sick at the airport.
- The Caesarian Section is a district in Rome.
- A super-saturated solution is one that holds more than it can hold.
- Christians go on pilgrimage to Lord's.
- The equator is a menagerie lion running around the earth through Africa.
- Where was the Magna Carta signed? – At the bottom.
- Mushrooms always grow in damp places and so they look like umbrellas.
- Momentum: what you give a person when they are going away.
- Planet: a body of earth surrounded by sky.
- Rhubarb: a kind of celery gone bloodshot.
- Who invented King Arthur's round table? – Sir Cumference.
- What is a seizure? – A Roman emperor.
- What is the fibula? – A small lie.

The geography teacher was giving a lesson on map reading, and trying to explain to his class about latitude and longitude, degrees and minutes. Towards the end of the lesson, he asked his students: 'Suppose I ask you to meet me for lunch at latitude 19 degrees, 7 minutes north and longitude 39 degrees, 13 minutes east?'

After a confused silence, one student volunteered: 'I guess you'd be eating alone, sir!'

His teacher was horrified to hear Little Johnny swearing in school.

'I never want to hear you using language like that again. Where on earth did you pick up such foul-mouthed talk?'

'From my Dad,' said Johnny.

'Well, he should be ashamed of himself,' said the teacher. 'And it's no reason for you to talk like that. Anyway, you don't even know what it means.'

'I do!' said Johnny. 'It means the car won't start.'

A college student took a part-time job delivering pizza. On his first day, he had to deliver to a renowned skinflint.
  'What's the usual tip?' growled the customer.
  'Well,' said the student, 'this is my first delivery, but the other guys said that if I got a quarter out of you, I'd be doing great.'
  'That so?' grunted the man. 'In that case, here's five dollars.'
  'Thank you, I'll put it in my college fund.'
  'Oh, what are you studying?'
  'Applied psychology.'

Teacher: Didn't you promise to behave?
Johnny: Yes, miss.
Teacher: And didn't I promise to punish you if you didn't?
Johnny: Yes, but since I broke my promise, you don't have to keep yours.

Teacher: In 1940, what were the Poles doing in Russia?
Johnny: Holding up the telegraph lines.

Teacher: I hope I didn't see you looking at Tommy's test paper.
Johnny: I hope you didn't see me either!

Teacher: I think you copied off Tommy in that test.
Johnny: What makes you think that?
Teacher: Because when Tommy wrote 'I don't know' next to question five, you put 'Neither do I'.

Teacher: Where's your homework?
Johnny: I couldn't do it. There was too much noise at home.
Teacher: Noise? All evening? What kind of noise?
Johnny: It was the television. It was too loud. I couldn't do my homework.
Teacher: Surely you could have asked them to turn the sound down?
Johnny: No, miss. There was no one else in the room.

Teacher: If coal is selling at $6 a ton and you pay your dealer $24, how many tons will he bring you?
Johnny: A little over three tons.
Teacher: Johnny, that's not right.
Johnny: I know, miss, but they all do it.

Signs That You're A Teacher:
- You believe the staff room should be equipped with a Valium salt lick.
- You find humour in other people's stupidity.
- You want to slap the next person who says, 'Must be nice to work 8 to 3.30 and have summers free.'
- You believe chocolate is a food group.
- You believe 'shallow gene pool' should have its own box in the report card.
- When out in public you feel the urge to snap your fingers at children you don't know in order to correct their behaviour.
- You believe in aerial Prozac spraying.
- You've had your profession slammed by someone who would 'never dream' of doing your job.
- When you mention 'vegetables', you're not talking about a food group.
- You think people should be required to get a government permit before being allowed to reproduce.
- You think caffeine should be available in intravenous form.
- Meeting a child's parent instantly answers the question: 'Why is this kid like this?'

The teacher noticed that Little Johnny had arrived for school wearing only one glove.

'Why have you only got one glove?' she asked.

'Well, miss,' explained Johnny, 'I was watching the weather forecast on TV last night, and it said it was going to be sunny but on the other hand it could get quite cold.'

Little Johnny was late for school and apologised to the teacher. 'I'm sorry I'm late, miss, but I had to make my own breakfast this morning.'

'Very well, Johnny,' said the teacher, 'I'll accept your excuse, but now that you're here, perhaps you can take part in our geography test. So, Johnny, do you know where the Scottish border is?'

'Yes, miss, in bed with my mom. That's why I had to make my own breakfast.'

Mother: Why are you home from school so early?
Johnny: I was the only one who could answer a question.
Mother: Oh really? What was the question?
Johnny: Who set Miss Walsh's dress on fire?

Little Johnny was asked by his mother what he had learned in Sunday School.

'Well, Mom, our teacher told us how God sent Moses behind enemy lines on a rescue mission to lead the Israelites out of Egypt. When he got to the Red Sea, he had his engineers build a pontoon bridge and all the people walked across safely. Then he used his walkie-talkie to radio headquarters for reinforcements. They sent bombers to blow up the bridge and saved the Israelites.'

'Is that really what your teacher taught you?'

'Well, no, Mom, but if I told it the way the teacher did, you'd never believe it.'

A junior school class was being tested on the Kings and Queens of England.

'Who followed Edward VI?' asked the teacher.

'Mary,' answered a little girl at the front.

'And who followed Mary?' asked the teacher.

A boy at the back called out: 'Her little lamb!'

A child told her mother: 'My teacher thinks I'm going to be famous. She said all I have to do is mess up one more time and I'm history!'

A group of students at medical school were struggling with a physics lecture and let the professor know of their disquiet. One student rudely interrupted the lecture to ask: 'Why do we have to learn this stuff?'

'To save lives,' replied the professor.

'How does physics save lives?' the student persisted sarcastically.

The professor shot back: 'It keeps idiots like you from graduating medical school.'

A father visited his son's college. Watching students in a chemistry class, he was told they were conducting experiments to discover a universal solvent.

'What's that?' he inquired.

'A liquid that will dissolve anything,' replied the students.

'It sounds good,' said the father. 'But when you find it, what kind of container will you keep it in?'

Teacher: Well, at least there's one thing I can say about your son.

Father: What's that?

Teacher: With grades like these, he couldn't have been cheating!

The children at school were asked to talk about a recent exciting event in their lives. One small boy put up his hand and said: 'Daddy fell down a well last week.'

'My goodness!' exclaimed the teacher. 'Is he all right now?'

'He must be,' replied the boy. 'He stopped yelling for help yesterday.'

When a student returned home for Christmas, his mother asked: 'How's your history paper coming along?'

'Well, my history professor suggested I use the Internet for research and it's been extremely helpful.'

'Really?'

'Yes. So far I've located fifteen people who sell them.'

A teacher asked her young class: 'Give me a sentence about a public servant.'

One boy wrote: 'The fireman came down the ladder pregnant.'

The teacher called the boy to one side to correct him. 'Jamie,' she said, 'do you know what pregnant means?'

'Yes,' replied Jamie breezily. 'It means carrying a child.'

When a woman decided to improve her computer skills, she threw herself into the task with enthusiasm, borrowing two or three instructional books from the library each week.

After about a month, the librarian commented: 'Wow! You must be getting really knowledgeable about this stuff.'

'Thanks. What makes you say that?'

'Well,' said the librarian, 'only one of the books you're taking out this week has "For Dummies" in the title.'

A professor was delivering a lecture to his philosophy class. He picked up a jar, filled it with golf balls and asked the students if they thought the jar was full. They agreed that it was. Then he picked up two handfuls of pebbles and poured them into the jar. As he shook the jar, the pebbles dropped into the gaps between the golf balls. He then asked the students if they thought the jar was full. They said it was. Next he picked up a tin of sand and poured that into the jar. Once again he asked the students if they thought the jar was full. They agreed that it was.

The professor then picked up two cans of beer and poured them into the jar. 'Right,' he said. 'I want you to appreciate that the contents of this jar represent your life. The golf balls represent the essential things – your family, your health, your friends. If everything else were lost and only they remained, your life would still be full. The pebbles represent the other important things, such as your house and your job. The sand represents everything else – the minutiae of everyday life, things about which we sometimes worry too much. If you put the sand into the jar first, there's no room for the pebbles or the golf balls. But finally, remember: no matter how full your life might seem, there's always room for a couple of beers.'

The schoolchildren had all been photographed and their teacher was trying to persuade them each to buy a copy of the group picture. 'Just think,' she said, 'how nice it will be to look at when you are all grown up and you can say, "There's Jenny, she's a lawyer" or "There's David, he's a doctor."'

A small voice piped up at the back of the room: 'And there's teacher, she's dead.'

The teacher asked her class whether anyone could remember the chemical formula for water.

'Sure,' said one student. 'It's HIJKLMNO.'

'It's what?' said the teacher angrily.

'Well, you told us last week it was H to O.'

Having seen their twelve-year-old son finish bottom of the class in every subject, a couple decided to send him to a special tutor. Six weeks later, they asked the tutor how he was doing.

'He's getting straight As,' said the tutor.

'That's great,' said the relieved parents.

'Mind you,' added the tutor. 'His Bs are still a bit wonky.'

A nursery school teacher was walking her class along the road when a fire engine roared past. Sitting in the front seat was a Dalmatian.

The children immediately started debating the dog's duties.

'They use him to keep the crowds back,' said one.

'No,' said another. 'The dog's for good luck.'

A third child brought the argument to a close. 'They use the dogs,' she said firmly, 'to find the fire hydrants.'

You Know You've Been At College Too Long When . . .

- You consider McDonald's to be 'real food'.
- You actually enjoy doing laundry at home.
- Two miles is not too far to walk to a party.
- You know the pizza delivery boy by name.
- You go to sleep when it's light and get up when it's dark.
- You live for getting mail.
- Rearranging your room is your favourite pastime.
- It feels weird to take a shower without shoes on.
- You start thinking and sounding like your roommate.
- Whole wars have taken place in the outside world without you noticing.
- You wear the same socks three days in a row and think nothing of it.
- Half the time you don't wake up in your own bed.
- Looking out the window is a form of entertainment.
- Prank phone calls become funny again.

A small boy was struggling with his maths homework. After a while, he turned to his father and said: 'Dad, can you help me?'

The father said: 'I could. But it wouldn't be right, would it?'

'Probably not,' said the boy. 'But you could at least give it a try.'

As a kindergarten class settled down to their colouring books, one little boy went up to the teacher and said: 'I ain't got no crayons, miss.'

'No, Ricky,' said the teacher, 'you mean, I don't have any crayons. You don't have any crayons. We don't have any crayons. They don't have any crayons. Do you see what I'm getting at?'

'Not really, miss. What happened to all them crayons?'

'What's your father's occupation?' asked the school secretary filling in the necessary forms on the first day of a new academic year.

'He's a magician,' said a new boy at school.

'How interesting! What's his favourite trick?'

'He saws people in half.'

'Gosh! Now, next question. Any brothers or sisters?'

'Yes. One half-brother and two half-sisters.'

A linguistics professor was lecturing his class. 'In English a double negative forms a positive. In some languages, however, such as Russian, a double negative is still a negative. But there is no language where a double positive can form a negative.'

A student at the back called out: 'Yeah, right.'

On the first day of college, the dean addressed the students. 'The female dormitory,' he stated, 'will be out of bounds for all male students, and the male dormitory to all female students. Anybody caught breaking this rule will be fined $20 the first time, $60 the second time and $150 the third time. Any questions?'

One male student asked: 'How much for a season ticket?'

A group of third, fourth and fifth graders accompanied by two teachers went on a field trip to the local racecourse to learn about thoroughbred racehorses. During the tour some of the children wanted to go to the toilet, so it was decided that the girls would go with one teacher and the boys would go with the other.

As the teacher assigned to the boys waited outside the men's toilet, one of the boys came out and told her that he couldn't reach the urinal. Having no choice, the teacher went inside and began hoisting the little boys up by their armpits, one by one. As she lifted one up by the armpits, she couldn't help but notice that he was unusually well-endowed for an elementary school child. 'I guess you must be in the fifth,' she said.

'No, ma'am,' he replied, 'I'm in the seventh, riding Silver Bullet. Thanks for the lift anyway.'

On his first day at a new school, a headmaster was making his rounds when he heard a terrible commotion from one of the classrooms. Marching in, he spotted one boy, taller than the others, who seemed to be making most of the noise. So he seized the lad, dragged him to the hall, and told him to wait there until he was excused.

Returning to the classroom, the headmaster restored order and lectured the class for ten minutes on good behaviour.

'Now,' he concluded. 'Any questions?'

One girl stood up timidly and asked: 'Please, sir. May we have our teacher back?'

'Yes, where exactly is your teacher?'

The girl replied: 'He's in the hall, sir.'

At a school careers' evening, a fifteen-year-old boy was asked what he wanted to do when he left school. 'I want to be a stamp collector,' he replied.

The careers advisor was sceptical. 'What about teaching? There's always a shortage of teachers.'

'No, I want to be a stamp collector.'

'Or how about studying law? There's good money to be made as a lawyer.'

'No, I want to be a stamp collector.'

'Or journalism? That can lead to all manner of different career opportunities – public relations, sports writing, a career in television . . .'

'No, I want to be a stamp collector.'

The careers advisor threw up his hands in despair. 'But don't you see, philately will get you nowhere!'

A boy was sitting a school test that consisted solely of either/or questions. As he hadn't done any revision, he decided that tossing a coin was as good a way as any of answering the questions. If the coin came up 'heads', he would tick answer 'A'; if it came up 'tails', he would tick answer 'B'.

Using this technique, he raced through the paper and chose to use the remaining time re-reading the paper, tossing the coin again, and occasionally cursing under his breath.

As the swearing became audible, the teacher came over to ask if there was a problem.

'It's OK,' said the boy. 'I finished the test a while back. Now I'm just checking my answers.'

The kindergarten teacher noticed a little puddle under Mary's chair. 'Oh, Mary!' said the teacher. 'You should have put your hand up.'

'I did,' said Mary. 'But it still trickled through my fingers.'

A small boy was dawdling all the way to school.

'Hurry up,' said his mother. 'You'll be late!'

'What's the rush?' he asked. 'They're open till 3.30.'

In junior school science class the teacher wanted to instruct his young pupils about the evils of alcohol, so he produced an experiment involving a glass of water, a glass of whiskey, and two worms.

'Now, children,' he said. 'Watch the worms.'

And with that he put the first worm into the glass of water and saw it writhe about. Then he put the second worm into the glass of whiskey and saw it contort in pain before sinking to the bottom, dead as a doornail.

'So what lesson can we learn from this experiment?' he asked.

A boy at the back raised his hand and said: 'Drink whiskey and you won't get worms!'

Families

A couple were admiring their garden from the kitchen window. The wife said: 'Sooner or later, you're going to have to make a proper scarecrow to keep the birds off the flower beds.'

'What's wrong with the one we've got?' asked the husband.

'Nothing. But mother's arms are getting tired.'

A boy promised his girlfriend: 'We're going to have a great time Saturday. I got three tickets for the big game.'

'Why do we need three?' she asked.

'One for your father, one for your mother, and one for your kid sister!'

A husband was late home from work one evening. 'I'm sure he's having an affair,' said his wife to her mother.

'Why do you always think the worst?' said the mother. 'Maybe he's just been in a car crash.'

An American man went on vacation to the Middle East with most of his family, including his mother-in-law. While they were visiting Jerusalem, the mother-in-law died. With the death certificate in hand, he went to the American Consulate Office to make arrangements to send the body back to the United States for proper burial. The Consul warned that to send a body back to the US for burial was an extremely expensive business and could cost as much as $10,000. 'In most cases,' advised the Consul, 'the person responsible for the remains normally decides to bury the body here. That would only cost $300.'

The man gave it some careful thought before answering: 'I don't mind how much it's going to cost to send the body back home; that's what I want to do.'

The Consul remarked: 'Considering the difference in price, you must have been extremely fond of your mother-in-law.'

'No, it's not that,' said the man. 'You see, there was a case many years ago of a person that was buried here in Jerusalem. On the third day he rose from the dead. I just can't take that chance!'

A modern mother was explaining to her little girl about the pictures in the family photo album. 'This is the geneticist with your surrogate mother and here's your sperm donor and your father's clone. This is me holding you when you were just a frozen embryo.'

'Mummy,' said the little girl. 'Who is the lady with the worried look on her face?'

'That's your aunt Kim. She's the family genealogist.'

Two men were walking down the street when one spotted six men kicking and punching his mother-in-law.

'Are you going to help?' asked his friend.

'No,' he said. 'Six should be enough.'

A little girl said: 'Daddy, you're the boss of the house, right?'

'Yes, sweetheart,' he said, 'I'm the boss of the house.'

'And I know why you're the boss of the house, Daddy.'

'Why's that?'

'Because Mummy put you in charge.'

A man answered the phone. 'Yes, Mother,' he sighed. 'Listen, I've had a long day. Jane has been in one of her awkward moods . . . Yes, I know I should be firmer with her, but it's not easy. You know what she's like . . . Yes, I remember you warned me . . . Yes, I remember you told me she was a vile creature who would make my life a misery . . . Yes, I remember you begged me not to marry her. You were right, OK? You want to speak to her? I'll put her on.'

He put down the phone and called to his wife in the next room: 'Jane, your mother wants to talk to you.'

A lawyer cabled his client overseas: 'Your mother-in-law passed away in her sleep. Shall we order burial, embalming or cremation?'

Back came the reply: 'Take no chances – order all three.'

A couple were going out for a rare night on the town. They put on their best clothes, called a cab, and put the cat out. The taxi arrived but as the couple walked out of the front door, the cat shot between their legs, back into the house and up the stairs. Knowing that the cat would wreck the house while they were gone, the husband ran upstairs to chase the cat out again while the wife waited in the taxi.

Since she didn't want the cab driver to know that the house would be left unoccupied, the woman explained to him: 'My husband is just going upstairs to say goodbye to my mother.'

A few minutes later, the husband reappeared and climbed into the taxi. 'Sorry I took so long,' he said. 'Stupid old thing was hiding under the bed, and I had to poke her with a coat hanger to get her to come out!'

A woman came from a large family of five sisters and four brothers. One day she was looking through the family photo album when she noticed that in picture after picture, all of the children were dressed in matching outfits. Later, she asked her mother why everyone – even the baby – was dressed identically.

Her mother replied: 'When we had just four children, I dressed you alike so that we wouldn't lose any of you. Then when the other six came along, I started dressing you alike so that we wouldn't pick up any that didn't belong to us!'

A little boy greeted his grandma with a hug and said: 'I'm so happy to see you, Grandma. Now maybe Daddy will do the trick he has been promising us.'

'What trick's that?' she asked.

'Well,' said the little boy excitedly, 'I heard Daddy tell Mummy that he would climb the walls if you came to visit us again.'

A big game hunter went on safari with his wife and mother-in-law. One evening, the husband and wife were sitting around the camp fire having supper when she realised that her mother was missing. The hunter picked up his rifle and, with his wife close behind, set off into the jungle to look for the missing woman. After searching for over an hour, they finally spotted her backed up against a cliff with a huge lion facing her.

'What are we going to do?' shrieked the wife.

'Nothing,' said the husband. 'The lion got himself into this mess . . .'

A little girl noticed that her mother had a few grey hairs appearing on her head. 'Why is that?' she asked.

'Because,' explained the mother, 'every time you do something naughty and make me unhappy, one of my hairs turns white.'

The child thought for a moment and said: 'Is that why all of Grandma's hair is white? You must have been really hard work!'

Reading a letter at the breakfast table, a wife suddenly looked suspiciously at her husband. 'Henry, I've just received a letter from my mother saying she isn't accepting our invitation to come and stay, as we don't appear to want her. What does she mean? I told you to write and say that she was to come at her own convenience. You did write, didn't you?'

'Er, yes,' said the husband. 'But I couldn't spell "convenience", so I made it "risk".'

The scoutmaster was surprised to see a young boy arrive for summer camp with an umbrella.

'Why did you bring an umbrella to camp?' he asked.

The boy sighed: 'Did you ever have a mother?'

A teenager had just passed his driving test and asked his father, who was a church minister, whether he could borrow his car.

'Yes, you may borrow my car, if you study the Bible, work hard at college and get your hair cut.'

A month later, the lad asked again whether he could borrow the car.

His father said: 'I'm very proud of you, son. You've been studying your Bible and your college results are excellent. But the only thing is, you still haven't had your hair cut.'

The lad replied: 'I've been thinking about that. You know, Samson had long hair, so did Moses, Noah, and even Jesus.'

'That's very true,' said the father. 'And they walked everywhere.'

Two fathers were discussing their daughters. 'I don't know whether to send my daughter to college or not,' said one. 'Is it worth it? What do you think?'

The other said: 'Well, it cost me $1,000 a year to send Debbie to college and it took her four years to find a husband. I spent $300 to send Kelly to the beach for two weeks and she came home married. I recommend the beach.'

Jim was plagued by his spiteful mother-in-law who, much to his dismay, lived with the family. Each morning, just as he was about to leave for work, the mother-in-law would take him to one side and hiss: 'If you don't treat my daughter right after I'm dead, I'll dig up from the grave and haunt you!'

It was the same when Jim came home for lunch. The mother-in-law would sidle up to him and whisper menacingly: 'If you don't treat my daughter right after I'm dead, I'll dig up from the grave and haunt you!'

And at night, she would collar him on his way to bed and snarl: 'If you don't treat my daughter right after I'm dead, I'll dig up from the grave and haunt you!'

He recounted his awful life with the old woman to a friend who, after not seeing Jim for a couple of months, asked him how his mother-in-law was feeling.

'She isn't feeling anything,' said Jim. 'She died three weeks ago.'

'Aren't you worried about her ominous threat?' asked the friend.

'Not really,' replied Jim, 'but just to be sure, I buried her face down. Let her dig!'

Two sisters came home from school in floods of tears. 'Whatever is the matter?' asked their mother.

The first sister sobbed; 'The kids at school make fun of my big feet.'

'There, there,' soothed the mother. 'Your feet aren't that big.' She turned to the second sister. 'Now why are you crying?'

'Because I've been invited to a ski party, and I haven't got any skis.'

'That's OK,' said the mother. 'You can borrow your sister's shoes.'

A census taker in a rural area went up to a farmhouse and knocked on the door. When a woman answered, he asked her the names and ages of her children.

She said: 'Let's see now, there are the twins, Billy and Bobby, they're seventeen. And the twins, Seth and Beth, they're sixteen. And the twins, Benny and Jenny, they're fifteen.'

'Wait a minute!' said the census taker. 'Did you get twins every time?'

'Heck no,' answered the woman. 'There were hundreds of times we didn't get nothin'.'

Fashion

Harry wanted a new suit so he bought a nice piece of cloth and tried to find a good tailor. The first tailor he visited looked at the cloth, measured Harry, then told him there was not enough cloth to make a suit.

Harry found this hard to accept, so he went to the tailor next door who measured both Harry and the cloth before announcing that there was enough cloth to make a three-piece suit.

A week later, Harry returned to collect his suit and noticed that the tailor's son was wearing trousers made of the same cloth. Puzzled, Harry asked: 'How come you have been able to make a three-piece suit for me and trousers for your son when the chap next door could not even make a suit?'

'Simple,' said the tailor. 'The guy next door has two sons.'

Did you hear about the second-hand Indian clothing store called Whose Sari Now?

An inventor took his latest idea to a bra manufacturer. He said. 'I've come up with a new bra, specially designed for middle-aged women. I call it the "sheepdog bra".'

'Why do you call it that?' asked the manufacturer.

'Because it rounds them up and points them in the right direction!'

A wife said to her husband: 'Darling, I need a new dress.'

'What's wrong with the one you've got?' he said.

'Well, it's too long and, besides, the veil keeps getting in my eyes.'

A woman tried to board a bus but her skirt was so tight that she couldn't make the step up. So she reached behind her, lowered her zip and tried again. Still the skirt was too tight. So again she reached behind her, lowered her zip a little more and tried to negotiate the step. But still the skirt was too tight. Determined to catch this bus, she once more reached behind her, lowered the zip a little and attempted to climb aboard. Then suddenly she felt two hands on her butt, helping her on to the bus.

She turned around angrily and told the man behind her: 'Sir, I don't know you well enough for you to behave in such a manner.'

The man replied: 'Lady, I don't know you well enough for you to unzip my fly three times either!'

Why do long dresses make women look shorter when short dresses make men look longer?

A man walked into a shoe shop and tried on a pair of shoes.

'How do they feel?' asked the sales assistant.

'A bit tight.'

The assistant bent down to check the shoes and said: 'Try pulling the tongue out.'

'They thtill feelth a bith tighth.'

On a day trip to Amsterdam, a young man fell madly in love with a Dutch girl and after a whirlwind romance they got married. For the first six months they were blissfully happy but then she was stricken down with a mysterious foot disease, which meant that she had to wear special inflatable Dutch shoes. Her husband hoped that the inflatable shoes would cure her illness but sadly her condition continued to deteriorate until one day he was devastated to learn that she had popped her clogs.

62

Where do socks go when they got lost in the dryer?

A man told his friend: 'My wife only has two complaints: nothing to wear and not enough closet space.'

The manager of a ladies' dress shop realised that it was time to give one of her sales staff a pep talk. 'Paula,' she said, 'your figures are the lowest in the department by a long way. In fact, unless you can improve your sales record soon, I'm afraid I'll have to let you go.'

'I'm sorry, ma'am,' said a humbled Paula. 'Can you offer me any advice on how to do better?'

'Well,' said the manager, 'there is an old trick I can tell you about. It sounds silly, but it's worked for me in the past. Get hold of a dictionary and go through it until you find a word that has particular power for you. Memorise it, work it into your sales pitch whenever it seems appropriate, and you'll be amazed at the results.'

Sure enough, Paula's sales figures shot up, and at the end of the month the manager called her in again, this time to congratulate her.

'Did you try my little trick?' she asked.

Paula nodded. 'It took me a whole weekend to find the right word, but I did in the end.'

'And what is it?'

'Fantastic.'

'Yes, that's an excellent word,' said the manager encouragingly. 'And how have you been using it?'

'Well, my first customer on Monday was a woman who told me her little girl had just been accepted at the most exclusive prep school in the city. I said, "Fantastic." She went on to tell me how her daughter always got straight As and was the most popular girl in class. I said, "Fantastic", and she bought $500 worth of clothing.

'My next customer said she needed a formal dress for the spring ball at the country club, which she was organising. I said, "Fantastic." She went on to tell me she had the best figure of anyone on the committee and that her husband makes the most money. "Fantastic", I said, and she not only bought a $2,000 designer gown, but hundreds of dollars of accessories. It's been like that all week: the customers keep boasting, I keep saying, "Fantastic", and they keep buying!'

'Excellent work, Paula,' said the manager. 'You're a credit to the department. Just as a matter of interest, what did you used to say to customers before you discovered your power word?'

Paula shrugged. 'It was usually, "Who gives a damn?"'

Did you hear about the man who put on a pair of clean socks every day?
– By the end of the week he couldn't get his shoes on.

A man said to his friend: 'How come you're only wearing one glove? Did you lose one?'

The friend said: 'No, I found one.'

If love is blind, why is lingerie so popular?

A man walked into a shoe shop and asked for a pair of shoes, size 8.

The sales assistant said: 'Are you sure, sir? You look like a size 12 to me.'

'Just bring me a size 8,' insisted the customer.

So the assistant fetched a pair of size 8 shoes and the man squeezed his feet into them with obvious discomfort. He then stood up in the shoes, but with considerable pain.

'Listen,' he explained, 'I've lost my house to the taxman, I live with my mother-in-law, my daughter ran off with my best friend, and my son just told me he's gay. The only pleasure I have left is to come home at night and take my shoes off!'

If leather jackets get ruined in the rain, why aren't cows affected when they are out in the rain a lot?

A young man went to a lake for a swim but when he got there, he realised he had forgotten his swimming trunks. Since there was nobody about, he decided to jump in naked. An hour later, he climbed out and was just about to get dressed when he saw two old ladies approaching. He hastily grabbed a small bucket, held it over his privates and breathed a huge sigh of relief. But when the old ladies started to stare at him, he felt decidedly awkward.

One said to him: 'You know, I have a special gift. I can read minds. And I bet I can read yours.'

The young man scoffed: 'So you reckon you know what I'm thinking, do you?'

'Yes,' she said. 'Right now, I bet you think that the bucket you're holding has a bottom.'

A man walked into an army surplus store and asked if they had any camouflage trousers.

'Yes, we have,' replied the assistant, 'but we can't find them!'

Food

A little-known fact about William Tell is that apart from being an expert with the crossbow, he was an accomplished chef. One day he had prepared a new dish for his Swiss friends, but, ever the perfectionist, he felt there was something missing with the sauce.

'More berries in the sauce?' he suggested.

'No, no,' they said. 'I think you have just the right amount of berries.'

'More salt, then?'

'No, the amount of salt is perfect,' they insisted.

'Herbs, that's it,' he said triumphantly. 'I should have put in more herbs. What do you think?'

'Hmm,' they pondered, tasting the sauce. 'Perhaps only thyme, Will Tell.'

Two sausages were sizzling in a pan. One looked at the other and said: 'It's hot in here.' The other one said: 'My God, a talking sausage!'

What do you get if you divide the circumference of a pumpkin by its diameter? – Pumpkin pi.

A family of tomatoes were walking down the street but after a while the little boy tomato started to lag behind. The father tomato turned round and called: 'Ketchup!'

An overweight woman was put on a diet by her doctor. He said: 'I want you to eat regularly for two days, then skip a day, and repeat the procedure for two weeks. The next time you come to me, you should have lost seven pounds.'

When the woman returned two weeks later, she had lost 19 pounds. The doctor was dumbfounded. 'Did you follow my instructions?' he asked.

'Yes,' she said, 'but I thought I was going to drop dead that third day.'

'From hunger, you mean?'

'No, from skipping.'

Good King Wenceslas rang his local pizza parlour. 'The usual, please,' he said. 'Deep pan, crisp and even.'

If you sent a cauliflower through the Internet, would it arrive as e-coli?

A millionaire was driving along in his stretch limo when he saw a humble man eating grass by the roadside. Ordering his chauffeur to stop, he wound down the window and called to the man: 'Why are you eating grass?'

'Because, sir, we don't have the money for real food.'

'Come with me then,' said the millionaire.

'But, sir, I have a wife and six children.'

'That's fine – bring them all along.'

The man and his family climbed gratefully into the limo. 'Sir, you are kind. How can I ever thank you for taking all of us with you, offering us a new home?'

'No, you don't understand,' said the millionaire. 'The grass at my home is four feet high. No lawn mower will cut it!'

What does cheese say when it has its picture taken?

A cannibal king in a remote jungle territory had a particular taste for missionaries. Somehow their meat always tasted sweeter. And the king was an expert on food, for there was nothing he enjoyed more than sitting down to a sumptuous banquet.

On one particular evening he was tucking in heartily to the huge platter of thinly sliced missionary before him. It was easy to see why he weighed in at over twenty-five stone. Whilst his people were happy to see the king enjoying himself – he had a ferocious temper when things did not meet with his approval – they were fervently hoping that there would be a few scraps left over for them. For whereas the king was decidedly rotund, his subjects were thin from near starvation. So with each slice of meat that he devoured, their hearts sank a little further. It was beginning to look as if there would be nothing left.

The natives began to mutter among themselves. 'It doesn't look good,' said the cannibal who had felled the missionary with a poison dart. 'He is going to eat the lot! It's always the same when we bring him back one of these religious types.'

'He certainly has a liking for these men of God,' agreed a fellow subject. 'There's obviously something about their delicate skin.'

'Well, it's simply not good enough,' said the first native, becoming increasingly irate. 'It's about time we followed the example of the Watumbabibi tribe down river and refused to hunt until the king shows us more consideration and allows us a fair helping of his missionary meals.'

'You mean,' queried his fellow cannibal, 'that we should ask him to implement some kind of Prophet-sharing scheme?'

A husband took his young daughter to the grocery store where, in addition to the carefully prepared list of healthy items, they bought a box of sugar-rich cookies.

When they arrived home and unpacked the items, his wife immediately glared at the cookies.

'It's OK, honey,' he said. 'This box of cookies has one-third fewer calories than usual.'

'How come?' she asked.

'Because we ate a third on the way home.'

When the plums dry on your tree, it's time to prune.

After a harrowing day, a housewife answered the phone and was relieved to hear a friendly voice on the other end. 'Oh, Mother,' she sobbed, 'I've had the most terrible day. I sprained my ankle this morning and so I haven't been able to do any shopping. The washing machine's broken, the baby won't eat, the house is a mess, and I'm supposed to be hosting a dinner party tonight.'

'Now, don't you worry about a thing. I'll be over in half an hour. I'll do the shopping, clean the house and cook your dinner. I'll feed the baby and I'll call a repairman to fix the washing machine. I'll do everything. And I'll call Ray at the office and tell him he ought to come home and help.'

'Ray? Who's Ray?'

'Ray – your husband! This is 466 3980?'

'No, this is 466 3880.'

'Oh.'

'Does this mean you're not coming over?!'

What cheese is made backwards? Edam.

Two students were talking about food.

'I've got a cookery book,' said one. 'But I've never been able to use it.'

'Why not?' asked the other. 'Were the recipes too complicated?'

'Not really, but each one began the same way: take a clean dish . . .'

If carrots help your eyesight, how come you see so many dead rabbits by the side of the road?

A man went into a butcher's shop and asked for half a rabbit.

'I'm sorry,' said the butcher. 'I don't want to split hares.'

What do you get if you cross a door knocker with some courgettes, tomatoes, onions, and garlic? – Rat-a-tat-a-touille.

Why did the raisin go out with the prune? – Because she couldn't find a date.

Two bags of crisps were striding along the road when a driver stopped to offer them a lift.

'No, it's OK,' they said, 'we're Walkers.'

In the window of a seafood restaurant, a man spotted a sign saying 'Lobster Tails $2 each.'

Sensing a bargain, he went inside and asked the waitress why they were so cheap. 'They must be very short tails for that price,' he suggested.

'No,' replied the waitress. 'They're normal length.'

'Then they must be pretty old.'

'No, they're fresh today.'

'There must be something wrong with them . . .'

'No, they're just regular lobster tails.'

'OK,' said the man, 'for two dollars I'll have one.'

So the waitress took the man's money, sat him down and said: 'Once upon a time there was a big red lobster . . .'

What did the grape say when it was trodden on? – Nothing. It just let out a little wine.

People who eat metal paper fastenings have a staple diet.

Fork: Who was that ladle I saw you with last night?

Spoon: That was no ladle. That was my knife.

Grossly overweight, a man was bullied by his work colleagues into going on a diet. For three weeks, he resisted temptation, even changing his route to work to avoid his favourite bakery. But then one day, to the horror of his workmates, he turned up at the office clutching a huge chocolate cake.

When his colleagues berated him, he was quick to offer an explanation. 'I accidentally drove by the bakery this morning and there were loads of tasty treats in the window. I felt this was fate, so I prayed to God, saying: "If you want me to have one of those delicious chocolate cakes, show me a sign – let there be a parking space directly in front of the bakery. And sure enough, the eighth time around the block, there it was!'

Did you know it takes 40 pigs to make 4,000 sausages? Isn't it amazing what you can teach them?

What food will reduce a woman's sex drive by 50 per cent? – Wedding cake.

When a clock is hungry, does it go back four seconds?

A husband was standing on the bathroom scales, desperately holding his stomach in.

His wife, thinking he was trying to reduce his weight, remarked: 'I don't think that will help.'

68

'It does,' he said. 'It's the only way I can read the numbers!'

What part of a fish is a fish stick?

Diner: I can't eat such a tough steak. Call the manager!
Waiter: It's no use. He won't eat it either.

'How were your sandwiches today, darling?' asked the wife as her husband returned home from work.
    'They were fine,' he replied.
    'Are you sure they tasted OK?'
    'Yes, they were really good.'
    'You don't feel ill at all?'
    'No, never felt better. Why?'
    'Oh, it's just that tomorrow you're going to have to clean your shoes with fish paste.'

A man went into a fishmonger's carrying a trout under his arm.
    'Do you make fishcakes?' he asked.
    'Yes, we do,' replied the fishmonger.
    'Great,' said the man. 'It's his birthday.'

A Zen Master walked up to a hot-dog seller and said: 'Make me one with everything.'

An ice cream man was found lying on the floor of his van covered in hundreds and thousands. Police say he topped himself.

One day a little girl was watching her mother prepare roast beef. The mother cut off the ends, wrapped it in string, seasoned it, and placed it in the roasting tin. The girl asked her mother why she always cut off the ends of the roast. She replied that she didn't really know why – but it was the way her mother had done it.
    That night, grandma came to dinner and the little girl and her mother asked her why she had always cut the ends off the roast before putting it in the oven. Grandma replied that she didn't know why – but that was the way her mother had done it.
    Great grandmother was very old and confined to a nursing home. But the next time the little girl, her mother and her grandma went to visit, they asked her the same question. 'Why did you cut the ends off the roast before cooking?'
    Great grandmother looked at them in surprise and explained simply: 'We were poor and had a small oven in those days. I cut off the ends so the roast would fit.'

wo biscuits were walking down the street when one was crushed by a passing car. The other said: 'Crumbs!'

A blacksmith living in a remote German village was cut off during a particularly harsh winter. With the roads impassable, he was unable to get to the nearest shops for food supplies. The weather showed no signs of abating and his plight became increasingly desperate. Eventually with no one else to turn to, he contacted his brother who lived over 200 miles away in Munich and asked him to send a food parcel by helicopter.

'What sort of food would you like me to send?' asked the brother.

'Some bread, some milk, oh, and some sausage. Definitely some sausage. It has been weeks since I have tasted a good German sausage.'

The brother promised to send the parcel immediately but two days later it had still to arrive. 'I don't know how much longer I can go on,' wailed the blacksmith. 'I am tired and frail, I have no gas or electricity, snow is piled against the front door, and the wurst is yet to come!'

A man ordered a takeaway pizza. The waiter said: 'Shall I cut it into six pieces or twelve?'

'Six please. I could never eat twelve.'

What is the best way to make an apple crumble? – Torture it for ten minutes.

Wife: The two things I cook best are meatloaf and apple pie.
Husband: And which is this?

Did you hear about the man who bought a plate with four corners so he could enjoy a square meal?

According to popular legend, Mrs Descartes was throwing a lavish New Year's Party to celebrate the arrival of 1630. She had been making preparations for weeks and had invited all the local dignitaries. Shortly before the guests began to turn up, she issued her philosopher husband Rene with strict instructions regarding the pastries on the pantry table. To make sure that the guests did not leave immediately after midnight, she insisted that the pastries should not be eaten until the early hours. In fact she decided that an hour into the New Year was the ideal time to allow the guests to tuck into her cooking and keep the party in full swing. Rene was given the job of guarding the pastries until that time. Although deep in thought, he agreed to mind the table.

As the party started to warm up, Descartes found himself involved in an absorbing philosophical discussion with Van Dyck about art and life in general. To hear each other better, they drifted away from the drawing room and towards the pantry. With Descartes lost in thought, Van Dyck helped himself to one of the precious pastries even though it was barely ten o'clock. When Descartes suddenly realised what the artist had done, he discreetly wrote a message on a napkin and handed it to Van Dyck so as not to attract his wife's attention. Van Dyck was eager to see what gem of inspiration Descartes' brilliant mind had come up with now. However before Van Dyck could read it, they were interrupted and he had to stuff the napkin in his pocket to read later.

The following morning Van Dyck opened the napkin to discover what thought-provoking message his friend had left him. Sure enough, there scrawled in Descartes' hand was an expression of timeless insight: 'I think they're for 1 am.'

Health

When a patient came round after an operation, the surgeon told her: 'I'm afraid we're going to have to open you up again. You see, unfortunately, I left my rubber gloves inside you.'

The patient said: 'Well, if that's all it is, I'd prefer you to leave me alone and I'll buy you a new pair.'

A man went to see his doctor to see if he could prescribe something for a heavy cold. The doctor gave him some tablets, but they didn't work. On his next visit, the doctor gave him an injection, but that didn't work either.

On his third visit, the doctor told the man: 'Go home and take a hot bath. As soon as you finish, open all the windows and stand in the draught.'

'But doctor if I do that, I'll catch pneumonia.'

'I know,' said the doctor. 'But I can cure pneumonia.'

A man accidentally swallowed all the tiles from a Scrabble set. His doctor said the problem would eventually sort itself out, but not in so many words.

Old Doctor Morris went to see a woman patient at her home. 'Could you fetch me a hammer from the garage?' he asked the woman's husband.

The husband fetched the hammer.

'Right,' said the doctor a couple of minutes later. 'Now I'd like you to get me some pliers, a screwdriver and a hacksaw.'

The husband became alarmed at the last request. 'Just exactly what are you going to do to my wife?' he asked.

The doctor replied: 'Nothing until I can get my medical bag open.'

How do you prevent a summer cold? – Catch it in the winter.

Feeling stressed out, a man decided to take a long hot bath, but just as he had made himself comfortable, the front doorbell rang. The man climbed out of the tub, wrapped a large towel around him, wrapped his head in a smaller towel, put on his slippers, and went to the door. It was a salesman trying to sell him brushes. Slamming the door, the man returned to his hot bath.

Two minutes later, the doorbell rang again. The man climbed out of the tub, wrapped a large towel around him, wrapped his head in a smaller towel, put on his slippers, and trudged downstairs to the door. It was an energy company trying to get him to change his power supply. Slamming the door, the man returned to his hot bath.

Five minutes later, the doorbell rang again. On went the slippers and towels, but as he made for the bathroom door, he slipped on a wet spot and hurt his back in falling against the hard porcelain of the tub.

Cursing under his breath, the man struggled into his street clothes and, with every move causing a stabbing pain, he drove to the doctor. After examining him, the doctor said: 'You know, you've been lucky. There are no bones broken. But you need to relax. Why don't you go home and take a long hot bath?'

A man walked into a doctor's office with a lettuce leaf sticking out of his ear.
     The doctor said: 'Hmmm, that's strange.'
     The man said: 'That's just the tip of the iceberg.'

A newly hired nurse listened while a hospital surgeon doing his rounds yelled: 'Typhoid! Tetanus! Measles!'
     'Why does he keep doing that?' she asked a colleague.
     'Oh, he just likes to call the shots around here.'

'Doctor, doctor, please hurry. My son swallowed a razor-blade.'
     'Don't panic, I'm coming immediately. Have you done anything yet?'
     'Yes, I shaved with the electric razor.'

'Doctor, doctor, I've got amnesia.'
     'Just go home and forget all about it.'

'Doctor, doctor, I suffer from attention deficit disorder.'
     'Sorry, what did you say?'

'Doctor, doctor, I can't stop stealing things.'
   'Take these pills for a week and if they don't work, get me a digital camera.'

'Doctor, doctor, my wife thinks she's a lift.'
   'Tell her to come in.'
   'I can't. She doesn't stop at this floor.'

'Doctor, doctor, I can't pronounce my Fs, Ts or Hs.'
   'You can't say fairer than that.'

'Doctor, doctor, I keep thinking I'm a packet of savoury biscuits.'
   'You must be crackers!'

'Doctor, doctor, I think I'm a yo-yo.'
   'Are you stringing me along?'

'Doctor, doctor, I keep thinking there are two of me.'
   'One at a time please.'

'Doctor, doctor, my baby's swallowed a bullet.'
   'Well, don't point him at anyone till I get there.'

'Doctor, doctor, I keep thinking I'm a spoon.'
   'Sit there and don't stir.'

'Doctor, doctor, I've just swallowed a pen.'
   'Sit down and write your name.'

'Doctor, doctor, I feel awful.'
   'What are the symptoms?'
   'It's a cartoon show with yellow people.'

'Doctor, doctor, my son has swallowed a pen, what should I do?'
   'Use a pencil till I get there.'

'Doctor, doctor, what does it mean if my feet smell and my nose runs?'
   'You're built upside down.'

Over a round of golf, two surgeons began talking about work.
   'I operated on Mr Goldberg the other day,' said one.
   'What for?'
   'About $19,000.'

'What did he have?'
'Oh, about $19,000.'

'Doctor, doctor, I've got a cricket ball stuck up my backside.'
  'How's that?'
  'Don't you start!'

'Doctor, doctor, I feel like a needle.'
  'Hmmm. I see your point.'

'Doctor, doctor, I think I'm a greyhound.'
  'Take one of these every two laps.'

'Doctor, doctor, I keep thinking I'm a bee.'
  'Buzz off, can't you see I'm busy?'

'Doctor, doctor, I think I'm a moth.'
  'Get out of the way, you're in my light.'

'Doctor, doctor, everyone thinks I'm a liar.'
  'I can't believe that.'

'Doctor, doctor, I can't get to sleep.'
  'Sit on the edge of the bed. You'll soon drop off.'

'Doctor, doctor, I think I'm a snail.'
  'Don't worry, we'll soon bring you out of your shell.'

'Doctor, doctor, I snore so loudly I keep myself awake.'
  'Hmm. Have you tried sleeping in another room?'

'Doctor, doctor, I think I may need glasses.'
  'Quite possibly. This is the greengrocer's.'

A woman went to the doctor's clutching the side of her face.
  'What seems to be the problem?' asked the doctor.
  'I don't know,' said the woman removing her hand. 'It's this pimple on my cheek. There's a small tree growing from it, and a table and chairs, and a picnic basket. What on earth can it be?'
  'It's nothing to worry about,' said the doctor reassuringly. 'It's only a beauty spot.'

A young woman had terrible toothache but was reluctant to go to the dentist because she was frightened of his drill. Eventually, however, she was in such discomfort that she decided to pluck up courage.

'I'm really scared,' she confided to the dentist as she entered the surgery. 'I don't know which is worse – having a tooth filled or having a baby.'

'Well,' said the dentist, 'make up your mind before I adjust the chair.'

Actual Answers By Medical Students:
- Before giving a blood transfusion find out if the blood is affirmative or negative.
- To remove dust from the eye, pull the eye down over the nose.
- For a nosebleed, put the nose much lower than the body until the heart stops.
- What is artificial respiration commonly known as? – The Kiss of Death.
- What are steroids? – Things for keeping the carpet on the stairs.
- What is a common treatment for a badly bleeding nose? – Circumcision.
- For drowning: climb on top of the person and move up and down to make artificial perspiration.
- For fainting: rub the person's chest or, if a lady, rub her arm above the hand instead. Or put the head between the knees of the nearest doctor.
- The alimentary canal is located in the northern part of Indiana.

A middle-aged man went to the doctor for a routine medical. The nurse began with the basics.

'How much do you weigh?' she asked.

'Oh, about twelve stone,' he answered.

The nurse put him on the scale. 'Fourteen stone, ten pounds. And your height?'

'Oh, about six feet,' he said.

The nurse measured him. 'Five feet eight inches.'

Then she took his blood pressure. 'It's very high,' she said, concerned.

'High!' he exclaimed. 'Of course it's high! When I came in here, I was tall and slim. Now I'm short and fat!'

A man walked into the doctor's office with a strawberry growing out of his head.

The doctor said: 'I'll give you some cream to put on it.'

How can you tell if your doctor's a quack? – By his large bill.

The doctor knocked at the door of the examination room before entering, and the woman patient called out for him to come in. The doctor then told her to take all her clothes off. He proceeded to give her a thorough physical examination – from head to toe, front and back – leaving no part of her body untouched. When he had finished, he said that she appeared to be in good health and asked whether she had any questions.

'Just one, doctor,' she replied.

'And what's that?' he asked.

She said: 'Why did you bother to knock?'

Two young boys were discussing their respective ailments in the hospital children's ward.

'Are you medical or surgical?' asked one who had been in for several days.

'What do you mean?' said the other.

'It's simple. Were you sick when you came in here, or did they make you sick when you got here?'

A woman phoned 911 to report that her sister had fallen down the stairs.

The emergency operator said: 'Do you know what caused the fall?'

'No,' said the woman. 'What?'

A speaker was about to address a public meeting when he realised that he had left his false teeth at home. He shuffled around anxiously for a few moments before informing the lady who was chairing the meeting that he would be unable to give his speech because he had forgotten his false teeth.

His predicament was overheard by a man in the front row of the audience who immediately produced a pair of false teeth from his pocket and said: 'Why don't you try these?'

The speaker put the set of false teeth in his mouth but they were too tight.

'By chance, I have another pair,' said the man. 'Try these.'

The speaker put the second set of teeth in his mouth but they were too loose. 'It's no good,' he said. 'I won't be able to do my speech.'

'Wait,' said the man. 'It so happens that I have one more set of false teeth in my pocket. Try these.'

The speaker did, and they fitted perfectly. 'Thank you,' he said. 'I've been looking for a good dentist.'

'I'm not a dentist,' said the man. 'I'm an undertaker.'

Concerned about the health of her aunt, a woman phoned her doctor. After consulting his case notes, the doctor said: 'There's no need for me to come out because your aunt isn't really ill at all – she just thinks she's sick.'

A week later, the doctor telephoned the house to check that his diagnosis was correct. 'And how's your aunt today?' he asked.

'Worse,' said the woman. 'Now she thinks she's dead!'

Two children were trying to figure out what game to play. One said: 'Let's play doctor.'

'Good idea,' said the other. 'You operate and I'll sue.'

In order to get to the valves, a mechanic carefully removed the engine parts from a car while the car owner – a surgeon – looked on. Afterwards the mechanic said to the surgeon: 'You know, I reckon my line of work is every bit as difficult and skilled as yours.'

'Perhaps,' said the surgeon, 'but I'd like to see you do it while the engine is running.'

A man went into the doctor's office for his annual check-up, and the doctor asked whether he had experienced any abnormalities over the past twelve months.

'Not really,' said the man, 'although I think my suit must have shrunk over the last year because it didn't fit when I went to put it on for a wedding three weeks ago.'

The doctor said: 'Suits don't shrink just hanging in a wardrobe. You've probably put on a few pounds.'

'That's just it, doctor, I know I haven't gained a single pound since the last time I wore it.'

'Well then,' said the doctor, 'you must have a case of furniture disease.'

'What in the world is furniture disease?'

'That's when your chest starts sliding down into your drawers.'

A man went to the doctor's for his annual physical. He told the doctor: 'I'm getting really forgetful. I forget where I live, I forget where I've parked my car, and I go into shops and can't remember what it is that I want. And when I do get to the checkout, I find I've forgotten my wallet. It's getting pretty bad. What can I do?'

The doctor thought for a moment and said: 'Pay me in advance.'

After a routine medical, a guy confessed to the doctor that he was thinking about getting a vasectomy.

'That's a pretty big decision,' said the doctor. 'Have you talked it over with your family?'

'Yes, and they're in favour fifteen to two.'

When a wealthy businessman choked on a sharp fish bone in a restaurant, he was fortunate that a doctor was seated at a nearby table. Springing into action, the doctor skilfully removed the bone and saved the businessman's life.

Recovering slowly, he thanked the doctor profusely and offered to pay him. 'Just name your fee,' he croaked gratefully.

The doctor thought for a moment and said: 'OK. How about half of what you would have offered when the bone was still stuck in your throat?'

A brown paper bag went to the doctor complaining of feeling unwell. The doctor took a blood sample and told the bag to come back the following week.

When the bag arrived for his follow-up appointment, the doctor said: 'I'm afraid I have some bad news. The results of your blood tests indicate that you have haemophilia.'

'How can I possibly have haemophilia? I'm a brown paper bag.'

'Yes,' replied the doctor, 'but it seems your mother was a carrier.'

At a naval barracks the enlisted men were being given a series of injections prior to going overseas. Afterwards one lad asked for a glass of water.

'Not feeling too good?' asked the medical officer.

'No, I'm just making sure I'm still watertight.'

A pharmacist was working in his room at the rear of the shop when there was suddenly a loud explosion. A minute or so later, he emerged into the shop, his white coat blackened and with sooty marks around his face. Handing a piece of scorched paper to a lady customer, he said: 'Would you ask your doctor to write your prescription again and this time *print it*?'

A woman went to see a psychiatrist. 'Doctor, I want to talk to you about my husband. He thinks he's a refrigerator.'

'That's not so bad,' said the psychiatrist. 'It's a fairly harmless contraption.'

'Well maybe,' she said. 'But he sleeps with his mouth open and the light keeps me awake.'

An old man woke up in the recovery room after an operation and said: 'Thank God that's over!'

'You're lucky,' said the guy in the next bed. 'They left a scalpel inside me and had to cut me open again.'

'How awful!' said the old man.

'They had to open me up again too,' said the guy on the other side. 'To find their sponge.'

'That's appalling,' said the old man.

Just then, the surgeon who had operated on the old man stuck his head around the door and asked: 'Has anybody seen my hat?'

The old man fainted.

A man went to see a psychiatrist and listed all the things that were wrong with his life – how he had no job, no money, and no love life. After listening to the patient's story, the psychiatrist said: 'I think your problem is low self-esteem. It's very common among losers.'

A grumpy grandmother was in hospital for the first time and hating every minute of it. Within two hours of her arrival, she had complained about everything – the food, the ward, the nurses, her bed, even her fellow patients.

On her first night there, she spotted a small button attached to a cord. 'What's that?' she demanded.

The intern explained: 'If you need anything in the middle of the night, just press that button.'

'What does it do? Ring a bell?'

'No, it turns on a light in the hall for the nurse on duty.'

'Look,' snapped granny, 'I'm the sick one around here. If the night nurse needs a light on in the hall, she can damn well get up and switch it on herself!'

A man walked into a psychiatrist's office with a pancake on his head, a fried egg on each shoulder and a piece of bacon over each ear.

'What seems to be the problem?' asked the psychiatrist.

The man said: 'I'm worried about my brother.'

Three nurses arrived at the Pearly Gates. St. Peter asked the first why he should admit her. She replied that she had been an emergency room nurse and had saved thousands of lives. St. Peter readily admitted her to heaven.

The second stated that she had worked in a children's ward and had helped improve the lives of thousands of sick youngsters. St. Peter immediately told her that she, too, could come into heaven.

The third nurse revealed that she had been a managed care nurse and had saved thousands of dollars for the insurance company.

St. Peter told her: 'OK. Come on in. But you can only stay for three days.'

Patient: 'Can you recommend anything for yellow teeth?'
Dentist: 'A brown tie.'

A man told a psychiatrist: 'I can't stop deep-frying things in batter. I've deep-fried my laptop, I've deep-fried my mobile, I've deep-fried my DVD player, and battered my jeans. What's wrong with me?'

The psychiatrist took a deep breath and said: 'It seems to me that you're frittering your life away.'

A football manager who had an ulcer visited his doctor's surgery for a check-up.

'Remember,' advised the doctor, 'don't get over-excited, don't get stressed out and forget all about football when you're not at the club. Just stay calm. Don't let people needle you.'

'Thanks, doc,' said the manager.

'By the way,' added the doctor, 'how come you spent ten million on that waste of space from Manchester United when you've got a perfectly good kid in the reserves? And don't you think it's about time you ditched the diamond formation in favour of 4-4-2?'

A mother took her young son to the doctor.

'Doctor,' she said, 'can an eight-year-old boy operate on himself and remove his own appendix?'

'Of course not,' said the doctor.

'See!' she said to the boy. 'Now put it back!'

A man had been seeing a psychiatrist for three years in an attempt to cure his fear that there were monsters lurking under his bed. But all the psychiatrist's efforts were in vain and the man was no nearer to being cured. Eventually the man decided that further sessions were a waste of time and money.

A few weeks later, the psychiatrist bumped into the man in a bar. The man was looking much happier.

'You look well,' remarked the psychiatrist.

'Yes,' beamed the man. 'That's because I'm cured. After all this time, I can finally go to sleep at night and not worry that there are monsters lurking under my bed.'

The psychiatrist was puzzled. 'How have you managed to get cured? Nothing I tried with you seemed to work.'

'I went to see a different doctor,' explained the man. 'He is a behaviourist and he cured me in one session.'

'In one session!' exclaimed the psychiatrist. 'How?'

'It was simple,' said the man. 'He told me to saw the legs off my bed.'

An old woman went to see the doctor about her constipation.

She told him: 'I haven't moved my bowels in a week.'

The doctor said: 'Have you done anything about it?'

'Well, yes, I sit in the bathroom for half an hour in the morning and again at night.'

'No,' said the doctor. 'I mean, do you take anything?'

'Sure,' replied the old lady. 'I take a book.'

After losing his own ear in a car crash, a man was given a pig's ear as a replacement. Six weeks after the transplant, he returned to the hospital for a check-up.

'Any problems?' asked the surgeon.

'Not really,' said the patient, 'although I do get a bit of crackling.'

A patient told his doctor: 'Those pills you gave me are great, but the only problem is, they make me walk like a crab.'

'Yes,' said the doctor. 'Those will be the side effects.'

A man walked into a doctor's surgery and the receptionist asked him what he had.

'Shingles,' he replied.

So she took down his name, address and medical insurance number, and told him to take a seat.

A few minutes later, a nursing assistant came out and asked him what he had.

'Shingles,' he answered.

So she took down his height, weight and complete medical history, and told him to wait in the examining room.

Ten minutes later a nurse came in and asked him what he had.

'Shingles,' he said.

So she gave him a blood test, a blood pressure test, an electrocardiogram, and told him to take off all his clothes and wait for the doctor.

Fifteen minutes later the doctor came in and asked him what he had.

'Shingles,' he replied.

'Where?' asked the doctor.

'Outside in the truck. Where do you want them?'

A woman went to the doctor and said: 'Every time I go to the bathroom, dimes come out.'

'Go home and relax,' he advised. 'I'm sure it's nothing to worry about.'

A week later, she was back. 'It's got worse, doctor. Now every time I go to the bathroom, quarters come out.'

'Just go home and relax,' he said. 'It's nothing serious.'

A week later, she returned again. 'Things are no better. Now every time I go to the bathroom, half-dollars come out. What's happening to me, doctor?'

'Relax,' he said. 'You're just going through your change!'

While making his rounds, a doctor pointed out an X-ray to a group of medical students.

'As you can see,' she said, 'the patient limps because his left fibula and tibia are radically arched. Peter, what would you do in a case like this?'

'Well,' pondered the student, 'I suppose I'd limp too.'

A doctor was driving his four-year-old daughter to preschool when she picked up a stethoscope that he had left on the back seat and began playing with it. Glancing in his mirror, he smiled at the thought that perhaps his daughter would eventually follow in his footsteps.

Then the child spoke into the instrument: 'Welcome to McDonald's. May I take your order?'

An old man in hospital became increasingly irritated by the patronising tone of one of the nurses. Every morning she would tuck in his sheets, pat him on the head and ask: 'And how are we today?'

He decided to take his revenge at breakfast. Having been given a urine bottle to fill, he instead emptied his apple juice into the container. When the nurse examined the supposed sample, she remarked: 'It seems we are a little cloudy today.'

To her horror, the old man snatched the bottle from her hand, drank the contents and said sarcastically: 'Well, I'll run it through the system again. Maybe I can filter it better this time!'

A husband and wife entered the dentist's office. The husband said: 'I want a tooth pulled. I don't want gas or Novocain because I'm in a terrible hurry. Just pull the tooth as quickly as possible.'

'You're a brave man,' said the dentist. 'Now, show me which tooth it is.'

The husband turned to his wife and said: 'Open your mouth, dear, and show the dentist which tooth it is.'

Home

A man called over to his neighbour one morning: 'Did you hear me thumping on the wall last night?'

'Oh, don't worry about it! We were making a fair bit of noise ourselves.'

Dave turned up unannounced at a friend's house late one evening and asked whether he could stay the night. The friend said: 'Sure. You can either sleep on the floor in the living room, or you can sleep in the room with Baby.'

'I think I'll sleep on the floor in the living room,' said Dave.

The next morning he went to the bathroom and bumped into a beautiful blonde. 'Hi, who are you?' he asked.

'I'm Baby,' she said. 'Who are you?'

'I'm stupid.'

A vacuum cleaner salesman wormed his way into the home of a woman in a remote Welsh valley.

'This machine is amazing,' he enthused in his finest sales patter before tipping a bag of dirt over the lounge floor carpet. 'Watch this. If this machine doesn't remove every last speck of that dirt, I'll lick it off the carpet myself!'

'Do you want ketchup on it?' asked the woman. 'Only we're not connected for electricity!'

A woman rang up a pet shop and asked for three hundred cockroaches.

The shop owner said: 'If you don't mind me asking, what on earth do you want three hundred cockroaches for?'

The woman replied: 'Well, I'm moving today, and my lease says I must leave the place in the same condition I found it.'

A woman was having trouble with her neighbour's child throwing stones into her garden. So she ordered her husband to erect a boundary around the garden. The husband didn't want to upset the neighbours but bowed to his wife's pressure and spent the day fixing thirty posts into the ground.

Still the wife wasn't happy. 'Why haven't you attached the panels to the posts?' she raged.

The husband said: 'I didn't want to cause a fence.'

Bill Gates bought a new house . . .

Bill: There are a few issues we need to discuss.

Contractor: You have your basic support option. Calls are free for the first ninety days and $75 a call thereafter. OK?

Bill: Uh, yeah. The first issue is the living room. We think it's a little smaller than we anticipated.

Contractor: Yeah. Some compromises were made to have it out by the release date.

Bill: We won't be able to fit all our furniture in there.

Contractor: Well, you have two options. You can purchase a new, larger living room, or you can use a stacker.

Bill: A stacker?

Contractor: Yeah, it allows you to fit twice as much furniture into the room. By stacking it, of course, you put the entertainment centre on the couch, the chairs on the table, and so on. You leave an empty spot, so when you want to use some furniture you can unstack what you need and then put it back when you're done.

Bill: Uh. I don't know. Issue two: the light fixtures. The bulbs we brought with us from our old home won't fit. The threads run the wrong way.

Contractor: Oh, that's easy! Those bulbs aren't plug and play. You'll have to upgrade to the new bulbs.

Bill: And the electrical outlets? The holes are round, not rectangular. How do I fix that?

Contractor: Just uninstall and reinstall the electrical system.

Bill: You're kidding!

Contractor: Nope. It's the only way.

Bill: Well . . . I have one last problem. Sometimes when I have guests over, someone will flush the toilet and it won't stop. The water pressure drops so low that the showers don't work.

Contractor: That's a resource leakage problem. One fixture is failing to terminate and is hogging the resources preventing access from other fixtures.

Bill: And how do I fix that?

Contractor: Well, after each flush, you all need to exit the house, turn off the water at the street, turn it back on, re-enter the house and then you can get back to work.

Bill: That's the last straw. What kind of product are you selling me?

Contractor: Hey, nobody's making you buy it.

Bill: And when will this be fixed?

Contractor: Oh, in your next house, which will be ready to release some time near the end of next year. It was due out this year, but we've had some delays . . .

Tom was continually plagued by his next-door neighbour asking to borrow things. One morning he saw the neighbour approaching his front door and so he was ready for him.

'Can I borrow your power-saw this morning?' asked the neighbour.

'Afraid not,' replied Tom gleefully. 'I'll be using it all day.'

'In that case, you won't be using your golf clubs. Mind if I borrow them?'

For once in his life, the real estate agent decided to be honest with a prospective house-buyer. 'This property has its good and bad points. There is a chemical plant one block to the north and a slaughterhouse one block to the south.'

'Well, what are its good points?' asked the client.

'You can always tell which way the wind is blowing.'

Two women were discussing their most unusual items of furniture. One said: 'I learned from an antiques expert that the "W.C." carved on our dining room table may indicate that it once belonged to Winston Churchill.'

'Well,' said her friend, 'I bought a bureau once and twenty people fell out.'

'Really?'

'Yes. It turned out it was a missing persons' bureau.'

Old college buddies Nat and Joey had not seen each other in years. When they finally got in touch, they had a lot of catching up to do, so Nat invited Joey to visit him in his new apartment. 'I have a wife and three kids and it would be great if you came to see us.'

'Sure. Why not?' said Joey. 'Where do you live?'

'The address is 68 Park Mansions,' said Nat. 'There's plenty of parking space behind the apartment. Park there and come round to the front door, kick it open with your foot, go to the elevator and press the button with your left elbow, then enter. When you reach the sixth floor, go down the hall until you see number 68. Then press the doorbell with your right elbow and I'll let you in.'

'Good,' said Joey. 'But tell me, what is all this business of kicking the front door open, then pressing elevator buttons with my right, then my left elbow?'

'Well, surely you're not coming empty-handed?'

When his computer printer began to print out faintly, a man called the repair shop.

The clerk said: 'From your description of the problem, the printer probably only needs cleaning. It will cost you $50 to have it cleaned here so really you'd be better off reading the manual and doing the job yourself.'

Pleasantly surprised by the clerk's honesty, the man said: 'Does your boss know that you discourage business?'

'Actually,' replied the clerk sheepishly, 'it's my boss's idea. We usually make more money on repairs if we let people try to fix things themselves first.'

An elderly lady called the police to complain about the behaviour of her next-door neighbour. When the officer came out, she told him that the man next door kept wandering around naked with the curtains open.

The officer took a look through the window. 'But I can't even see into next door's house from here,' he said.

'No,' said the old lady. 'You have to climb on the dresser and look out of the skylight.'

When a husband arrived home, his wife told him that the maid whom they had recently dismissed had stolen two of their towels as a parting gesture.

'How dare she!' stormed the husband.

'I know,' said his wife, 'and they were our two best towels – you know, the ones we got from the Hilton Hotel on holiday last year.'

Insults

Any similarity between you and a human being is purely coincidental.

You are depriving a village somewhere of its idiot.

Your inferiority complex is totally justified.

Is there no beginning to your talents?

You're nobody's fool. Let's see if we can get someone to adopt you.

If I put my ear to your head, I can hear the ocean.

You're a gross ignoramus – 144 times as dim as an ordinary ignoramus.

Are you the first in your family to be born without a tail?

It's difficult to believe you beat a million other sperm.

You're a difficult man to forget – but well worth the effort.

With training you could be a good paperweight.

You used to be rude and obnoxious, but now you're the opposite – obnoxious and rude.

You will never be able to live down to your reputation.

You let your mind wander, and it hasn't come back yet.

What do you use for contraception? Your personality?

You're a man of hidden shallows.

They say no woman ever made a fool out of you. So who did?

After hearing you speak, I now know that the dead do contact us.

Are you always so stupid or is today a special occasion?

The only place you're ever invited is outside.

You always have your ear to the ground. So how is life in the gutter?

You're the reason that siblings shouldn't marry.

You have a 20-watt intellect.

You drank from the Fountain of Knowledge but didn't like the taste and spat it out.

When you took an IQ test, the results were negative.

You are so two-faced that any woman married to you would be a bigamist.

I used to think you were a pain in the neck. Now I have a much lower opinion of you.

I hear you were born on a farm. Any more in the litter?

You started at rock bottom and went downhill from there.

You got into the gene pool while the lifeguard wasn't watching.

Nice suit. Were you there for the fitting?

You have a good family tree, but the crop is a failure.

You're about as much use as a chocolate teapot.

I'd like to leave you with one thought – but I'm not sure you' place to put it.

Ordinarily people live and learn. You just live.

Keep repeating, 'Socks first, then shoes.'

Sit down and give your mind a rest.

The glow of your intellect wouldn't light the inside of a thimble.

Bacteria outscore you on IQ tests.

Is your name Amazon? You're so wide at the mouth.

Don't you realise there are enough people to hate in the world already without your working so hard to give us another?

As an outsider, what do you think of the human race?

Have you considered suing your brains for non-support?

You've obviously mistaken me for someone who gives a damn.

I know you're a self-made man – and it's good of you to take the blame.

I knew one day you'd leave me for my best friend. So here's his lead, water bowl and chew toys.

People say you are outspoken, but not by anyone I know.

The porch lights are on but nobody's home.

You're not the sharpest tack in the box.

You're a few chocolate chips short of a cookie.

You've got a photographic memory but with the lens cap on.

There was something about you that I liked, but you spent it.

You have a mechanical mind – it's a shame you forgot to wind it up this morning.

We all sprang from the apes but you didn't spring far enough.

I don't think you're an idiot. But then what's my opinion against thousands of others?

If you were any more stupid, you'd have to be watered twice a week.

If I gave you a penny for your thoughts, I'd get change.

You're a prime candidate for natural deselection.

Did you fall out of the family tree?

Your brain is so powerful no thoughts can penetrate.

The more I think of you, the less I think of you.

If brains were dynamite you wouldn't have enough to sneeze.

If you ever had a bright idea, it would be beginner's luck.

Your mouth's in gear, but your brain's in neutral.

The wheel is turning, but the hamster is dead.

You donated your brain to science before you'd finished using it.

When they handed out brains, you thought they said 'drains' and didn't want one.

The brightness knob is set to low.

Your brain probably feels as good as new, seeing that you've never used it.

I see you in my dreams – if I eat too much.

On the road of life you're the one going the other way.
If what you don't know can't hurt you, you're invulnerable.
You're not a perfect idiot – nobody's perfect.
You'd be out of your depth in a paddling pool.
There's nothing wrong with you that reincarnation won't cure.
I like your approach. Now let's see your departure.

Law and Order

The cross-eyed judge looked at the three defendants in the dock and said to the first one: 'How do you plead?'

'Not guilty,' said the second defendant.

'I wasn't talking to you,' boomed the judge.

'I never said a word,' replied the third defendant.

A doctor and a lawyer were talking at a party, but their conversation was constantly interrupted by people describing their ailments and asking the doctor free medical advice. After an hour of this, the exasperated doctor asked the lawyer: 'What do you do to stop people asking you for legal advice when you're out of the office?'

The lawyer said: 'I give it to them and then I send them a bill.'

Although shocked by this, the doctor agreed to give it a try.

The next day the doctor, acting on the lawyer's suggestion, was reluctantly putting a number of bills into his mailbox when he found a bill addressed to him. It was from the lawyer.

The defendant stood defiantly in the dock and said to the judge: 'I don't recognise this court.'

'Why?' rapped the judge.

'Because you've had it decorated since the last time I was here.'

Two new prisoners were shown to their cell.

'How long are you in for?' asked the first.

'Eighteen years,' replied the second. 'How about you?'

'Twenty-five years. So since you're getting out first, you'd better have the bed by the door.'

Why did the escaped convict saw the legs off his bed? – He wanted to lie low.

In prison for the first time, George was puzzled by a strange ritual that was carried out at night immediately after the lights were turned off. Someone from another cell called out 'Thirty-seven' and the whole block burst out laughing. A few moments later another distant voice called out 'Sixty-one' and again everyone laughed.

'What do the numbers mean?' George asked his cellmate.

'Down in the prison library there's a big joke book. We've memorised all the jokes. So now when anybody wants to tell a joke, they just have to shout out the page number from the book.'

George was intrigued and the next day he studied the joke book in the prison library, writing down the numbers of a few good jokes so that he could join in the fun that evening.

That night, George decided to take the initiative. Once the lights had gone off, he called out 'Fifty-five.' But instead of laughter there was silence. So he tried again. 'Eighty-seven.' Again there was an eerie silence.

He asked his cellmate: 'Why is it that when I call out the numbers, nobody laughs?'

His cellmate said: 'It's the way you tell them.'

Prosecutor: Did you kill the victim?
Defendant: No, I did not.
Prosecutor: Do you know what the penalties are for perjury?
Defendant: Yes, I do. And they're a lot less than the penalty for murder.

A truck driver hated lawyers with such a vengeance that whenever he saw any walking by the side of the road he would deliberately swerve his truck into them and run them down. The resounding thud as truck hit lawyer made it all worthwhile.

One day the truck driver saw a priest hitchhiking at the side of the road. Always ready to offer a helping hand to a man of the cloth, he asked: 'Where are you going to, Father?'

'To St. Michael's Church ten miles along the road,' replied the priest.

'Hop in,' said the truck driver and he set off in the direction of St. Michael's.

A mile on, the truck driver saw a lawyer walking along the side of the road and instinctively swerved to hit him. Then he remembered that he was carrying a priest in his truck, so at the last minute he swerved back into the middle of the road, narrowly missing the lawyer. But he still heard a thud. Puzzled, he glanced in his mirrors and when he didn't see anything, he turned to the priest and said: 'I'm sorry, Father, I almost hit that lawyer.'

'Don't worry,' replied the priest. 'I got him with the door!'

A man chosen for jury duty tried in vain to get out of serving. He pleaded sickness, prior commitments, pressure of work, the death of a distant cousin, but when all else had failed, he made one last desperate attempt just as the trial was about to begin. Having been granted permission to approach the bench, he told the judge: 'Your honour, I must be excused from this trial because I am prejudiced against the defendant. I took one look at the man in the blue suit with those beady eyes and that dishonest face, and I said straight away: "He's a crook. He's guilty." So you see, your honour, there is no way that I can be on that jury and guarantee a fair trial.'

'Get back in the jury box,' barked the judge impatiently. 'That man is his lawyer!'

A robber burst into a bank brandishing a gun and yelled at the teller: 'Give me the money. One false move and you're geography!'

The teller said: 'Don't you mean history?'

The robber screamed: 'Don't change the subject!'

A judge grew tired of seeing the same town drunk in front of his bench week after week. One day he glared down at the intoxicated defendant and thundered: 'It is the sentence of this court that you be taken from here to a place of execution and there hanged by the neck until dead.'

The drunk immediately fainted and while the bailiff attempted to revive him, the judge simply shrugged and said: 'I've always wanted to do that.'

Did you hear about the psychic dwarf who escaped from prison? – The newspaper headline read: 'Small Medium At Large.'

The jurors in a multi-billion-dollar lawsuit against the tobacco industry were ordered by a judge not to see a new movie called *Smoking Kills* in case it influenced their verdict. He also told them not to see *The House on Haunted Hill*.

The prosecutor was mystified. He said to the judge: 'I can understand why you have instructed the jurors not to watch *Smoking Kills*, but why have you told them not to watch *The House on Haunted Hill*?'

The judge leaned forward and said: 'Because I got it on video last night, and it stinks!'

Lawyer: Your honour, I wish to appeal my client's case on the basis of newly discovered evidence.

Judge: And what is the nature of this new evidence?

Lawyer: I discovered that my client still has $500 left.

A man was walking along the street when he noticed a bottle lying in the gutter. He picked up the bottle and decided to rub it for good luck. To his amazement, a genie appeared.

'I will grant you three wishes,' said the genie, 'but I must warn you, there is a catch. For each wish I grant, every lawyer in the world will receive double what you ask for. Do you understand?'

'I think so,' said the man.

'Right,' said the genie. 'What is your first wish?'

'My first wish,' replied the man, 'is for a Rolls-Royce. I've always wanted a Rolls-Royce.'

'Then you shall have a Rolls-Royce,' answered the genie, 'and all the lawyers in the world will be given two Rolls-Royces. Now what is your second wish?'

'I could use a million dollars,' said the man.

'Very well,' said the genie. 'You shall have a million dollars. But you do realise that means that every lawyer in the world will become two million dollars richer? Now what is your third wish?'

The man thought for a moment. 'Well, I've always wanted to donate a kidney.'

Finding a window in his busy schedule, a prison governor agreed to listen to the pleas of a woman who was desperate for her husband to be released from jail.

'What was he convicted of?' asked the governor.

'Stealing bread,' said the woman.

'I see. And is he a good husband?'

The wife shifted awkwardly in her seat. 'To be honest, no, he's not a particularly good husband. He shouts at the kids, he hits me when he gets drunk, and he's been unfaithful on at least three occasions that I know of.'

'Well,' said the governor, 'it sounds to me as if you're better off without him. Why on earth do you want him out of jail?'

'We've run out of bread again.'

A wizened old prisoner was introduced to his new cellmate. 'Look at me,' said the old man, 'I'm way past it. You'd never believe that I used to lead the life of Riley. I wintered on the French Riviera, had a boat, four cars, a string of beautiful women, and ate at the finest restaurants.'

'So what went wrong?' asked the newcomer.

The old lag sighed: 'One day Riley reported his credit cards missing!'

A lady customer in a Post Office was puzzled to see a man spraying scent on a huge pile of Valentine's envelopes before posting them.

'What are you doing?' she asked.

He replied: 'I'm sending out a thousand Valentine's cards signed "Guess who?"'

'Why do you want to do that?' she queried.

'It's simple,' he replied. 'I'm a divorce lawyer.'

Judge: I thought I told you I never wanted to see you in here again.

Defendant: Your honour, that's what I tried to tell the police, but they wouldn't listen.

A farmer's truck had been involved in a road accident with a police patrol car, as a result of which the farmer had decided to sue the police for the injuries he sustained. In court, he came up against a smart police lawyer.

'Is it not the case,' began the lawyer, 'that immediately after the accident you told patrol officer Kelly that you felt fine? And yet here you are suing the police for injuries sustained.'

'Well, you see,' said the farmer, 'I had loaded my favourite mule, Maisie . . .'

The lawyer interrupted him. 'With all due respect, the court is not interested in your mule. I want to know why you told the officer you felt fine immediately after the crash and are now claiming compensation.'

The farmer started again. 'I had loaded my favourite mule, Maisie . . .'

Again the lawyer pounced. 'What has your mule to do with the fact that you told the officer at the scene of the accident that you felt fine, yet you are now seeking compensation?'

The farmer looked towards the judge for help. 'You may tell your story,' said the judge.

The farmer started again. 'I had loaded my favourite mule, Maisie, on to the back of the truck and I had driven five miles down the road when a police car came straight out of a side turning and ploughed into the side of my truck. I was badly cut and dazed and lying in the road. I could see Maisie was limping a little. The next thing I knew, officer Kelly had gone up to her and shot her between the eyes. Then he came over to me and said: 'Your mule didn't look too well, so I had to shoot her. How are you feeling?'

A woman celebrating her eightieth birthday was surprised to receive a notice for jury duty. So she called the clerk's office to remind them that she was exempt because of her age.

'You need to come in and fill out the exemption forms,' they said.

'I have done,' she protested. 'I did it last year.'

'You have to do it every year,' they insisted.

'Why? Do you think I'm going to get younger?'

Did you hear about the new sushi bar that caters exclusively for lawyers? – It's called Sosumi.

A man was in court on a charge of selling drugs. To determine the exact quantity of illegal substance allegedly sold, the judge asked the prosecutor how many grams there were in an ounce. While both attorneys

92

checked their notes, the defendant, who had yet to enter a plea, announced helpfully: 'There are 28.3 grams in an ounce, your honour.'

At this, his lawyer leaned over to him and said: 'I think you might as well plead guilty.'

NASA was interviewing professionals to be sent to Mars. Only one could go, and it would be a one-way journey. Despite this stipulation, there were three applicants.

First up was a naturalist. Asked how much he wanted to be paid for going, he answered: 'A million dollars because I want to donate it to the World Wildlife Fund.'

Asked the same question, the next applicant, a doctor, replied: 'Two million dollars. I want to give a million to my family and leave the other million for the advancement of medical research.'

The last applicant was a lawyer. When asked how much money he wanted for going to Mars, he whispered in the interviewer's ear: 'Three million dollars.'

'Why so much more than the others?' queried the interviewer.

The lawyer replied: 'If you give me three million dollars, I'll give you one million, I'll keep one million, and we can send the naturalist!'

A driver caught speeding was brought before a judge. The judge said: 'What will you take, thirty days or $100?'

The defendant said: 'I think I'll take the money.'

A lawyer's wife died. At her funeral, the mourners were appalled to see that the headstone read: 'Here lies Mary, wife of Spencer, L.L.D., Wills, Divorce, Malpractice, Personal Injury. Reasonable Rates.'

Suddenly Spencer burst into tears. His brother said: 'So you should be crying, pulling a disgraceful stunt like this!'

Spencer sobbed: 'No, you don't understand. They left off the phone number!'

A defence lawyer told his client: 'I've got good news and bad news. The bad news is your blood test came back and your DNA matches the blood found on the victim, the murder weapon and the getaway car.'

'Oh no!' said the client. 'I'm finished! What's the good news?'

'Your cholesterol is down to 140.'

Lawyer: Now would you mind telling the jury why you shot your husband with a bow and arrow?

Defendant: I didn't want to wake the children.

A young lawyer defending a wealthy businessman in a complex lawsuit

93

feared that the evidence was against his client. So he asked the senior partner of the law firm whether it would be appropriate to send the judge in the case a box of expensive cigars.

The partner was appalled by the suggestion. 'The judge is an honourable man, and I can guarantee that if you do that, you will lose the case.'

Six weeks later, the judge ruled in favour of the lawyer's client. Congratulating his colleague, the senior partner said: 'Aren't you glad you didn't send those cigars to the judge?'

'But I did send them. I just enclosed the plaintiff's lawyer's business card!'

Having drunk too much, a lawyer was involved in a car crash on his way home from a bar when he rear-ended the car in front at traffic lights. In his most pompous manner, he got out of the car, marched over to the innocent driver and sneered: 'Boy, are you in trouble! I'm a lawyer!'

The other driver said: 'No, you're in trouble. I'm a judge.'

A judge was hearing a drink-driving case but the defendant, who had a history of driving under the influence, demanded a jury trial. It was nearly four o'clock in the afternoon and getting a jury would take some time, so the judge called an adjournment and went out in the hall looking to recruit anyone available for jury duty. In the main lobby he found a dozen lawyers and told them that they were a jury. The lawyers thought this would be a novel experience and followed the judge back into the courtroom.

The trial itself was over in about ten minutes and it was obvious that the defendant was guilty. The jurors retired to their room, and the judge, thinking that they would be back with their verdict in a matter of minutes, prepared to go home. But after three hours, the jury was still out. The judge was furious and sent the bailiff into the jury room to find out what was delaying the verdict.

When the bailiff returned, the judge said impatiently: 'Well, have they reached a verdict yet?'

The bailiff shook his head and said: 'Verdict? They're still arguing over who should be foreman!'

A man phoned a law firm and asked to speak to Mr Kennedy, his ex-wife's lawyer.

'I'm sorry,' said the secretary, 'but Mr Kennedy died last night.'

Ten minutes later the phone rang again. The same voice asked: 'Can I speak to Mr Kennedy, my ex-wife's lawyer?'

'I'm afraid that's not possible,' said the secretary. 'As I told you a few minutes ago, Mr Kennedy died last night.'

Ten minutes later the phone rang again. The same voice said: 'I'd like to speak to Mr Kennedy, my ex-wife's lawyer.'

'Look,' said the secretary. 'I've told you twice. Mr Kennedy is dead. Why do you keep phoning? Don't you understand?'

'Sure I understand,' said the caller. 'I just enjoy hearing you say it over and over.'

A lawyer was talking to a client who had just been found guilty of murder.

'There's good news and bad news,' said the lawyer. 'The bad news is, you're getting the electric chair. The good news is, I got the voltage lowered.'

The judge told the witness: 'Do you understand that you have sworn to tell the truth?'

'I do.'

'And do you understand what will happen if you are not truthful?'

'Sure. My side will win.'

A middle-aged woman was called to serve for jury duty, but asked to be excused because she didn't believe in capital punishment and feared that her personal views might prevent the trial from running its proper course. However, the prosecution lawyer liked her thoughtfulness and quiet assurance, and tried to convince her that she would make an excellent juror.

'Madam,' he explained, 'this is not a murder trial! It's a simple civil lawsuit. A wife is bringing this case against her husband because he gambled away the $12,000 with which he had promised to buy her a new kitchen.'

'Well, OK,' agreed the woman, 'I'll serve. I guess I could be wrong about capital punishment after all.'

Marriage

A newly married man came home from work to find his young wife stretched out on the sofa, wearing a sexy negligee.

'Guess what I've got planned for dinner?' she purred seductively. 'And don't you dare tell me you had it for lunch today!'

A husband and wife were chatting with friends when the subject of marriage counselling was raised. The husband said: 'Oh, we'll never need that. My wife and I have a great relationship. She has a communications degree and I have a degree in theatre arts. She communicates really well and I just act like I'm listening.'

A woman collared her husband as he stumbled through the door. 'What's the big idea coming home half drunk?'

'Sorry, honey. I ran out of money.'

When does a man know that he can count on his wife? – When she wears beads.

A man asked his wife what she would like for her birthday. 'I'd love to be eight again,' she said.

So he pulled out all the stops to make her dream come true. He whisked her off to Disneyland, made her go on all the scariest roller coasters, and force-fed her candyfloss and ice cream. Then he took her to McDonald's for a special kids' meal before rounding the day off with a trip to the cinema to see a two-hour cartoon carnival.

That night she slumped into bed, feeling exhausted and queasy.

'So what was it like being eight again?' asked her husband.

'Actually,' she said, 'I meant my dress size!'

The Invisible Man married an invisible woman. The kids were nothing to look at.

A wife was still in a foul mood the morning after a party. She told her husband crossly: 'You certainly made a fool of yourself last night. I just hope nobody realised you were sober.'

Did you hear about the x-ray specialist who married one of his patients? – Everybody wondered what he saw in her.

Carl lamented to his friend Larry that all the excitement had gone out of his marriage.

'That often happens when people have been married for ten years, like you,' said Larry. 'Have you ever considered having an affair? That might put a bit of spark back into your relationship.'

'No, I couldn't,' said Carl, shocked.

'Get real,' said Larry. 'This is the 21st century. These things happen all the time.'

'But what if my wife found out?'

'No problem. Be upfront. Tell her about it in advance.'

Overcoming his initial misgivings, Carl plucked up the courage and broke the news to his wife the next morning.

'Honey,' he said hesitantly, 'I don't want you to take this the wrong way . . . and please remember that I'm only doing this because I love you, otherwise I would never dream of being unfaithful . . . but I think an affair might bring us closer together.'

'Forget it,' said his wife. 'I've tried it, and it's never worked.'

Once upon a time there was a prince who, through no fault of his own, was put under a spell by an evil witch. The curse was that the prince could speak only one word each year. However, he could save up the words from one year to the next so that if he did not speak for a whole year, he was allowed to speak two words the following year.

One day he met and fell madly in love with a beautiful princess who had golden hair, sapphire eyes and ruby lips. With the greatest difficulty he decided to refrain from speaking for two whole years so that he could look at her and say, 'My darling'. But at the end of the two years he wished to tell her that he loved her. Consequently, instead of speaking, he chose to remain silent for another three years, thus allowing himself the luxury of five words.

But at the end of those five years he was so madly in love with her that he wanted to ask her to marry him, so he decided to wait another four years without speaking.

Finally as the ninth year of silence ended, his joy knew no bounds. Leading the lovely princess to the most secluded and romantic spot he knew, the prince placed a hundred red roses on her lap, knelt before her, and, taking her hand in his, said huskily: 'My darling, I love you! Will you marry me?'

The princess tucked a strand of golden hair behind a dainty ear, opened her sapphire eyes in wonder, and, parting her ruby lips, said: 'Pardon?'

Arriving home drunk one night, a husband cut himself when he walked into an overhanging shelf in the garage. With blood trickling from facial wounds, he went straight upstairs to the bathroom to carry out repairs.

The next morning, his wife said: 'You came home drunk last night, didn't you?'

'No,' he replied, mustering all the sincerity at his disposal.

'Then perhaps you can explain to me why there are plasters all over the bathroom mirror . . .'

Husband: I think our son got his brain from me.
Wife: I think he did – I've still got mine with me.

Two children were playing weddings. One was overheard saying: 'You have the right to remain silent, anything you say may be held against you, you have the right to an attorney, you may kiss the bride.'

A husband and wife were out shopping when the husband eyed up a shapely young woman in a short, tight skirt. Without looking up from the item she was examining, the wife said: 'Was it worth the trouble you're in?'

A husband and wife were going through a rocky phase and were giving each other the silent treatment. One day, at the height of hostilities, he realised that he needed his wife to wake him at 5 a.m. so that he could catch an early morning business flight. Not wanting to be the first to break the silence, he wrote on a piece of paper: 'Please wake me at 5 a.m.'

The next morning, he woke to discover that it was 9 a.m. and that he had missed his flight. Furious, he was about to confront his wife when he noticed a piece of paper on his pillow.

The paper read: 'It is 5 a.m. Wake up.'

A mother travelled 2,000 miles around the world to be with her only son on the day he received his Air Force Wings and also got married.

'Thank you for coming,' he said afterwards. 'It meant so much to me.'

'I wouldn't have missed it,' she said. 'After all, it's not every day a mother watches her son get his wings in the morning and have them clipped in the afternoon.'

Wife: Why don't you ever wear your wedding ring?
Husband: It cuts off my circulation.
Wife: It's supposed to.

A husband was feeling sorry for himself and in a rare moment of candour, confessed to his wife: 'Sometimes I think I'm nothing but an idiot.'

His wife held his hand tenderly and said: 'Don't worry, darling. Lots of people feel like that. In fact, virtually everyone we know thinks you're an idiot.'

A woman with fourteen children, aged between one and fourteen, decided to sue her husband for divorce on grounds of desertion.

'When did he desert you?' asked the judge.

'Thirteen years ago,' she answered.

The judge was baffled. 'If he left thirteen years ago, where did all the children come from?'

'He kept coming back to say he was sorry.'

John brought his new work colleague, Robert, home for dinner. As they arrived at the door, his wife rushed up, threw her arms around John and kissed him passionately.

'Wow!' said Robert. 'And how long have you two been married?'

'Twenty-four years,' replied John.

'You must have a terrific marriage if your wife greets you like that after all those years.'

'Don't be fooled,' said John. 'She only does it to make the dog jealous.'

Deciding to wash his sweatshirt, a husband asked his wife: 'What setting do I use on the washing machine?'

'It depends,' she replied. 'What does it say on your shirt?'

'University of Oklahoma.'

A friend asked a woman: 'What's in that locket, a memento of some sort?'

'Yes,' replied the woman. 'It's a lock of my husband's hair.'

'But your husband is still alive!'

'I know, but his hair's all gone.'

Enjoying a nice refreshing shower, a wife was interrupted when her husband poked his head in to ask: 'What shall I give Lucy for lunch?'

Although he was always very good with their baby daughter, there were times when the wife wanted him to think for himself without always bothering her. This was one such occasion. 'It's up to you,' she replied disinterested. 'There's plenty of food in the house. I'll tell you what, why don't you pretend that I'm not at home?'

'OK,' he said and went away.

A few minutes later, her mobile phone rang. Her husband's voice said: 'Hi, honey, how are you? What shall I give Lucy for lunch?'

As Carla was getting to know John and his family, she was particularly impressed by how much his parents seemed to love each other. 'They're so thoughtful and considerate towards each other,' said Carla. 'Why, your dad even brings your mom a cup of hot coffee in bed every morning.'

Soon Carla and John became engaged, and then married. On the way from the wedding to the reception, Carla again remarked on John's loving parents and his mother's morning coffee in bed. 'Tell me,' said Carla, 'does it run in the family?'

'It sure does,' said John. 'But I think you should know – I take after my mother.'

At the height of an argument, the husband said: 'Admit it, Cheryl, the only reason you married me was because my grandfather left me $10 million.'

'Don't be ridiculous,' she said. 'I don't care who left it to you.'

A woman woke up one morning and said to her husband: 'I had the most vivid dream last night. I dreamed you bought me a really expensive diamond ring for my birthday. I've never had a dream like that before. What do you think it means?'

'You'll know tonight, darling,' he said.

Hardly able to contain her excitement all day, she eagerly awaited her husband's arrival home from work. Sure enough, he was carrying a small, beautifully wrapped package, which he then handed to her.

Thrilled, she opened it . . . and found a book entitled *The Meaning of Dreams*.

A man asked his friend: 'How has marriage changed things for you?'

'Well,' said the friend sadly. 'Before we got married, I caught her in my arms. Now I catch her in my pockets!'

Deciding to throw a fortieth birthday party for his wife, a man ordered a huge cake from the bakery. Over the phone he said: 'The message I want is "You are not getting older, you are getting better."'

The baker's assistant said: 'That's a lot of words. How should we arrange it?'

After a moment's thought, the man said: 'Put "You are not getting older" at the top, "You are getting better" at the bottom.'

'OK,' said the assistant, making a note of the inscription to give to the baker.

Come the day of the party, friends and family travelled from far and wide. At the height of the celebrations, the birthday cake was unveiled. The wife was greatly embarrassed to read the message on it: 'You are not getting older at the top, you are getting better at the bottom.'

A doctor and his wife were sunbathing on a beach when a beautiful young woman in a skimpy bikini strolled by. The near-naked woman looked at the doctor, smiled, and said in a sexy voice: 'Hi there, handsome. How are you doing?'

She then wiggled her backside and walked off.

'Who was that?' demanded the doctor's wife.

'Er . . . just a woman I met professionally,' he replied.

'Oh yeah?' snarled his wife. 'Whose profession? Yours or hers?'

Why did the polygamist cross the aisle? – To get to the other bride.

John: 'I hear you got married again, Ken.'
Ken: 'Yes, for the fourth time.'
John: 'What happened to your first three wives?'
Ken: 'They all died.'
John: 'Oh I'm sorry, I didn't know. That's terrible. How did they die?'
Ken: 'The first ate poisonous mushrooms.'
John: 'How awful! What about the second?'
Ken: 'She ate poison mushrooms.'
John: 'Oh no. What about the third? Did she die from poisonous mushrooms too?'

100

Ken: 'No, she died of a broken neck?'
John: 'I see, an accident.'
Ken: 'Not exactly – she wouldn't eat her mushrooms.'

Three weeks after her wedding, a new bride called her priest in a state of great anxiety.

'Father,' she said, 'John and I had the most dreadful fight. It was really awful. I just don't know what to do next.'

'Calm down, my child,' said the priest. 'It's not as bad as you think. Every marriage has to have its first fight.'

'I know, I know,' she said. 'But what am I going to do with the body?'

A guy in an office revealed to his co-workers that, in a moment of tender romance, he had asked his girlfriend to marry him.

'What did she say?' asked one.

'I don't know. She hasn't e-mailed me back yet.'

The Differences Between Men and Women:
- A man will pay $2 for a $1 item he wants; a woman will pay $1 for a $2 item that she doesn't want.
- A woman worries about the future until she gets a husband; a man never worries about the future until he gets a wife.
- A successful man is one who makes more money than his wife can spend; a successful woman is one who can find such a man.
- To be happy with a man you must understand him a lot and love him a little; to be happy with a woman you must love her a lot and not try to understand her at all.
- Men wake up as good-looking as when they went to bed; women somehow deteriorate during the night.
- A woman marries a man hoping he will change, but he doesn't; a man marries a woman hoping that she won't change, but she does.
- A woman has the last word in any argument; anything a man says after that is the beginning of a new argument.

On their first day at home after their honeymoon, the new bride said: 'If you make the toast and pour the juice, breakfast will be ready.'

'Great,' said the husband. 'What are we having?'

'Toast and juice.'

Two men were sitting in a bar, complaining about their wives. 'It really annoys me,' said one. 'Whenever we have a row, she gets historical.'

'Don't you mean "hysterical"?' queried his friend.

'No, I mean historical. Every time we argue, she says: "I still remember the time that you . . ."'

A new bride was embarrassed at being known as a honeymooner. So when she and her husband pulled up to the hotel, she asked him if there was any way they could make it appear that they had been married a long time.

'Sure,' he said. 'You carry the suitcases.'

A couple had been married for forty-seven years during which time they had raised twelve children and been blessed with twenty-four grandchildren. When asked the secret of how they had managed to stay together for so long, they said: 'Years ago we made a promise to each other: the first one to pick up and leave had to take all the kids.'

On their silver wedding anniversary, a woman turned to her husband and said: 'Darling, will you still love me when my hair turns grey?'

'Why shouldn't I?' he replied. 'I stuck with you through the other six shades.'

A man said to his friend: 'My wife's a peach.'

'Why? Because she's so soft and juicy?'

'No, because she has a heart of stone.'

What do you call a woman who knows where her husband is every night? – A widow.

On the way home from a party, a wife said to her husband: 'Have I ever told you how sexy and irresistible to women you are?'

'I don't believe you have,' he replied, flattered.

'Then what in hell's name gave you that idea at the party?'

Two husbands were drowning their sorrows in a bar. One said: 'Why do you and your wife fight all the time?'

The other replied: 'I don't know. She never tells me.'

Wife: When we got married, you said you had an ocean-going yacht.
Husband: Just shut up and row!

Husband: Put your coat on, honey, I'm going to the bar.
Wife: Are you taking me out for a drink?
Husband: Don't be silly, woman. I'm turning the heating off!

Husband: I hear you've been telling everyone that I'm stupid.
Wife: Sorry, I didn't realise it was a secret.

A jealous husband hired a private detective to check on his wife's movements. The husband demanded more than just a written report – he wanted a video of his wife's activities.

A week later, the detective returned with a tape and sat down to watch it with the husband. As the tape played, he saw his wife meeting another man. He saw the two of them laughing in the park. He saw them enjoying themselves at an outdoor café. He saw them having a playful fight in the street. He saw them dancing in a dimly lit nightclub.

When the tape ended, the distraught husband said: 'I can't believe this!'

'What's not to believe?' asked the detective. 'It's right up there on the screen. The camera never lies.'

The husband replied: 'What I mean is, I can't believe my wife is so much fun!'

Two husbands were in a bar discussing the state of their marriages.

One said: 'My wife always complains that I don't help with the housework.'

The other said: 'Mine constantly complains that I never listen to her – or something like that.'

A woman was taking a shortcut through a cemetery when she spotted a man sobbing uncontrollably beside a grave.

'Why did you have to go?' he cried. 'Why, oh why?'

The woman put a comforting hand on his shoulder. 'I don't wish to intrude on your grief, but I'm so sorry for your loss. Is this your wife's grave?'

'No,' sniffled the man. 'It's her first husband's.'

On their honeymoon night, the husband was surprised and a little disappointed to see his new wife gazing out of the window.

'Aren't you coming to bed, honey?' he asked.

'No,' she sighed dreamily. 'My mother told me this would be the most magical night of my life, and I don't want to miss a single minute of it.'

A woman arrived home to find her house had been ransacked, but she didn't report it until the following day. When a police officer came round to investigate, he asked her the reason for the delay.

She said: 'To tell you the truth, officer, I didn't know I'd been robbed. When I saw the place in such a state, I simply assumed my husband had been looking for some clean socks.'

After a furious row with his wife, a husband tried to make the peace.

'Why don't you meet me halfway on this?' he suggested. 'I'll admit you're wrong if you admit I'm right.'

103

Men

Mary and Jane were old friends. Both had been married to their husbands for a long time. Mary was upset because she thought her husband no longer found her attractive. 'You poor thing,' said Jane. 'I'm lucky. As I get older my husband says I get more beautiful every day.'

'Yes,' replied Mary, 'but he's an antique dealer.'

A Woman's Guide to Manspeak:
He says: 'You deserve someone better than me.'
He means: 'I've found someone better than you.'

He says: 'Is that a new dress?'
He means: 'I've taped over your only copy of *Sliding Doors*.'

He says: 'It's probably my fault.'
He means: 'It's definitely my fault but there's no way I'm going to apologise and the football's about to start.'

He says: 'Football's finished.'
He means: 'Get 'em off!'

He says: 'We all need our own space.'
He means: 'I'm up to something.'

He says: 'What's wrong?'
He means: 'What meaningless, self-inflicted psychological trauma are you going through now?'

He says: 'I love you too.'
He means: 'There, I've said it. Now can we get on with the sex.'

He says: 'It'd take too long to explain.'
He means: 'I've no idea how it works.'

He says: 'Take a break, love – you're working too hard.'
He means: 'I can't hear the TV over the vacuum cleaner.'

He says: 'I really want to get to know you better.'
He means: 'So I can tell my friends about it.'

He says: 'I don't know if I like her.'
He means: 'She won't sleep with me.'

He says: 'I've got my reasons for what I'm doing.'
He means: 'I hope I think of some pretty soon.'

He says: 'I can't find it.'
He means: 'It didn't fall into my hands, so I'm completely clueless.'

He says: 'No reason at all – I just remembered how much you like flowers.'
He means: 'Forgive me, partner, for I have sinned.'

He says: 'You're the only girl I've ever cared about.'
He means: 'You're the only girl who hasn't rejected me.'

He says: 'That's women's work.'
He means: 'I don't understand how to do it.'

He says: 'Let's not bother with potatoes.'
He means: 'I can't find the user instructions for the potato peeler.'

He says: 'I'm a romantic.'
He means: 'I'm poor.'

He says: 'You look terrific.'
He means: 'Please don't try on any more outfits – I'm dying for a pint.'

He says: 'There's only one cookie left.'
He means: 'What are you going to have?'

He says: 'Do you need a hand with dinner?'
He means: 'Why the hell isn't it on the table yet?'

He says: 'Haven't I seen you before?'
He means: 'Nice ass.'

He says: 'Of course I'm listening.'
He means: 'What did you just say?'

He says: 'I'll give you a call.'
He means: 'I'd rather have my arm ripped off by wild dogs than see you again.'

He says: 'I've been thinking a lot.'
He means: 'You're not as attractive as when I was drunk.'

He says: 'I'm hungry.'
He means: 'Fix me something to eat.'

He says: 'Of course your bum doesn't look big in that.'
He means: 'Get out of the way, I can't see the screen.'

He says: 'I'm not lost. I know exactly where we are.'
He means: 'No-one will ever see us alive again!'

A man was married to the worst cook in the world. One evening he came home from work to find her in floods of tears.

'It's a disaster,' she wailed. 'The cat's eaten your dinner!'

'Never mind,' said the husband. 'I'll buy you a new cat.'

The doctor told a man waiting in a surgery: 'I've got good news and bad news. The bad news is that you have an inoperable brain tumour. The good news is that our hospital has just been awarded a certificate to perform brain transplants and, by chance, there has been an accident right out front in which a young couple have been killed. You can have whichever brain you like. The man's brain is $100,000 and the woman's brain is $30,000.'

The patient said: 'If you don't mind me asking, doctor, why is there such a large difference between the price of a male and female brain?'

The doctor explained: 'The female brain is used.'

Men are like mascara – they usually run at the first sign of emotion.
Men are like blenders – you need one, but you're not quite sure why.
Men are like plungers – they spend most of their lives in a hardware store or the bathroom.
Men are like mini skirts – if you're not careful, they'll creep up your legs.
Men are like copiers – you need them for reproduction, but that's about it.
Men are like coolers – load them with beer and you can take them anywhere.
Men are like place mats – they only show up when there's food on the table.
Men are like high heels – they're easy to walk on once you get the hang of it.
Men are like bike helmets – they're handy in an emergency, but otherwise they just look silly.
Men are like curling irons – they're always hot and always in your hair.
Men are like bananas – the older they get, the less firm they are.
Men are like coffee – the best ones are rich, warm, full-bodied, and can keep you up all night.

Men are like used cars – they're easy to get, cheap, and they prove to be unreliable.

Men are like chocolate bars – they're sweet, smooth, and they usually head right for your hips.

Men are like horoscopes – they always tell you what to do and are usually wrong.

Men are like noodles – they're always in hot water, they lack taste and they need dough.

NOTICE: Classes for men at our local learning centre for adults will be starting soon. Due to the high level of difficulty, each course will accept a maximum of ten applicants.

Topic 1: How To Fill Up The Ice Cube Trays. Step-by-step, with slide presentation.

Topic 2: The Toilet Paper Roll: Do They Grow On The Holders? Round table discussion.

Topic 3: Is It Possible To Urinate Using The Technique Of Lifting The Seat Up And Avoiding The Floor And Walls? Group practice.

Topic 4: Fundamental Differences Between The Laundry Basket And The Floor. Pictures and explanatory graphics.

Topic 5: The After-Dinner Dishes And Cutlery: Can They Levitate And Fly Into The Dishwasher? Examples on video.

Topic 6: Loss Of Identity: Losing The Remote To Your Partner. Helpline and support groups.

Topic 7:Real Men Ask For Directions When Lost. Real-life testimonials.

Topic 8: Is It Genetically Impossible To Sit Quietly While She Parallel Parks? Driving simulation.

Topic 9: How To Be The Ideal Shopping Companion. Relaxation exercises, meditation and breathing techniques.

Topic 10: How To Fight Cerebral Atrophy: Remembering Birthdays, Anniversaries, Other Important Dates And Calling When You're Going To Be Late.

A bald man was neurotic about his lack of hair. He had tried all sorts of treatments, but without success. Then one day he passed a barber's shop with a sign in the window that read: 'Bald Men. Your Problems Solved Instantly. You Too Can Have a Head of Hair Like Mine For $1,000.' And beneath the sign was a photo of the barber with his flowing mane of hair.

So the bald man went into the shop and asked the barber: 'Can you guarantee that for $1,000 my hair will instantly look like yours?'

'Absolutely,' said the barber. 'It'll take just a few seconds for us to look exactly alike.'

'Right then,' said the bald man, handing over $1,000. 'Let's go for it.'

The barber took the money and shaved his own hair off.

James Bond once slept through an earthquake. He was shaken, not stirred.

What's the difference between a man and childbirth? – One can be really painful and almost unbearable while the other is just having a baby.

Male Code of Conduct:

1. Under no circumstances may two men share an umbrella.
2. Any man who brings a camera to a bachelor party may be legally beaten and killed by his fellow partygoers.
3. You may exaggerate any anecdote told in a bar by 50 per cent without recrimination.
4. If you've known a guy for more than 24 hours, his sister is off-limits forever.
5. The maximum amount of time you have to wait for another guy who's running late is five minutes. For a girl, you are required to wait ten minutes for every point of hotness she scores on the classic 1-10 scale.
6. Moaning about the brand of free beer in a friend's refrigerator is unacceptable. Only complaints about the temperature are permissible.
7. Before dating a friend's ex-girlfriend, you are required to ask his permission.
8. Women who claim they 'love to watch sport' must be treated as spies until they demonstrate knowledge of the game and, more importantly, the ability to pick a chicken wing clean.
9. No man is ever required to buy a birthday present for another man.
10. The universal compensation for friends who help you move home is beer.
11. It is permissible to consume a fruity cocktail only when you're sunning yourself on a tropical beach.
12. Unless you're in prison, never fight naked.
13. A man in the company of a provocatively dressed woman must remain sober enough to fight.
14. If a buddy is already singing along to a song in the car, you must never join in.
15. Never hesitate to reach for the last beer or the last slice of pizza, but not both. That's just plain mean.
16. If a man's zipper is down, that's his problem; you didn't see anything.

What's the one thing that all men in singles bars have in common? – They're married.

After a row with her husband, a woman went to her mother for moral support.

'Men are only good for one thing,' said the wife.

'Exactly,' said her mother. 'And how often do you have to double park?'

What can you tell about a well-dressed man? – His wife chooses his clothes.

Reasons For Men To Stay Single:
- Cooking your own meals would be an adventure, not a punishment.
- You wouldn't have to explain why you're wearing that shirt with those trousers.
- You could leave the toilet seat in any position you like.
- You could actually tell the bartender, 'If anyone calls, I'm here.'
- You could be painting the town instead of the house.
- You'd get to see what your paycheck looks like.
- You'd get to see what your credit cards look like.
- You wouldn't have to watch German films with sub-titles.
- You could use your own name at hotels.
- You could go home drunk to sleep, instead of under a bridge.

One day in the Garden of Eden, Eve called out to God: 'Lord, I have a problem.'

'What's the problem, Eve?' asked God.

'Lord, I know you've created me and have provided this beautiful garden and all of these wonderful animals, but I'm just not happy.'

'Why is that, Eve?'

'I am lonely, Lord. And I'm sick to death of apples.'

'Well, Eve, in that case, I have a solution. I shall create a man for you.'

'What's a man, Lord?'

'This man,' said God, 'will be a flawed creature, with aggressive tendencies, an enormous ego and an inability to empathise or listen to you properly. All in all, he'll give you a hard time. But he'll be bigger and faster and more muscular than you. He'll be really good at fighting, kicking a ball about, and hunting fleet-footed ruminants, and he will help populate the Earth.'

'Sounds great,' said Eve, with an ironically raised eyebrow.

'Anyway, you can only have him on one condition.'

'What's that, Lord?'

'You'll have to let him believe that I made him first.'

Adam said to God: 'When you created Eve, why did you make her body so curvy and tender, unlike mine?'

God replied: 'I did that, Adam, so that you could love her.'

'And why,' asked Adam, 'did you give her long, shiny, beautiful hair, but not me?'

'So that you could love her,' answered God.

'Then why did you make her so stupid?' asked Adam. 'Certainly not so that I could love her?'

'No, Adam,' said God. 'I did that so that she could love you.'

The Different Qualities of Men and Women:

Women are honest, loyal and forgiving. They are smart, knowing that knowledge is power. But they still know how to use their softer side to make a point. Women want to do the best for their family, their friends, and themselves. Their hearts break when a friend dies. They have sorrow at the loss of a family member, yet they are strong when they think there is no strength left. A woman can make a romantic evening unforgettable. Women drive, fly, walk, run or e-mail you to show how much they care about you. Women do more than just give birth. They bring joy and hope. They give compassion and ideals. They give moral support to their family and friends. And all they want back is a hug and a smile. The heart of a woman is what makes the world spin.

Men are good at lifting heavy stuff and killing spiders.

Money

Once there was a millionaire who collected alligators, which he kept in the pool at the back of his mansion. He also had a beautiful daughter who was single.

One day the millionaire threw a lavish party, during which he issued a challenge to every male guest: 'My friends,' he said, 'I will give one million dollars, or my daughter, to the man who can swim across this pool full of alligators and emerge unharmed!'

No sooner had he finished than there was the sound of an almighty splash in the pool. A man was swimming across the pool as fast as he possibly could, cheered on by the crowd. Finally he reached the other side unharmed.

The millionaire walked over and shook him warmly by the hand. 'I'm truly impressed. That was amazing. I really didn't think anybody would do it. Now I must keep my side of the deal. Do you want my daughter or the one million dollars?'

The man caught his breath, then said: 'Listen, I don't want your money. And I don't want your daughter. All I want is whoever pushed me in the pool!'

A Hollywood movie producer was lying by the pool at the Beverly Hills

Hilton when his business partner arrived in a state of high excitement.

'How did the meeting go?' asked the first guy.

'Great,' said his associate. 'Tarantino will write and direct for eight million, Tom Hanks will star for nine, and we can bring in the whole picture for under fifty million.'

'Fantastic!' said the guy by the pool.

'There's just one snag,' warned his partner.

'What's that?'

'We have to put up five thousand in cash.'

Why is it that by the time you can make ends meet, they move the ends?

Six men were playing poker when Norman lost $750 on a single hand. The shock was so great that he suffered a heart attack and dropped at the table. Showing respect for their fallen comrade, the other five counted their chips standing up.

Arthur looked around and said sombrely: 'Who is going to tell his wife?' They drew straws. Maurice picked the short one.

The others urged Maurice to be discreet and not to add to the poor woman's pain. Maurice promised that discretion was his middle name.

Arriving at Norman's house, Maurice composed himself and knocked on the door. Norman's wife answered and asked him what he wanted.

Maurice said: 'Your husband just lost $750 playing cards.'

The wife said: 'Well then, I hope he drops dead!'

Maurice said: 'I'll tell him.'

A man walked into a bank and asked to borrow the sum of $2,000 for a month. The loan officer asked what collateral the man had. He replied: 'I've got a Rolls-Royce. Keep it until the loan is paid off. Here are the keys.'

So the loan officer arranged for the car to be driven back into the bank's underground parking for safe keeping and gave the man the $2,000.

A month later, the man walked back into the bank, paid back the $2,000 loan plus $10 interest and regained possession of his Rolls-Royce. The loan officer was mystified. 'Tell me, sir,' he said, 'why would someone who drives a Rolls-Royce need to borrow $2,000?'

The man replied: 'I had to go abroad for a month, and where else could I store a Rolls-Royce for that length of time for $10?'

Why is a tax loophole like a good parking spot? – As soon as you see one, it's gone.

A mother decided her daughter should have something practical for her tenth birthday and suggested opening a savings account. The girl thought this was an excellent idea and so they went along to the bank to fill in the necessary form.

'Since it's your account,' said the mother, 'and you're so grown up now, you can fill in the form. But if there's anything you don't understand, I'm right here.'

The girl did fine until she came to the space for 'Name of your previous bank' and, after a moment's hesitation, she put 'Piggy'.

Why is it that in order to get a loan you must first prove you don't need it?

A small boy asked a wealthy old man how he had made his fortune.

'Well, son,' he replied, 'let me tell you a little story. It was back in the 1930s during the Great Depression. I was down to my last nickel and I invested that nickel in an apple. I spent the rest of the day polishing that apple so that it sparkled in the sun and at the end of the day I sold the apple for ten cents. The next morning, I invested those ten cents in two apples. I spent the entire day polishing them and then sold them for twenty cents. I carried on like that, and by the end of two weeks I had $1.20 in my pocket. Then my aunt died and left me five million dollars . . .'

Tom was broke. His business had gone bust and in desperation he prayed to God to make him win the lottery. But he was out of luck and had to sell his car. The next week he again prayed to God to make him win the lottery, but once more he was out of luck and had to sell his house. With his wife about to leave him, Tom made one last plea to God to make him win the lottery. God came back to him and said: 'Listen, Tom, meet me halfway on this – buy a ticket.'

Why is it that nothing in the known universe travels faster than a bad cheque?

A window salesman phoned a customer. 'I'm calling, sir,' he said, 'because our company replaced all the windows in your house with our triple-glazed weather-tight windows over a year ago, and you still haven't sent us a single payment.'

The customer replied: 'But you said they'd pay for themselves in twelve months!'

A man went into a bank and withdrew $3,000 in cash. To keep the bills together, he bound them with a rubber band. Then he stuffed the wad of money in his pocket and headed for the door. But he had only gone a few yards down the street when he noticed to his horror that the money was missing. Certain that he hadn't had his pocket picked, he assumed that the bundle of bills must have simply fallen out of his pocket.

As he rushed back into the bank, he collided with an elderly customer.

'Have you lost some money tied in a rubber band?' asked the old man.

'Yes, I have!'

'Well, I've found the rubber band.'

Only in America could a letter offering a million dollar prize be considered junk mail.

Bidding at an auction was proceeding vigorously until the auctioneer suddenly announced: 'A gentleman in this room has lost a wallet containing $10,000. If it is returned, he will pay a reward of $2,000.'

There was a moment's silence before a voice at the back of the room called out: '$2,500!'

Several men were sitting around in the locker room of a private club after exercising. Suddenly a mobile phone on one of the benches rang. One of the men picked it up.

'Hello?'

'Honey, it's me. Are you at the club?'

'Yes.'

'Great! I am at the mall two blocks from where you are. I just saw a beautiful mink coat. It's absolutely gorgeous. Can I buy it?'

'What's the price?'

'Only $1,500.'

'Well, OK, go ahead and get it if you like it that much.'

'Oh, and I also stopped by the Mercedes dealership and saw the 2005 models. There was one I really loved. I spoke with the salesman, and he gave me a really good price, and since we need to trade in the BMW that we bought last year . . .'

'What price did he quote you?'

'Only $80,000.'

'OK, but for that price I want it with all the options.'

'Great! But before we hang up, something else.'

'What?'

'It might sound like a lot, but I was studying our bank balance and . . . I stopped by the real estate agent this morning and saw the house we looked at last year. Remember, the one with the pool, two acres of ground, beach-front property? Well, it's on sale again!'

'How much are they asking?'

'Only $750,000 – a terrific price, and we've got more than enough in the bank.'

'OK then, go ahead and buy it, but just bid $750,000, understand? No more.'

'Yeah, darling. Oh, thank you. See you later. I do love you.'

'Bye . . . I do too.'

The man hung up, closed the phone's flap, and, raising his hand while still holding the phone, asked all those present: 'Does anyone know who this phone belongs to?'

Why is the man who invests all your money called a broker?

A building contractor was being paid weekly. As he opened his wage packet one week, he said to the site manager: 'But this is $200 less than we agreed on.'

'I know,' said the manager, 'but last week I overpaid you by $200 and you never complained.'

'Well,' explained the contractor, 'I don't mind an occasional mistake, but when it gets to be a habit, I feel I have to call it to your attention.'

Norm went up to his neighbour and said: 'I bet you $100 that I can jump higher than your house.'

The neighbour eyed him up carefully before concluding that with his short legs and beer belly, Norm appeared incapable of any astounding athletic feat. 'OK,' he said. 'You're on.'

So Norm prepared himself mentally before jumping all of nine inches off the ground. The neighbour roared with laughter until Norm said: 'Right. It's your house's turn now.'

A regular theatregoer was dismayed to find that he had a seat near the rear of the house for the performance of an eagerly awaited mystery thriller. With half an hour to go before curtain up, he summoned an usher and said: 'Could you possibly help me? I have been looking forward to this play for weeks, but I am not happy with my seat. You see, my eyesight and hearing are not what they were and, in order to be able to follow the intricate plot and work out the clues, I need a seat nearer the front of the house. If you can get me a better seat, I'll give you a handsome tip.'

The usher promised to do what he could and after twenty-five minutes of delicate negotiations, he was finally able to offer the man a seat right in the middle of the front row. The man took his seat, thanked the usher, and handed him a quarter by way of a tip.

The deflated usher took one look at the quarter and then whispered in the man's ear: 'The butler did it with the candlestick in the ballroom.'

114

A guy walked into a bank and said to the female teller at the window: 'I want to open a bloody account.'

'I beg your pardon,' said the teller. 'What did you say?'

'Listen, damn you,' snarled the man. 'I said I want to open a bloody account right now.'

'I'm terribly sorry, sir,' said the teller, 'but I am afraid we do not tolerate that kind of language in this bank.'

And with that, she left her window and reported the customer's behaviour to the manager. A few moments later, the manager returned to confront the man.

'Now what seems to be the problem?' asked the bank manager.

'There's no damn problem,' said the man. 'I just won sixty million in the lottery and I want to open a bloody account in this damn bank.'

'I see,' said the manager, 'and this bitch is giving you a hard time?'

A blackjack dealer and a player with thirteen in his hand were arguing about whether or not it was appropriate to tip the dealer.

The player said: 'When I get bad cards, it's not the dealer's fault. And when I get good cards, the dealer obviously has nothing to do with it. So why should I tip him?'

The dealer countered: 'When you eat out, do you tip the waiter?'

'Of course.'

'Well then, he serves you food, and I'm serving you cards. So you should tip me.'

'I see your point,' said the player, 'but the waiter gives me what I ask for . . . I'll take an eight.'

A man hired a taxi to take him to court for his bankruptcy trial. 'I'm in terrible debt,' he told the driver. 'I owe money to everyone – the taxman, my suppliers, the electric company, the gas company, the water company, a catering firm, two bookmakers, the council, and an office furnishing company.' As the taxi pulled up outside the court, he turned to the driver and added: 'Well, I suppose you might as well come in too.'

The queue at the bank stretched right back to the door. A woman customer decided to save time by filling in a withdrawal slip while she was waiting, but she couldn't remember the date.

So she turned and asked the woman behind: 'What's the date today?'

'It's the seventh.'

A man at the very back of the queue piped up: 'Don't write it in yet!'

Signs That You're Broke:
• American Express calls and says: 'Leave home without it.'
• At communion you go back for seconds.

115

- You receive care packages from Europe.
- You finally clean your house, hoping to find change.
- You think of a lottery ticket as an investment.
- You give blood every day – for the orange juice.
- McDonald's supplies you with all your kitchen condiments.
- The neighbourhood dogs have stopped sniffing at your pockets.

A stockbroker was 'cold calling' about a penny stock and found an interested client. 'I think this one will really move,' said the broker. 'It's only $1 a share.'

'Buy me 1,000 shares,' said the client.

The next day the stock was at $2, prompting the client to call the broker and say: 'You were right, give me 5,000 more shares.'

The next day the client looked in the newspaper and saw that the stock had risen to $4. The client ran to the phone and called the broker. 'Get me 10,000 more shares.'

'Great,' said the broker.

The next day the client looked in the paper and the stock was standing at $9. Seeing what a sizeable profit he had in just a few days, he phoned the broker and told him: 'Sell all my shares.'

The broker said: 'To whom? You were the only one buying that stock.'

A balding man went into a barber's shop and asked how much it would be for a haircut.

'Twenty-five dollars,' said the barber.

'Twenty-five dollars, that's outrageous!' said the man. 'I've hardly got any hair. How can it be that expensive?'

The barber explained: 'It's five dollars for the actual cut, and twenty dollars for the search fee.'

A woman was having a bad day at the casino. Down to her last $50, she exclaimed in exasperation: 'What lousy luck I've had today! What on earth am I going to do now? How can I turn it around?'

A man standing next to her at the roulette table suggested: 'I don't know. Why don't you play your age?' The man then wandered off.

But moments later his attention was grabbed by a great commotion at the roulette table. He rushed back and pushed his way through the crowd. The woman was lying limp on the floor with the table operator kneeling over her. The man was stunned.

'What happened?' he asked. 'Is she all right?'

The operator replied: 'I don't know. She put all her money on 29, and 36 came up. Then she just fainted!'

A one-dollar bill and a twenty-dollar bill met in a till. 'Where have you been?' asked the one-dollar bill. 'I haven't seen you around in ages.'

'I've been all over the world,' said the twenty-dollar bill. 'I've been hanging out at casinos, I went on a Mediterranean cruise and did the rounds of the ship, I came back to the US for a while, I went to a couple of baseball games, to the shopping mall, all kinds of places. What about you?'

The one-dollar bill said: 'Oh, you know, the same old stuff – church, church, church.'

A man complained to his friend: 'My wife is always asking me for more money. A month ago she asked me for $100, two weeks ago she said she wanted $200, and yesterday it was $400.'

'What does she do with it all?' asked the friend.

'I don't know. I never give her any.'

A young woman told her father tearfully: 'Dad, you know you told me to put all my money in an account with that big bank? Well, that bank is now in trouble, and I don't know what I'm going to do!'

'That bank can't be in trouble,' said the father. 'It's one of the major players in the financial world. You must have got it wrong.'

'I don't think so,' she sobbed. 'They just returned one of my cheques with a note saying, "Insufficient Funds".'

On his first day with a finance company, a man was sent to try and sort out the firm's toughest client. To the amazement of his boss, he returned with the $10,000 debt paid in full.

'How did you manage that?' asked the boss. 'We've been trying to get him to settle up for nine months.'

'It was easy. I simply told him that if he didn't pay us, I'd tell all his other creditors that he had!'

A man went into a bank and asked the cashier to check his balance. So the cashier pushed him over.

A shipping magnate decided to conduct a tour of his business to see how things were going. Going down to the docks, he noticed a young man leaning against the wall doing nothing.

Disgusted at this inactivity, the magnate walked up to the young man and said: 'How much do you make in a day, son?'

He replied: '$150.'

The magnate pulled out his wallet, gave him $150 and told him to clear off and never come back.

A few minutes later the shipping clerk came over to the magnate and asked: 'Have you seen that UPS driver? I asked him to wait here for me.'

A banker fell overboard while taking a cruise on a friend's yacht. The friend grabbed a lifebelt, held it up, and, not knowing if the banker could swim, shouted: 'Can you float alone?'

'Of course I can!' yelled the banker. 'But this is a heck of a time to talk business!'

Motoring

A woman was out driving when she stalled at a red light. Hard though she tried, she was unable to restart the engine and soon a long queue began to form. The male driver immediately behind her was particularly impatient, honking his horn continuously.

Finally she got out, went up to the driver behind and said: 'I can't seem to get my car started. Would you be a sweetheart and see if you can get it started for me? I'll stay here in your car and lean on your horn for you!'

A car was speeding along the road when it suddenly crashed through the guard rail, rolled down a cliff, bounced off a tree and landed upside down in a gully, wheels spinning wildly.As the driver clambered dazed from the wreckage, a passer-by asked: 'Are you drunk?'

'Of course,' said the motorist. 'What the hell do you think I am – a stunt driver?'

A man was driving down a country lane when his car ground to a halt. As he lifted the bonnet to study the engine, a brown and white cow from an adjoining field lumbered over to the car and stuck her head under the bonnet next to the man's. After a moment or two, the cow turned to the man and said: 'Looks like a dodgy carburettor to me.' Then she walked back into the field and resumed her grazing.

Amazed, the man walked up to the farmhouse and asked the farmer: 'Is that your cow in the field?'

'The brown and white one? Yes, that's old Buttercup.'

'Well,' continued the man, 'my car's broken down, and she just said: "Looks like a dodgy carburettor to me."'

The farmer shook his head and said: 'Don't mind old Buttercup. She don't know a thing about cars.'

A drunk phoned the police to report that thieves had been in his car. 'They've stolen the dashboard, the steering wheel, the brake pedal, even the accelerator,' he moaned.

Five minutes later the phone at the police station rang again. It was the same drunk. 'Sorry,' he slurred. 'I just realised I got in the back seat by mistake.'

A car mechanic received a repair order that read: 'Check for clunking sound when going around corners.' So he took it out on a test drive and, sure enough, whenever he went round a corner, he heard a clunk.
However, he quickly located the problem and returned the repair order to the service manager with the notation: 'Removed bowling ball from trunk.'

A Californian man has invented a robotic parking attendant. He's calling it the Silicon Valet.

While working on a car, a mechanic accidentally swallowed some brake fluid. To his surprise, he quite liked the taste. The next day he decided to have another swig and enjoyed it so much that he told his friend.
His friend said: 'You shouldn't be drinking brake fluid. It's bad for you.'
But the mechanic was becoming hooked, each day increasing his intake of brake fluid. His friend became seriously concerned.
'You've got to give it up,' he insisted. 'Brake fluid is poisonous.'
'Don't worry,' said the mechanic. 'I can stop any time.'

A guy driving a Yugo pulled up at a stop sign alongside a Rolls-Royce. The Yugo driver wound down his window and called across: 'Hey, buddy, that's a nice car. You got a phone in your Rolls? I've got one in my Yugo.'
'As a matter of fact I do have a phone,' replied the Rolls driver nonchalantly.
The Yugo man went on: 'Have you got a fridge in your Rolls, because I've got one in the back seat of my Yugo?'
'Yes, I do have a refrigerator.'
'What about a TV? Have you got a TV in your Rolls, because I've got one in the back of my Yugo?'
'Yes, of course I have a television set in my car,' replied the Rolls driver, irritated.
'How about a bed?' persisted the Yugo driver. 'Have you got a bed in your Rolls, because I've got one in the back of my Yugo?'
Annoyed that he didn't have a bed, the Rolls driver sped off and arranged to have one fitted that same day. The following morning, he sought out the Yugo, finally tracking it down to a side street where it was parked with all the windows steamed up. The Rolls driver stepped out of his car and banged on the door of the Yugo. There was no reply, so he

banged again. Eventually the Yugo driver stuck his head out. His hair was soaking wet.

The Rolls driver announced loftily: 'I now have a splendid bed in my Rolls.'

The Yugo driver glared back. 'You got me out of the shower to tell me *that*?'

If you smuggle cars into the country, are you trafficking?

When her car broke down, a woman called out a local mechanic to repair it. He lifted up the hood, looked in the engine, whacked something with a hammer and said: 'Try it now.'

To her amazement, the car started straight away.

'That's incredible,' she said. 'You've been here less than a minute and you've managed to fix it. I'm so grateful.'

'All part of the job, madam. That'll be $250.'

The smile vanished from the woman's face. 'How much? How can you charge $250 when all you did was hit it with a hammer?'

'I can write you out an itemised bill if you like.'

'Yes, please,' she said firmly.

So he wrote out the bill and handed it to her. It read: 'Hitting engine with hammer – $10. Knowing where to hit it – $240.'

What do you call a country where everyone has to drive a pink car? – A pink car nation.

A father was driving his son to school when he inadvertently made an illegal turn at some traffic lights. Realising his mistake, he said: 'Oops, I just made an illegal turn.'

'It's OK, Dad,' said his son. 'The police car behind us did the same thing.'

A motorist accidentally hit and killed a calf that was crossing the road. Feeling guilty about the incident, he asked the farmer how much the animal was worth.

'About $300 today,' replied the farmer, 'but in six years it would have been worth $900. So realistically I'm $900 out of pocket. That's what I want as compensation.'

The motorist wrote out a cheque and handed it to the farmer. 'Here is the cheque for $900,' he said. 'It is postdated six years from today.'

An angry motorist went back to the garage where he had purchased an expensive battery for his car six months earlier. He told the garage owner: 'When I bought that battery, you said it would be the last battery my car would ever need. Now six months later, it's dead!'

'Sorry,' said the garage owner, 'I didn't think your car would last longer than that.'

A juggler was driving to a show when he was stopped by a traffic cop. The cop peered inside the car, looked at the back seat and asked suspiciously: 'What are matches and lighter fuel doing in your car?'

'I'm a juggler,' replied the driver.

'Oh yeah?' said the cop, unconvinced. 'Let's see you prove it.'

So the driver collected his props and began juggling three blazing torches at the roadside. Just then an elderly couple drove by. The husband turned to his wife and said: 'I'm glad I quit drinking. Look at the test they're giving now!'

A man stood by the side of the road hitch hiking on a very dark night in the middle of a storm. The thunder was rolling and no cars passed. The rain was so torrential that he could barely see a few feet ahead. Then suddenly he saw a car come towards him and stop.

Instinctively, the man climbed into the car and shut the door, only to realise that there was nobody behind the wheel! The car started slowly. He peered through the windscreen at the road ahead and, to his horror, saw a tight corner. Scared to death, he said a silent prayer. He was still in shock when, a few yards before the corner, a hand appeared through the window and turned the wheel. The man, paralysed with terror, watched how the hand appeared every time he approached a corner. Finally he summoned the strength to escape from the moving car and run to the nearest town. Wet and shaking, he found a bar where he started telling everyone about the terrible experience he had been through.

About half an hour later, two men walked into the bar, and one said to the other: 'Look, Denzil, that's the guy who climbed into the car while we were pushing it.'

Three men – Don, Pete and Eric – were killed in a car crash and made their way up to heaven. St Peter was waiting for them and described the facilities that heaven had to offer. He announced: 'For the purposes of travelling around heaven, each of you will be given a means of transportation appropriate to your past deeds.'

First, St Peter turned to Don and said: 'Don, you cheated on your wife on five different occasions. You will drive around heaven in a battered old Dodge.'

Next, St Peter turned to Pete and said: 'Peter you cheated on your wife twice. You will be given a Toyota station-wagon.'

Finally, St Peter turned to Eric and said: 'Eric, you have led a blameless life. You never cheated on your wife and you always treated her

121

with kindness and consideration. As a reward for your loyalty, I grant you a top-of-the-range Ferrari.'

Eric was thrilled and drove around heaven in a shiny red Ferrari. Don and Pete were envious until, two months later, they spotted Eric crying at the wheel of his car.

'What's the problem?' they asked. 'You've got everything you could possibly want – the best car in heaven.'

'I know,' sobbed Eric, 'but I just saw my wife go by on a skateboard.'

A scoutmaster was driving along a country lane one morning when a truck suddenly pulled out in front of him. He tried to sound his horn to warn the truck driver, but no noise came out and so he was forced to slam on his brakes. Fortunately his brakes were in good working order and a collision was avoided, but the scoutmaster thought he had better get the broken horn fixed. So he took the car to the nearest garage and explained the problem.

'The horn simply isn't working,' the scoutmaster told the mechanic. 'I can't get a sound out of it – not a honk, a toot or even a gentle beep. I'm on my way to weekend scout camp and I'm already running late, so is there any chance you could get some sort of sound out of it by lunchtime, even if it's just a patched up job?'

'OK,' said the mechanic, 'I'll have a look at it. Come back in a couple of hours.'

The mechanic fiddled with the wiring and eventually managed to get the horn to make a sound. It was by no means a loud blast, more a beep, but he thought that would satisfy the scoutmaster for the time being.

When the scoutmaster returned to collect his car, the mechanic was out at lunch. But he had left a note on the windscreen. It read: 'Beep repaired.'

Driving along a busy street, a man became aware of an impatient woman who was tailgating him. She was so close that when he had to brake to allow some children to use a pedestrian crossing, she almost crashed into him. Furious at being delayed, she sounded her horn and began waving her fists in a disgraceful exhibition of road rage.

Before she could move off, she felt a tap on her window. It was a police officer who ordered her to step out of the car. He then asked her to come down to the station where she was searched, fingerprinted, photographed, and put in a cell. A couple of hours later, after vehicle checks had been carried out, she was told that she could collect her valuables and that she was being released without charge.

The woman was extremely indignant at her arrest and demanded an apology. The officer responsible explained the reason for the mistake. 'You see, madam, I pulled up behind your car while you were sounding your horn and loudly cursing the driver in front of you. Then I noticed the "Follow Jesus, Not Me" sticker on the rear window, the "God Is Love" sticker, and the chrome-plated Christian fish emblem on the boot. Naturally, I assumed that you had stolen the car . . .'

One cab driver said to another: 'Why have you got one side of your cab painted red and the other side painted blue?'
'Well, when I get in an accident, the police always believe my version of what happened, because all the witnesses contradict each other.'

Bogged down in a huge, mud-filled hole in the road, a motorist paid a passing farmer $5 to pull him out with his tractor.
Once back on dry ground, the grateful motorist said: 'If that's all you charge, I bet you're pulling people out of the mud day and night.'
'Can't,' said the farmer. 'At night I haul water for the hole.'

Although he had hardly ever driven in his life, a man always dreamed of owning a sports car, so when he inherited a large sum of money from a dead relative, he headed straight for the car showroom and bought himself a Porsche. Within half an hour he was on a quiet country road putting his new car through its paces. Faster and faster he went until suddenly, at top speed, there was an almighty bang and smoke began pouring from the engine.
Towed back home, he immediately called the car salesman and told him what had happened. The salesman was at a loss for an explanation but, because the customer was so wealthy, he agreed to swap the Porsche for a Lotus. The next day, the man took the Lotus out on its first run, but as he hit 100mph, the same thing happened. The car juddered to a sudden halt and the engine exploded.
Highly dissatisfied, the man phoned the car salesman once again and told him what had happened. Eventually the salesman agreed to exchange the Lotus for a Ferrari, but only on condition that he joined the customer on a test drive to see what the problem was.
Together they set off into the country. Soon the customer was picking up speed and going through the gears from fourth to fifth and up to sixth. As he accelerated still more, the car suddenly shook violently and the engine went bang.
'What did you do?' asked the salesman, shaken.
'Well,' said the driver, 'I was going faster and faster, and I ran out of numbered gears. So I put it into R for "Race".'

An actuary quoted an extremely low premium for an automobile 'fire and theft' policy. When asked why it was so cheap, he said: 'Who'd steal a burnt car?'

A guy asked a passer-by: 'What's the quickest way to York?'
'Are you walking or driving?'
'Driving.'
'That's the quickest way.'

Genuine Excuses for Speeding:
- I had passed out after seeing flashing lights, which I believed to be UFOs in the distance. The flash of the camera brought me round from my trance.
- I had to rush my dying hamster to the vet's.
- I was in the airport's flight path and I believe the camera was triggered by a jet overhead, not my car.
- A violent sneeze caused a chain reaction where my foot pushed down harder on the accelerator.
- I had a severe bout of diarrhoea and had to speed to a public toilet.
- There was a strong wind behind my car, which pushed me over the limit.
- My friend had just chopped his fingers off and I was rushing the fingers to hospital.
- The only way I could demonstrate my faulty clutch was to accelerate madly.
- The vibrations from the surfboard I had on the roof rack set off the camera.

A traffic cop pulled over an elderly lady driving her little old car too slow on the highway. 'This is a 70 m.p.h. highway, ma'am,' he said. 'How come you're only doing about 20? You're a danger to other vehicles.'

'I'm sorry, officer,' she said, 'but I saw a lot of signs that said 20 not 70.'

'That's not the speed limit,' explained the cop. 'That's the name of the highway.'

Just then he looked in the back of the car and saw two more little old ladies trembling with fear. 'What's the matter with them?' he asked.

The driver replied: 'We've just come off Highway 127.'

Man: My wife drives like lightning.
Friend: You mean fast?
Man: No, she hits trees.

A wild drinking party in the woods was prematurely curtailed by a sudden storm – thunder, lightning and torrential rain. Two young men, much the worse for drink, were forced to run for ten minutes in the driving rain before eventually reaching the sanctuary of their car. Just

124

then the rain began to ease off and, although neither was in a fit state to drive, they decided to head for home. So the driver started the engine and put his foot down – the sooner they got home, they thought, the less chance there was of being stopped by the police.

They had been driving for about a minute when an old man's face suddenly appeared at the passenger window. The young men were startled, not least because the speedometer showed they were doing about 40mph.

'What do you want?' they shouted, swigging beer as the old man tapped on the window. The driver put his foot down but when the old man kept tapping, the scared passenger wound the window down partway.

'Do you have any tobacco?' asked the old man quietly.

The passenger looked aghast at the driver. 'He wants tobacco!'

'Well, give him a cigarette, quick!' shouted the driver, accelerating up to 60 m.p.h.

The passenger fumbled around with the packet, handed the old man a cigarette and yelled to the driver 'Step on it!' before quickly winding the window up.

'God, that was spooky!' said the passenger, taking another swig of beer.

'You're not kidding!' agreed the driver. 'Let's get home – fast!'

But moments later, with the speedometer touching 80 m.p.h., there was another tap at the passenger window.

'I don't believe it!' screamed the passenger. 'It's him again!'

'See what he wants now,' yelled the driver.

The terrified passenger wound the window down a little and the old man asked politely: 'Have you got a light?'

The passenger tossed a lighter out of the window, wound up the window and again ordered the driver to put his foot down.

They were now doing 100 m.p.h. and still guzzling beer, trying to forget what they had just seen, when all of a sudden there was more knocking.

'Oh my God! He's back!'

The passenger, shaking with fear, wound down the window and, in a trembling voice, asked the old man what he wanted this time.

The old man replied softly: 'Do you want some help getting out of the mud?'

Genuine statements made on insurance claim forms:
- I had been shopping for plants all day and was on my way home. As I reached an intersection a hedge sprang up obscuring my vision and I did not see the other car.
- I started to turn and it was at this point I noticed a camel and an

elephant tethered at the verge. This distraction caused me to lose concentration and hit a bollard.

- On approach to the traffic lights the car in front suddenly broke.
- I didn't think the speed limit applied after midnight.
- Windscreen broken. Cause unknown. Probably Voodoo.
- When I saw I could not avoid a collision I stepped on the gas and crashed into the other car.
- The accident happened when the right front door of a car came round the corner without giving a signal.
- My car was legally parked as it backed into another vehicle.
- I told the police that I was not injured, but on removing my hat found that I had a fractured skull.
- The indirect cause of the accident was a little guy in a small car with a big mouth.
- I had been learning to drive with power steering. I turned the wheel to what I thought was enough and found myself in a different direction going the opposite way.
- The accident occurred when I was attempting to bring my car out of a skid by steering it into the other vehicle.
- I was backing my car out of the driveway in the usual manner, when it was struck by the other car in the same place it had been struck several times before.
- I saw her look at me twice. She appeared to be making slow progress when we met on impact.
- No one was to blame for the accident but it would never have happened if the other driver had been alert.
- I was unable to stop in time and my car crashed into the other vehicle. The driver and passengers then left immediately for a vacation with injuries.
- The pedestrian ran for the pavement, but I got him.

Out driving with his wife, a man sped along a country lane in an increasingly reckless fashion.

'Can't you slow down when you're turning corners?' she complained. 'You're scaring the life out of me.'

'Do what I do,' he replied. 'Shut your eyes.'

Over lunch in a fast-food restaurant, a woman was telling her friend about a recent accident in which a teenage boy had driven into the back of her car. 'The boy blamed me and called me every rude, dirty name in the book!'

Two small boys had been listening at the next table and one turned to the other and said wide-eyed: 'There's a book?'

A driver was speeding along a twisty country lane when he turned a corner and, to his horror, saw two farmhands standing chatting in the middle of the road. He swerved violently to avoid them but the car ran up an embankment, did a triple somersault and landed in an adjacent field.

One farmhand turned to the other and said: 'That was a stroke of luck. I reckon we got out of that field just in time.'

When a man arrived home from work, his wife was waiting for him. She sat him down and told him she had good news and bad news about the car.

'Right,' he said. 'What's the good news?'

She said: 'The air bag works.'

Two old ladies were out driving in a big car. Both could barely see over the dashboard. They were cruising along at a steady twenty-six miles an hour when they came to a junction and although the light was red, they went straight through. The woman in the passenger seat thought to herself: 'I must be losing it, I could have sworn we just went through a red light.'

Three hundred yards further down the road, they approached another junction. Again the light was red, but again they went through it. The woman in the passenger seat thought to herself: 'I must be seeing things because I'm sure we just went through another red light.'

A couple of minutes later they went through a third red light. This time she turned to the other woman and said: 'Mildred! Don't you know we just went through three red lights! You could have killed us!'

'Oh,' said Mildred. 'Am I driving?'

Music

A tourist in Europe was walking through a graveyard when he suddenly heard music. With nobody around, he began searching for the source. He finally located the origin and discovered that it was coming from a grave with a headstone that read: Ludwig van Beethoven, 1770-1827. Then he realised that the music was the Ninth Symphony and that it was being played backwards. Puzzled, he left the graveyard and persuaded a friend to return with him.

By the time they arrived back at the grave, the music had changed. This time it was the Seventh Symphony but, like the previous piece, it was being played backwards. Curious, the men agreed to consult a music scholar. When they returned with the expert, the Fifth Symphony was playing, again backwards.

The expert noticed that the symphonies were being played in the reverse order to which they were composed – the Ninth, then the Seventh, then the Fifth. By the next day word of this strange phenomenon had spread, and a small crowd had gathered around Beethoven's grave. They were all listening to the Second Symphony being played backwards.

Just then the caretaker of the graveyard ambled up to the group. Someone in the crowd asked him if he had an explanation for the music.

'Oh, it's nothing to worry about,' said the caretaker. 'He's just decomposing.'

A Scotsman visited London on holiday but complained that the locals were unfriendly. He told his friends: 'At four o'clock every morning they hammered on the door of my hotel room, and on the walls, the floor and the ceiling. They hammered so loud I could hardly hear myself playing the bagpipes!'

Why do pipers march when they play? – To get as far away from the music as possible.

How are playing the bagpipes like throwing a javelin blindfold? – You don't have to be very good to get people's attention.

How can you tell if the bagpipes are out of tune? – Someone is blowing into them.

Following a late-night gig, an accordion player woke up in the morning and realised he had left his accordion on the back seat of his car, which was parked out in the street. Convinced that the instrument would have been stolen overnight, he dashed out in his pyjamas and, sure enough, saw that the side rear window of the car had been smashed. When he looked into the back seat, he saw that somebody had thrown in two more accordions.

If you drop an accordion, a set of bagpipes and a viola off a twenty-storey building, which one crashes to the ground first? – Who cares?

How can you tell that there's an accordionist at your front door? – He doesn't stop knocking even after you answer.

Why are an accordionist's fingers like lightning? – They rarely strike the same spot twice.

What is an accordion good for? – Learning how to fold a map.

Genuine answers given by music students in exams:
- The principal singer of 19th century opera was called pre-Madonna.
- Sherbet composed the Unfinished Symphony.
- A virtuoso is a musician with real high morals.
- Contralto is a low sort of music that only ladies sing.
- A harp is a nude piano.
- Refrain means don't do it. A refrain in music is the part you'd better not try to sing.
- Rock Monanoff was a famous post-romantic composer of piano concerti.
- Johann Sebastian Bach wrote a great many musical compositions and had a large number of children. In between he practised on an old spinster which he kept up in his attic.

Two intrepid explorers met in the heart of the Amazon jungle.

One said: 'I'm here to commune with nature in the raw, to contemplate the eternal truths and to widen my horizons. And what about you?'

The other said: 'I came because my daughter has started cello lessons.'

What's the range of a cello? – Twenty yards if you've got a good arm.

What's the difference between a cello and a chainsaw? – The grip.

An explorer in Indonesia was seeking out a remote tribe thought to be hostile to strangers. He sought the services of a local guide to act as translator and, if necessary, peacemaker.

At dusk on the first day the pair were sitting around a campfire when they heard the sound of tribal drums in the distance. The drums got louder. The guide admitted: 'I don't like the sound of those drums.'

As dusk turned to evening, the drums got even louder. The guide said: 'I really don't like the sound of those drums.'

Evening turned to dead of night and still the drums got louder. It was obvious that they were very close. The guide repeated: 'I really do not like the sound of those drums.'

Suddenly the drums stopped and a voice from the darkness cried out: 'Hey, man, he's not our regular drummer!'

Why are orchestra intermissions limited to twenty minutes? – So you don't have to retrain the drummers.

What's the difference between a drum kit and a lawnmower? – The neighbours are upset if you borrow a lawnmower and don't return it.

What's the difference between a pizza and a drummer? – A pizza can feed a family of four.

What's the difference between a drummer and a vacuum cleaner? – You have to plug one of them in before it sucks.

How is a drum solo like a sneeze? – You can tell it's coming, but you can't do anything about it.

If a drummer and a bass guitarist caught a cab, which one would be the musician? – The cab driver.

Why is a drum machine better than a drummer? – Because it can keep a steady beat and won't sleep with your girlfriend.

What's the last thing a drummer says in a band? – 'Hey, guys, why don't we try one of my songs?'

What did the drummer get on his IQ test? – Drool.

In a bid to keep his customers entertained, a bar owner hired a pianist and a drummer. However, after discovering that the drummer had stolen some valuables from the upstairs accommodation, the owner was forced to call in the police.

Desperate for a replacement drummer, the bar owner then rang a friend who knew some musicians.

'What happened to the drummer you had?' asked the friend.

'I had him arrested.'

The friend said: 'How badly did he play?'

What's the difference between a dead trombone player lying in the road and a dead squirrel lying in the road? – The squirrel might have been on his way to a gig.

How do you know when there's a trombonist at your door? – His hat says 'Domino's Pizza'.

A guy playing trombone in the opera was suddenly offered an unexpected gig at a prestigious jazz club on one of the days that he was supposed to be performing at the opera house. The gig was just too good to turn down, so he tried to find a fellow trombonist to replace him at the opera. Unable to find anyone, as a last resort he persuaded his accountant to stand in for him.

'I'll give you my other trombone,' he said. 'All you have to do is copy what the guy next to you is doing. It'll be fine.'

130

The next day he asked the accountant how it went.

'Terrible. Your colleague also sent his accountant to replace him!'

What's the definition of perfect pitch in a piccolo? – When you throw it in the toilet and it doesn't hit the rim.

Why are harps like elderly parents? – They're both unforgiving and hard to get in and out of cars.

An anthropologist visited a remote tropical island to investigate the natives. Accompanied by a guide, he travelled upriver to a clearing and pitched camp. Ominously, in the distance he began to hear drums.

'What are those drums?' he asked the guide.

The guide turned to him and said: 'Drums OK, but when drums stop, very bad.'

Three hours later the drumming suddenly stopped. Mindful of the guide's warning, the anthropologist began to panic. 'The drums have stopped,' he yelled. 'What happens now?'

The guide crouched down, covered his head with his hands and said: 'Bass solo.'

What's the difference between a French horn and a '57 Chevy? – You can tune a '57 Chevy.

What's the definition of an optimist? – A folk musician with a mortgage.

A girl went on a date with a trumpet player. When she got home, her roommate wanted to know how it went.

'Did his embouchure make him a great kisser?'

'No, that dry, tiny, tight little pucker was no fun at all.'

The next night she went out with a tuba player. When she got home, her roommate asked what he was like as a kisser.

'Horrible. Those huge rubbery, slobbering lips were gross.'

The following night she went out with a French horn player. When she got home, her roommate was eager to hear all the details.

'Was he a good kisser?' she asked.

'His kissing was so-so, but I just loved the way he held me!'

Why are conductors' hearts so coveted for transplants? – They've had so little use.

Why is a conductor like a condom? – It's safer with one, but more fun without.

A conductor was having a lot of trouble with one drummer. He talked and talked with the drummer, but his performance showed no sign of improving. Finally, in front of the whole orchestra, the conductor declared sarcastically: 'When a musician just can't handle his instrument and doesn't improve when given help, they take away the instrument, give him two sticks, and make him a drummer!'

A voice from the percussion section whispered loudly: 'And if he can't handle that, they take away one of his sticks and make him a conductor.'

Conductor: You should have taken up the viola earlier.
Viola student: Why, do you think the practice would have made me really good?
Conductor: No, but you might have given up by now.

A viola player came home late at night to find police cars and fire trucks outside his house. The chief of police intercepted him.

'I'm afraid I have some terrible news for you,' said the chief. 'While you were out, the conductor came to your house, killed your family and burned your house down.'

The viola player was stunned. 'You're kidding! The conductor came to my house?'

What do a lawsuit and a viola have in common? – Everyone is much happier when the case is closed.

During a concert, a fight broke out between the oboe player and the viola player. At the interval, the orchestra leader went to investigate.

'He broke my reed,' protested the oboe player.

'He undid two of my strings,' countered the viola player, 'but he won't tell me which ones!'

What's the difference between a violinist and a dog? – A dog knows when to stop scratching.

While a small boy was practicing the violin in the living room, his father was desperately trying to read the paper. But as the boy scraped away tunelessly at the instrument, the family dog howled incessantly. Finally the father lost patience and said to the boy: 'Can't you play something the dog doesn't know?'

A woman answered the door to find a workman, complete with tool box, standing on the porch.

'I'm the piano tuner, madam,' he announced.

'But I didn't send for a piano tuner!'
'I know, but your neighbours did!'

Why is a bassoon better than an oboe? – A bassoon burns longer.

What is a burning oboe good for? – Setting a bassoon on fire.

How do you get a lead guitarist to stop playing? – Put sheet music in front of him.

How many baritones does it take to change a light bulb? – None. They can't get up that high.

How can you tell there's a singer at your front door? – She forgot the key and doesn't know when to come in.

What happens if you play country music backwards? – Your wife returns to you, your dog comes back to life, and you get out of prison.

Three men died and went up to heaven where they found themselves in a queue at the Pearly Gates. The angel responsible for admissions on this particular day warned that, because a few undesirables had managed to sneak in recently, the rules for entry had been tightened and she now had to ask each applicant their profession and annual salary.
The first man in line announced: 'I made $150,000 last year as a bank manager.'
'Very good,' said the angel. 'In you go.' And he was admitted to heaven.
The second man stated: 'I made $95,000 last year as a head teacher.'
'Yes, that's fine,' said the angel. 'Through you go.'
The third man said: 'My annual salary last year was $8,000.'
'Cool,' said the angel. 'Which instrument do you play?'

A movie director was testing Sylvester Stallone and Arnold Schwarzenegger for a new film about classical composers.
The director said to Stallone: 'Who do you fancy playing, Sly?'
Stallone looked down the list of characters and said: 'I'd like to play Mozart.'
Then the director turned to Schwarzenegger. Arnie said simply: 'I'll be Bach.'

Names

What do you call a man with a shovel in his head? – Doug

What do you call a man without a shovel in his head? – Douglas

What do you call a man lying in a ditch? – Phil

What do you call a woman with a toothpick in her head? – Olive

What do you call a woman with one leg longer than the other? – Eileen

What do you call a woman with both legs the same length? – Nolene

What do you call a man lying at your front door? – Matt

What do you call two men hanging outside your window? – Kurt n Rod

What do you call a man in a catapult? – Chuck

What do you call a man with a government subsidy? – Grant

What do you call a woman with a keyboard on her head? – Cynth

What do you call a man in the middle of an oilfield? – Derek

What do you call a man with one leg longer than the other? – Tip

What do you call a man with a pile of leaves on his head? – Russell

What do you call a man with a wooden head? – Edward

What do you call a man with a rabbit up his butt? – Warren

What do you call a man with his legs chopped off at the knees? – Neil

What do you call an Italian with a rubber toe? – Roberto

What do you call a man in a fast-flowing stream? – Eddy

What do you call a man with a car on his head? – Jack

What do you call a man who runs up large debts? – Owen

What do you call a man with a seagull on his head? – Cliff

What do you call a man holding up the wheels of your car? – Axel

What do you call a man hanging on a wall? – Art

What do you call a woman between two tall buildings? – Ali

What do you call a woman hanging from a washing line? – Peg

What do you call a woman at the end of a long March? – April

What do you call a girl on a barbecue? – Patty

What do you call a woman with a turtle on her head? – Shelley

What do you call a woman with a frog on her head? – Lily

What do you call a man who wears two raincoats? – Max

What do you call a man who has been buried in the ground for 2,000 years? – Pete

What do you call a man who works out? – Jim

What do you call a man with cat scratches all over him? – Claude

What do you call a man who does odd jobs and lives just around the corner? – Andy

What do you call a man in a cooking pot? – Stu

What do you call a man on a stage? – Mike

What do you call a woman who goes fishing? – Annette

What do you call a female magician? – Trixie

What do you call a woman tied to a jetty? – Maud

What do you call a man who cuts himself shaving? – Nick

What do you call a man who has had his car stolen? – Carlos
What do you call a man with a horse on his head? – Orson
What do you call a man carrying a spear? – Lance
What do you call a man carrying several spears? – Lancelot
What do you call a man in your letterbox? – Bill
What do you call a woman who puts Bill in the fireplace? – Bernadette

Newspaper Headlines

Prosecutor Releases Probe Into Undersheriff
Grandmother of Eight Makes Hole in One
Deaf Mute Gets New Hearing in Killing
Police Begin Campaign To Run Down Jaywalkers
House Passes Gas Tax Onto Senate
Milk Drinkers Are Turning To Powder
Explosion of Professors at Universities
Safety Experts Say School Bus Passengers Should Be Belted
Iraqi Head Seeks Arms
Queen Mary Having Bottom Scraped
Stiff Opposition Expected To Casketless Funeral Plan
Two Convicts Evade Noose, Jury Hung
Two Soviet Ships Collide – One Dies
Prostitutes Appeal to Pope
New Housing For Elderly Not Yet Dead
Panda Mating Fails – Veterinarian Takes Over
William Kelly Was Fed Secretary
Two Sisters Reunite After Eighteen Years At Checkout Counter
Nicaragua Sets Goal To Wipe Out Literacy
If Strike Isn't Settled Quickly It May Last a While
Complaints About NBA Referees Growing Ugly
Man Minus Ear Waives Hearing
War Dims Hope For Peace
Cold Wave Linked To Temperatures
Child's Death Ruins Couple's Holiday
Blind Woman Gets New Kidney From Dad She Hasn't Seen in Years
Man Is Fatally Slain
Hospitals Are Sued By Seven Foot Doctors
Scientists Prove Sterility Is Inherited
Ten Revolting Officers Executed
18 Hurt in Cheese Roll
20-Year Friendship Ends At Altar
Sex Education Delayed, Teachers Request Training
Something Went Wrong in Jet Crash, Experts Say
Death Causes Loneliness, Feeling of Isolation.
Lawmen From Mexico Barbecue Guests

Miners Refuse To Work After Death
British Union Finds Dwarves in Short Supply
Local High School Dropouts Cut in Half
New Vaccine May Contain Rabies
Bridge Sets 60mph Limit For Pedestrians
Steals Clock, Faces Time
Ability To Swim May Save Children From Drowning
Drunk Gets Nine Months in Violin Case
Survivor of Siamese Twins Joins Parents
Lung Cancer in Women Mushrooms
Bulge in Trousers Was Ecstasy
Caribbean Islands Drift To Left
Dead Man Gets Job Back
Police Discover Crack in Australia
Smokers Are Productive, But Death Cuts Efficiency
Never Withhold Herpes Infection From Loved One
Judges To Rule On Nude Beach
Women's Movement Called More Broad-Based
Stud Tires Out
Eye Drops Off Shelf
Stolen Painting Found By Tree
Arson Suspect Is Held in Massachusetts Fire
Chef Throws His Heart Into Helping Needy
Alcohol Ads Promote Drinking
Antique Stripper To Display Wares at Store
Babies Used To Sneak Drugs Into Prison
Autos Killing 110 a Day – Let's Resolve To Do Better
Killer Sentenced To Die For Second Time
Red Tape Holds Up New Bridge
Man Struck By Lightning Faces Battery Charge
Dr Ruth To Talk About Sex With Newspaper Editors
Organ Festival Ends In Smashing Climax
New Study of Obesity Looks For Larger Test Group
Astronaut Takes Blame For Gas in Spacecraft
Kids Make Nutritious Snacks
Reagan Wins On Budget, But More Lies Ahead
Shot Off Woman's Leg Helps Nicklaus
Plane Too Close To Ground, Crash Probe Told
Juvenile Court To Try Shooting Defendant
Squad Helps Dog Bite Victim
Enraged Cow Injures Farmer With Ax
Dealers Will Hear Car Talk At Noon

Occupations

A social worker asked a colleague: 'What time is it?'

The other one answered: 'Sorry, I don't know, I'm not wearing a watch.'

'Never mind,' said the first. 'The main thing is that we talked about it.'

What is the difference between God and a social worker? – God doesn't pretend to be a social worker.

A social worker was walking home late at night when she was confronted by a mugger with a gun.

'Your money or your life!' snarled the mugger.

'I'm sorry,' she replied. 'I'm a social worker, so I have no money and no life.'

A priest, a vicar and a consultant were travelling by plane when it suffered total engine failure. It was obvious that the plane was going to crash and all three would be killed. The priest began to pray and finger his rosary beads, the vicar began to pray and read the Bible, and the consultant began to organise a committee on air traffic safety.

A tourist was browsing around a pet shop when a customer came in and said: 'Have you got a C monkey?'

The shopkeeper nodded, went over to a large cage at the side of the shop and took out a monkey. Fitting a collar and leash to the monkey, he told the customer: 'That will be $5,000.' The customer paid and left with the monkey.

Startled, the tourist went over to the shopkeeper and said: 'That was a very expensive monkey – most of them are only priced at a few hundred dollars. What was so special about it?'

The shopkeeper replied: 'That monkey is invaluable to computer buffs. It can program in C with very fast, tight code, no bugs. Believe me, it's well worth the money.'

The tourist started to look at the other monkeys in the shop. Pointing at the same cage, he said to the shopkeeper: 'That monkey's even more expensive, $10,000. What does it do?'

'Oh,' said the shopkeeper, 'that one's a C++ monkey. It can manage more complex programming, even some Java, all the really useful stuff.'

Then the tourist spotted a third monkey, in a cage of its own. The price tag around its neck said $50,000. 'What on earth does that one do,' he asked, 'to justify that sort of price?'

The shopkeeper said: 'I don't know if it actually does anything. But it says it's a consultant.'

At the construction site of a new church, the contractor stopped to chat with one of his workmen.

'Paddy,' he said, 'didn't you once tell me you had a brother who was a bishop?'

'That I did,' said Paddy.

'And yet you are a bricklayer. It sure is a funny old world. Things in life aren't divided equally, are they?'

'That they're not,' agreed Paddy as he proudly slapped the mortar along the line of bricks. 'My poor brother couldn't do this to save his life!'

Jim was fired from his construction job.

'What happened?' asked his friend Ken.

'Well,' explained Jim. 'You know what a foreman is? The one who stands around watching the other men work?'

'Yes. What of it?'

'Well, he got jealous of me. Everyone thought I was the foreman!'

What kind of aftershave do genetic scientists wear? – Eau de clone.

A farmer received a visit from a government official over allegations that he was paying his staff less than the minimum wage. The official asked him for a list of his employees and details of their pay.

'All right,' said the farmer. 'I have a hired man, been with me for three years. I pay him $600 a week, plus room and board. There's a cook – she's been here six months. She gets $500 a week, plus room and board.'

'Anybody else?' asked the official as he scribbled on a pad.

'Yeah,' said the farmer. 'There's one guy here is none too bright. He works about eighteen hours a day. I pay him ten dollars a week and a bit of beer money.'

'Aha!' roared the official. 'That's the man I want to talk to!'

'Speaking,' said the farmer.

How careers end:
Electricians are delighted
Far Eastern diplomats are disoriented
Alpine climbers are dismounted
Artists' models are deposed
Cooks are deranged
Office clerks are defiled
Mediums are dispirited
Programmers are decoded
Accountants are discredited
Holy people are disgraced
Perfume makers dissent

Butterfly collectors are debugged
Students are degraded
Bodybuilders are rebuffed
Underwear models are debriefed
Painters are discoloured
Gamblers are discarded
Mathematicians are discounted
Tree surgeons disembark

Two advertising executives – one junior and one senior – had lunch together. Part-way through the meal, the junior executive asked: 'What's happened to Joel Kulowsky? I haven't seen him around lately.'

'Haven't you heard?' said the senior. 'Joel died last week – he's gone to that great ad agency in the sky.'

'How terrible!' exclaimed the younger man. 'He was only 55. What did he have?'

'Nothing much,' replied the senior. 'A small shampoo account, a couple of discount stores, nothing worth going after.'

Preparing for the most important presentation of his life, a sales representative went to see a psychiatrist.

'I'll implant a hypnotic suggestion in your mind,' said the doctor. 'Just say "one-two-three" and you'll give your best-ever presentation. However, do not say "one-two-three-four" because it will cause you to freeze and make a complete fool of yourself.'

The sales rep was delighted. He tried it at home and gave a fabulous presentation. He tried it at work and received a standing ovation. Then came the big day. Everything was set up in the boardroom and the managing director signalled him to start.

The sales rep whispered under his breath: 'One-two-three.'

Then the managing director asked: 'What did you say "one-two-three" for?'

A man trained in origami for eight years and opened a shop in London. But the business folded.

All through veterinary school, an aspiring vet made ends meet by working nights as a taxidermist. When he finally graduated, he decided to combine the two vocations in the hope not only of providing a more comprehensive service to his customers but also of doubling his income. So he opened his own offices with a sign on the door saying: 'Dr Brunskill: Veterinary Medicine and Taxidermy – Either Way You Get Your Dog Back!'

The head of admissions at a school of agriculture asked a prospective student: 'Why have you chosen this career?'

The student replied: 'I dream of making a million dollars from farming, like my father.'

The head was impressed. 'Your father made a million dollars from farming?'

'No, but he always dreamed of it.'

An engineer, a psychologist and a theologian were hunting in the wilderness of northern Canada. Suddenly the temperature dropped and a fierce snowstorm was upon them. Through the blizzard, they spotted an isolated cabin and, having been told that the locals were hospitable, they knocked on the door in the hope of obtaining respite from the weather. Nobody answered their knocking but when they tried the door, they found that it was unlocked and so they ventured inside.

The cabin was of basic layout, with nothing out of the ordinary except for the stove. It was large, pot-bellied and made of cast iron but what made it so unusual was its location – it was suspended in midair by wires attached to the ceiling beams.

'Fascinating,' said the psychologist. 'It is obvious that this lonely trapper, isolated from humanity, has elevated this stove so that he can curl up under it and vicariously experience a return to the womb.'

'Nonsense!' replied the engineer. 'The man is practicing the laws of thermodynamics. By elevating his stove, he has discovered a way to distribute heat more evenly throughout the cabin.'

'With all due respect,' interrupted the theologian, 'I'm sure that hanging his stove from the ceiling has religious significance. Fire lifted up has been a religious symbol for centuries.'

The three debated the point for several hours without resolving the issue. When the cabin owner finally returned, they immediately asked him why he had hung his heavy, pot-bellied stove from the ceiling.

He answered simply: 'Had plenty of wire, not much stove pipe.'

Two nuclear physicists got married recently. The ceremony was beautiful – she was absolutely radiant, and he was glowing too. Even the bridesmaids shone.

Three boys were standing in the school playground bragging about their fathers.

One said: 'My dad scribbles a few words on a piece of paper, he calls it a poem, and they give him $500.'

The second said: 'That's nothing. My dad scribbles a few words on a piece of paper, he calls it a song, and they give him $1,000.'

The third said: 'I got you both beat. My dad scribbles a few words on a piece of paper, he calls it a sermon, and it takes eight people to collect all the money.'

The boss on a building site ordered one of his men to dig a hole six feet deep. After the job was done, the boss returned and explained that there had been a mistake and the hole wouldn't be needed after all. So he ordered the man to fill it in.

The worker did as he was told, but couldn't get all the soil packed back into the hole without leaving a mound on top. He went back to the office and explained his problem.

The boss snorted: 'Honestly! What sort of idiots do we employ these days? Obviously you didn't dig the hole deep enough!'

A sales assistant reported for his first day at work at a major department store. The sales manager showed him around and was passing through the gardening department when he heard a customer asking for a packet of grass seed.

'Will you be needing a hose to water your new lawn?' interrupted the sales manager.

'I suppose I will,' said the customer. 'Thank you. I'll take a hose as well.'

'And what about fertiliser,' suggested the sales manager, 'to make the grass grow green and strong?'

'Good idea,' said the customer. 'I'll take some fertiliser.'

'But no matter how thorough your preparation, there are always those difficult weeds,' continued the sales manager. 'So you'll be needing a bottle of weed-killer to keep them down. The large bottles work out the most economical.'

'Right,' said the customer, 'I'll take some weed-killer too.'

'And how about a nice new lawn mower to do your grass justice?' said the sales manager. 'We've just had a delivery. One of these will give your lawn perfect stripes.'

'Why not?' replied the customer. 'Add a lawn mower to the bill.'

As the customer paid for the goods, the sales manager took the young assistant to one side and said: 'See, that's how it's done. That customer only came in for one item, but ended up leaving with five. That's good sales technique. That's what you must try to emulate.'

The assistant's first posting at the store was to the pharmaceutical department. A man came in and asked for a pack of tampons.

The assistant seized his opportunity. 'Are you sure you wouldn't like to buy a lawn mower as well?'

'Why would I want to do that?' asked the man.

'Well,' said the assistant, 'your weekend's ruined, so you might as well mow the lawn.'

On his first day working part-time at the Post Office, a young man was given the job of sorting the mail. He sifted through the sacks of mail in record time, a feat which did not go unnoticed by his supervisor who said at the end of the day: 'Well done. You're one of the quickest workers we've ever had.'

The young man said: 'Thank you. And tomorrow I'll try to do even better.'

The supervisor was staggered. 'How could you possibly better what you have achieved today?'

The young man replied: 'Tomorrow I'm going to read the addresses.'

A doctor phoned a plumber in the middle of the night. 'What are you ringing me for at this hour?' asked the plumber.

'It's an emergency,' said the doctor. 'If it was the other way round, you'd expect me to come out, wouldn't you? So put yourself in my shoes.'

'OK,' said the plumber. 'What's the problem?'

'The pipe under the kitchen sink is leaking.'

'All right,' said the plumber. 'Give it two aspirin and call me again in the morning if it's not better.'

Why don't actors stare out the window in the morning? – Because if they did, they'd have nothing to do in the afternoon.

On land by the Cheyenne River an enterprising Native American founded a business manufacturing crepe paper. Using modern equipment and Internet marketing techniques, he established a reputation for quality paper printed with traditional tribal designs.

As word of this unique product spread, it reached the ears of a New York gourmet who was planning a retirement party for a friend. Logging on to the Internet, he ordered what he thought was going to be twenty sets of designer-pattern crepe paper. However, when the shipment arrived, it turned out that the order had been incorrectly entered as twenty cases of crepe paper.

Assuming his habitual restaurant demeanour, he bellowed at an assistant: 'Send this back. The Crepe Sioux Sets have been grossly overdone!'

A wealthy woman was throwing a lavish garden party attended by the cream of local society. While dignitaries and minor celebrities enjoyed themselves, two gardeners were busy weeding a flower border behind a low hedge.

As a guest watched, one gardener suddenly leaped high and did the splits in mid-air. Impressed by the spring in his heels and his obvious athleticism, the guest remarked to the host: 'That man is such a talented dancer. I'll pay him $500 to dance at my next party.'

When the host mentioned the suggestion to the other gardener, he called over to his colleague: 'Hey, Ted, do you think for $500 you could step on that rake again?'

An accountant was walking along the street when he spotted a tramp begging for money.

'Spare some change, sir?' asked the tramp.

'And why should I do that?' replied the accountant.

'Because I'm completely broke without a penny to my name and I haven't had a proper meal in three months.'

'Hmm,' said the accountant, 'and how does this compare to your last quarter?'

An unemployed man was desperate to support his family. His wife did nothing but watch TV all day while his three teenage kids had dropped out of high school to hang around with the local troublemakers. His options limited, he applied for a janitor's job at a large company and easily passed the aptitude test.

The human resources manager told him: 'You will be hired at a minimum wage of $5.05 an hour. Let me know your e-mail address so that we can get you in the loop. Our system will automatically e-mail you all the forms, and advise you when to start and where to report on your first day.'

But the man pointed out that he was too poor to afford a computer, and that therefore he didn't have an e-mail address. The manager replied icily: 'Surely you must realise that to a company like ours, not having an e-mail address means that you virtually cease to exist. Without e-mail you can hardly expect to be employed by a hi-tech firm. Good day.'

Stunned and dismayed, the man left. Not knowing which way to turn and with just $10 left in his wallet, he walked past a market wholesaler and saw a trader selling 25lb crates of beautiful red tomatoes. So he bought a crate, carried it to a busy street corner and began selling them. In less than two hours he sold all the tomatoes and made a 100 per cent profit. Repeating the process several more times that day, he finished up with nearly $100 and arrived home that night with several bags of groceries for his hungry family.

Not surprisingly, he decided to repeat the tomato business the next day, and by working long hours he quickly multiplied his profits. By the second week he had invested in a cart and two weeks later he bought a broken-down pickup truck. At the end of the year he owned three trucks. His two sons had left their neighbourhood gangs to help him with the tomato business, his wife was buying the tomatoes, and his daughter was

143

taking night courses in accountancy at the local college so that she could keep his books.

After five years, he owned a fleet of trucks and a warehouse, which his wife supervised, plus two tomato farms managed by the boys. The tomato company's payroll gave work to hundreds of homeless and jobless people. His daughter reported that the business grossed a million dollars. Planning for the future, he decided to buy some life insurance and, with the help of an insurance adviser, he picked a plan that suited his newfound wealth. Then the adviser asked him for his e-mail address in order to send the final documents electronically.

When the man replied that he didn't have time to mess with a computer and had no e-mail address, the insurance advisor was stunned. 'What? No computer? No Internet? No e-mail? Just think where you would be today if you'd had all of that five years ago!'

'Ha!' snorted the man. 'If I'd had e-mail five years ago, I would be sweeping floors at a multinational computer company and making $5.05 an hour.'

Two construction workers were toiling away on a swelteringly hot day. Pointing to the supervisor, Mick said to Dave: 'How come we do all the work while he sits in the shade under the tree and gets all the money?'

Dave replied: 'I don't know. Why don't you go and ask him?'

So Mick went over to the supervisor and said: 'Hey, how come we do all the work while you sit in the shade under the tree and get all the money?'

The supervisor answered simply: 'Intelligence.'

Mick looked bemused. 'What do you mean, intelligence?'

The supervisor said: 'I'll show you.' He put his hand on the bark of the tree and said: 'Hit my hand as hard as you can.'

Mick summoned up all his strength and pent-up frustration and prepared to land the hardest punch he could muster. But just before he made contact, the supervisor pulled his hand away, leaving Mick to crash his fist into the tree.

As Mick nursed his sore hand, the supervisor smiled: 'That's intelligence.'

Still smarting, Mick went back to Dave who asked: 'What did he say?'

With a wry grin, Mick promised to explain. He looked around for a tree but couldn't find one. So he put his hand on his face and said: 'Hit my hand as hard as you can . . .'

A woman attending evening computer classes was relieved to find that she had a female teacher instead of the male head of department.

When she relayed this information to the teacher, the latter was flattered, if a little surprised. 'My colleague is far more experienced than me,' she admitted.

'Yes,' said the woman, 'but I feel much more comfortable with you – I get nervous around really smart people.'

A team of archaeologists were excavating in Israel when they found a cave with the symbols of a woman, a donkey, a shovel, a fish, and a Star of David on the wall.

Pointing to the first drawing, the head of the team declared: 'This indicates that these people were family oriented and held women in high esteem. The donkey shows that they were intelligent enough to use animals to till the soil. The shovel means that they were able to forge tools. Even further proof of high intelligence is the fish: if famine hit the land, they would take to the sea for food. The last symbol is the Star of David, telling us they were Hebrews.'

However, one of his fellow archaeologists begged to disagree. 'Hebrew is read from right to left,' he explained. 'The symbols say: "Holy Mackerel, Dig the Ass on that Chick!"'

A salesman was demonstrating an unbreakable comb in a department store. After twisting it and pulling it, he tried to show how amazingly flexible it was by bending it completely in half. Unfortunately the comb immediately snapped in two with a resounding crack. Without missing a beat, the salesman held up both halves of the supposedly unbreakable comb for everyone to see, and said bravely: 'And this, ladies and gentlemen, is what an unbreakable comb looks like on the inside . . .'

A farmer was ploughing his field when his well-meaning but somewhat inept son came to help him.

'Dad, I'd like to do some ploughing.'

'I don't know, son. It takes a steady hand.'

'Please, I want to help.'

The farmer reluctantly agreed and handed the boy some tools but when he came to check the work an hour later, he found that the line was very erratic.

'Your line is as crooked as can be,' said the farmer.

'But I was watching the plough to make sure that I kept straight,' said the son.

'That's the problem. Don't look at the plough. You have to watch where you're going. Look at the other end of the field, pick out one object, head straight for it and you'll cut a straight line every time. I'm going to get a drink of water, so can you handle it now?'

'Sure, dad.'

When the farmer returned, he saw to his horror that the son had cut the

145

worst row he had ever seen. It went all over the field in curves and circles. The farmer ran up to his son and stopped him.

'What happened?' he yelled. 'I've never seen a worse looking field in my life. There's not one straight line!'

'But I did what you said,' insisted the son. 'I fixed my sights on that dog playing on the other side of the field.'

What is the definition of an extroverted accountant? – One who looks at your shoes while he's talking to you instead of his own.

A mechanical engineer, a chemical engineer, an electrical engineer and a computer engineer were travelling along the road when their car broke down.

The mechanical engineer said: 'Sounds to me like the pistons have seized. We'll have to strip down the engine before we can get the car working again.'

The chemical engineer begged to differ. 'It sounded to me as if the fuel might be contaminated. I think we should clear out the fuel system.'

'Well, I think it might be a grounding problem,' said the electrical engineer, 'or maybe a faulty plug lead.'

Having offered their opinions, the three turned to the computer engineer who was strangely silent on the matter. 'What do you think?' they asked.

'Hmmm,' said the computer engineer. 'Perhaps if we all get out of the car and get back in again?'

Joel and Stanley had started out with only $500 between them, but they had built up a computer business with sales in the millions. Their company employed over 300 staff, and the two executives lived like princes.

But almost overnight things changed. Sales dropped alarmingly, major customers deserted them and the company plunged into freefall. Eventually personal debts forced both men into bankruptcy. Joel and Stanley each blamed the other for their predicament, and the parting of the ways was distinctly acrimonious.

Five years later, Joel drove up to a decrepit roadside diner and stopped for a cup of coffee. As he was discreetly wiping some crumbs from the table, a waiter approached. Joel looked up and gasped.

'Stanley!' he said, shaking his head in a patronising manner. 'It's a terrible thing, seeing you working in a place as bad as this.'

'Yeah,' said Stanley, smiling thinly. 'But at least I don't eat here.'

A guy was telling a friend about his time working at a large company. 'I tell you, it didn't matter if it was the managing director, the vice presidents or whatever, I always told those guys where to get off.'

'What was your job again?' asked the friend.

'I was the lift operator.'

Did you hear about the man who started writing poetry as soon as he got up in the morning? – He went from bed to verse.

A man was employed as a security guard at a factory where there had been a spate of thefts by workers on the night shift. Every morning when the night shift workers passed through his gate, it was his job to check their bags and pockets to make sure that nothing was being stolen.

On the first night, all was quiet until a man pushing a wheelbarrow full of newspapers came through his gate. The guard's suspicions were aroused at once. Convinced that the man was hiding something beneath the newspapers, he searched beneath them but found nothing. Nevertheless he still felt that the man was acting strangely, so he questioned him further about the cargo.

The man said: 'I get a little extra money from recycling newspapers, so I go into the canteen and pick up all the ones that people have discarded.'

The guard accepted the explanation for the time being, but resolved to keep a close eye on him in future.

The next night it was the same, and the night after that. Week after week it went on. The same guy would push the wheelbarrow of newspapers past the guard's checkpoint. The guard would always check the contents and find nothing. Then one night, about a year later, the guard reported for work only to find a message had been left ordering him to go straight to the supervisor's office. He walked into the office but before he could say a word, the supervisor shouted: 'You're fired!'

'Fired?' he asked, stunned. 'Why? What have I done wrong?'

'It was your job to make sure that no one stole anything from this plant, and you have failed miserably. So you're fired.'

'Hang on, what do you mean – failed? Nobody has stolen anything from this place while I've been on duty.'

'Oh, really?' said the supervisor. 'Then how do you account for the fact that there are 365 missing wheelbarrows?'

Do bakers with a sense of humour make wry bread?

Two postmen were standing outside the sorting office at the end of their rounds when one spotted a snail crawling by. Suddenly he stamped on the snail, brutally squashing it into the ground.

'That was a bit cruel,' said his colleague.

'That snail had it coming. It's been following me around all day.'

An architect, an artist and an accountant were discussing whether it was better to spend time with a wife or a mistress. The architect said he enjoyed time with a wife, building a solid foundation for an enduring relationship. The artist said he enjoyed time with a mistress, because of the passion and mystery. The accountant said he liked both.

'Both?' chorused the others.

'Yes,' he explained. 'If you have a wife and a mistress, they will each assume you are spending time with the other woman, which means you can go to the office and get some work done.'

How do you drive an accountant insane? – Tie him to a chair, stand in front of him and fold up a road map the wrong way.

A mathematician and a farmer were on a train journey. As they passed a flock of sheep in a field, the mathematician announced confidently: 'There are 797 sheep out there.'

The farmer said: 'That's incredible! It so happens I know the owner and that figure is exactly right. But how did you count them so quickly?'

The mathematician said: 'Easy. I just counted the number of legs and divided by four.'

When the CIA lost track of one of their operatives, they called in one of their top spy hunters. The CIA boss said: 'All I can tell you is that his name is Jones and that he's in a small town somewhere in Wales. If you think you've located him, tell him the code words, "The forecast is for mist on the hills." And if you've got the right man, he will say, "But I hear it's sunny in the valleys."'

So the spy hunter set off for Wales and found himself in a small town. Reasoning that the local pub was the centre of the community, he gradually engaged the barman in conversation. Eventually he said: 'Maybe you can help me. I'm looking for a guy named Jones.'

The barman said: 'You're going to have to be more specific because around here there are hundreds of men named Jones. There's Jones the bread, who runs the baker's shop over the road; Jones the nail, who runs the hardware shop two doors down; not to mention Jones the bank, Jones the steam and Jones the fish. And as a matter of fact, my name is Jones, too.'

Hearing this, the spy hunter figured he might as well try the code words on the barman, so he leaned over the bar and whispered: 'The forecast is for mist on the hills.'

The barman replied: 'Oh, you're looking for Jones the spy. He lives at number 44, halfway up the hill.'

A muscular young man working on a construction site kept bragging that he was the strongest member of the gang. After a while his boasting began to irritate the older workers to the point that one issued him with a challenge.

'It's time to put your money where your mouth is,' said the older worker. 'I'll bet a week's wages that I can haul something in a wheelbarrow over to that outbuilding that you won't be able to wheel back.'

'You're on,' said the young man, already mentally counting his winnings.

So the older worker grabbed a wheelbarrow by the handles and said to the young man, 'OK. Get in . . .'

Did you hear about the mathematician who turned off his heating because he wanted to be cold and calculating?

A Microsoft support technician went to a firing range and shot six bullets at a target thirty metres away. After checking the target, the scorers called out that all six shots had missed completely. Unable to believe that he had failed to register a single hit, the technician demanded that his score be checked again, but the answer was the same. So he fired a shot into the ground right by his feet. He then shouted to the scorers: 'It's working fine here. The problem must be at your end.'

After his wife walked out on him, a man became so depressed that he went to see a psychiatrist.

'My life isn't worth living,' he wailed. 'Everything is so empty without her.'

The psychiatrist said: 'The best thing I can suggest is for you to occupy your time fully so that you don't have time to dwell on your unhappiness. Try and submerge yourself in your work. What do you do for a living?'

'I clean out septic tanks.'

An engineer, an accountant, a pharmacist and a civil servant were arguing over whose dog was the smartest. To settle the argument, each dog was required to perform its best trick.

The engineer's dog used a compass to draw a perfect circle on a sheet of paper; the accountant's dog divided a pile of biscuits into four equal parts; and the pharmacist's dog poured exactly half a carton of milk into a measuring jug.

Finally it was the turn of the civil servant's dog. It sauntered over, peed all over the drawing paper, ate the biscuits, drank the milk, had sex with the other three dogs, claimed a back injury as a result and applied for compensation before going on sick leave.

A woman applying for a job in a lemon grove seemed over-qualified. The foreman said to her: 'Have you any actual experience in picking lemons?'

'As a matter of fact, I have,' she answered. 'I've been divorced three times.'

How did the butcher introduce his wife? – Meat Patty.

A clergyman was walking along a country road when he saw a young farmer struggling to load a huge pile of hay back onto a cart after it had fallen off.

'It's a baking hot day,' said the clergyman, 'and the sweat's pouring off you. Why don't you rest for a while?'

'No, I can't,' said the farmer. 'My father wouldn't like it.'

And he continued re-loading the hay.

'But surely,' continued the clergyman, 'everyone is entitled to a break. Here, have a drink of water.'

'I'd better not,' said the farmer. 'My father wouldn't like it.'

And he continued re-loading the hay.

'Your father must be a real slave driver,' said the clergyman. 'Tell me where he is and I'll give him a piece of my mind!'

'He's under the load of hay.'

Why did the man clean shoes for a living? – Because he really took a shine to it.

A bar was so convinced that its bartender was the strongest man in the town that the owner offered a $1,000 bet that nobody could match his strength. The bartender would squeeze a lemon until all the juice ran into a glass and then hand the lemon to a customer. Anyone who could squeeze out another drop would win the money.

Dozens tried and failed. Lumberjacks, professional sportsmen, builders, farmers: all were unable to squeeze another drop out of the lemon. Then a skinny little man said he would like a go. The large crowd that had gathered roared with laughter at the prospect of this weedy fellow succeeding where the toughest guys in town had failed. But their jeers turned to cheers when he did indeed manage to squeeze one last drop out of the lemon.

The stunned bartender said: 'What the hell do you do for a living? Are you a lumberjack or a weightlifter?'

'No,' replied the little man, 'I'm a tax inspector.'

A plumber was called to a house to fix a leaking pipe. As he set to work, the attractive lady of the house began flirting with him. He needed no encouragement and soon they ended up in bed. He was really turned on by her but just as they were about to have sex, the phone rang.

'That was my husband,' said the woman. 'He's on his way home, but he's going out again at seven, so if you come back around 7.30, we can finish what we've started.'

The plumber looked at her in disbelief. 'What?' he said. 'In my own time?'

An accountant was having difficulties sleeping at night, so he went to see his doctor.

The doctor said: 'Have you tried counting sheep?'

'That's the trouble,' said the accountant. 'I make a mistake and then spend three hours trying to find it!'

A statistician was walking along a corridor when he felt a sudden pain in his chest. Immediately he ran to the nearest staircase and threw himself down the stairs.

His friend came to visit him in hospital and asked him why he had thrown himself down the stairs.

The statistician replied: 'Because the chances of suffering a heart attack while falling downstairs are much lower than the chances of just having a heart attack.'

Experiencing teething troubles with their new computer, a couple called the Help Desk. But the guy there insisted on talking to the husband in complex computer jargon, none of which seemed to make much sense.

Eventually in frustration, the husband said: 'Look, you know what you're talking about but I don't. So can you treat me like a four-year-old and explain it to me that way?'

'OK, son,' said the computer technician, 'put your mommy on the phone.'

A research scientist dropped a piece of buttered toast on the floor and was amazed to see that it landed butter-side up, thereby disproving the long-held theory that toast always lands butter-side down. Thinking that he might have made an important breakthrough that could lead to the rewriting of science textbooks, he took the slice of toast to a colleague for his observations.

'How could it be that when I dropped this slice of toast, it landed butter-side up when all previous knowledge suggests that the opposite should have occurred?'

'It's easy,' said the colleague. 'You must have buttered the wrong side.'

151

A farmer who grew watermelons was being plagued by local children who would sneak into his patch at night and eat the produce. After weeks of putting up with this, he devised what he thought was a foolproof plan to deter the trespassers. He put up a sign, which read: 'Warning! One of the watermelons in this field has been injected with cyanide.'

Sure enough, when the kids read the sign they headed straight home but instead of giving up altogether, they prepared a sign of their own, which they planted right next to the farmer's.

The following day when the farmer inspected the field, he was pleased to find that none of his watermelons were missing. But then he spotted the new sign next to his. It read: 'Now there are two.'

Three schoolboys were boasting about how fast their respective fathers could run.

The first, the son of an Olympic archer, said: 'My father can run the fastest. He can fire an arrow, start to run, and reach the target before the arrow!'

The second boy said: 'You think that's fast! My dad is a hunter. He can shoot his gun and be there before the bullet!'

'That's nothing,' said the third boy. 'My dad is a civil servant. He stops working at 4.30 and he's home by 3.45!'

In preparation for starting a new office job, a young accountant spent a week with the retiring accountant whom he was replacing. He hoped to pick up a few tips from the old master and studied his daily routine intently.

Every morning the experienced accountant began the day by opening his desk drawer, taking out a frayed envelope and removing a yellowing piece of paper. He then read it, nodded his head sagely, returned the envelope to the drawer and started his day's work.

After the old man retired, the new boy could hardly wait to read for himself the message in the drawer, particularly since he felt somewhat inadequate about stepping into such illustrious shoes. Surely, he thought to himself, the envelope must contain the secret to accounting success, a pearl of wisdom to be treasured forever. The anticipation was so great that his hands were actually trembling as he opened the drawer and took out the mysterious envelope. And there, inside, on that aged piece of paper he read the following message:

'Debits in the column nearest the potted plant; credits in the column towards the door.'

An efficiency expert concluded his lecture with the warning: 'Don't try these techniques at home.'

'Why not?' asked a member of the audience.

'I watched my wife's routine at breakfast for twenty-two years,' he explained. 'She made up to ten trips between the fridge, the cooker, the toaster and the table, almost always carrying just a single item at a time. One day I told her: "You're wasting too much time. Why don't you try carrying several things at once?"

'And did it save time?' asked the man in the audience,

'Yes it did,' replied the expert. 'It used to take her twenty minutes to make breakfast. Now I do it in ten.'

A shepherd was patiently herding his flock in a remote field when a Jeep Cherokee pulled up in a cloud of dust. Out stepped a young man dripping in designer labels from his Ray-Ban sunglasses to his Gucci shoes.

'Hey, mister,' he called over to the shepherd, 'if I can tell you exactly how many sheep you have in your flock, will you let me have one?'

The shepherd was baffled by the proposition, but agreed to go along with it.

So the flash young man stepped out of his Jeep with his laptop under his arm. He hooked himself up to the Internet, consulted endless data and spreadsheets, before announcing: 'You have 986 sheep.'

'That's right,' said the shepherd. 'Fair enough. You can take one of my sheep.'

And he watched while the man made his selection and loaded it into the Jeep.

'Before you go,' said the shepherd, 'how about letting me have a go? If I can tell you exactly what your job is, will you give me my sheep back?'

'Sure,' said the young man.

'You're a consultant,' said the shepherd.

'That's right. How did you know that?'

'Easy,' said the shepherd. 'You turned up here uninvited. You wanted to be paid for telling me something I already knew. And you don't know anything about my business because you took my dog!'

A sales manager and an operations manager went bear hunting. While the operations manager remained in the cabin, the sales manager went looking for a bear. He eventually found one and took aim, but merely succeeded in wounding the animal, which proceeded to chase him back to the cabin. The bear was closing with every stride until just as he reached the cabin door, the sales manager tripped and fell flat on his face. Too close behind to stop, the bear vaulted over him and landed in the cabin.

The sales manager quickly jumped up, closed the cabin door and yelled to his friend inside: 'You skin this one while I go and get another!'

153

The chickens in a large hen house began to peck out each other's feathers. As the quarrelling escalated, a number died every day. The concerned farmer rushed to a consultant and asked for a solution to the problem.

'Add a little sugar to the hens' food,' he advised. 'It will keep them sweet and help them to calm down.'

A week later the farmer called on the consultant again. 'The sugar has had no effect. My chickens are still dying. What shall I do?'

'Add pear juice to their drinking water,' he suggested. 'That will help for sure.'

A week later the farmer was back once more. 'My chickens are still quarrelling,' he told the consultant. 'Do you have any more advice?'

'I can offer you more and more advice,' replied the consultant. 'The real question is whether you have any more chickens.'

A marketing manager married a woman who had previously been married nine times but still claimed to be a virgin. She explained her virginity thus:

'My first husband was a sales representative who spent our entire marriage telling me: "It's gonna be great!"

'My second husband worked in software services. He was never quite sure how it was supposed to function, but he said he would send me the instructions.

'My third husband was an accountant. He said he knew how to, but he just wasn't sure whether it was his job to.

'My fourth husband was a teacher. He simply remarked: "Those who can, do; those who can't, teach."

'My fifth husband was an engineer. He told me that he understood the basic process but needed three years to research, implement and design a new state-of-the-art method.

'My sixth husband was a psychiatrist, and all he ever wanted to do was talk about it.

'My seventh husband was a professional builder, but he never finished anything he started.

'My eighth husband was a help-desk coordinator, and he kept teaching me how to do it myself.

'My ninth husband was in technical support, and he kept saying, "Don't worry, it'll be up any minute now."

'And now I am married to you, my darling, a marketing manager.'

The husband looked at her and said nervously: 'I know I have the product, I'm just not sure how to position it.'

Old Age

An elderly couple were lying in bed one night. The husband was falling asleep but the wife was feeling romantic and was eager to talk.

'You used to hold my hand when we were courting,' she said coyly.

Wearily he reached across, held her hand for a second and tried to get back to sleep.

A few moments later she said: 'Then you used to kiss me.'

Mildly irritated, he reached across, gave her a peck on the cheek and settled down to sleep.

Shortly afterwards she said: 'Then you used to bite my neck.'

Angrily, he threw back the bedclothes and climbed out of bed.

'Where are you going?' she asked.

'To get my teeth!'

After years of regular church attendance, a 105-year-old man suddenly stopped attending. When the vicar happened to see him in the street, he asked why, after decades of never missing a Sunday service, he had given up going to church.

The old man whispered: 'When I got to 90, I expected God to take me any day. But then I got to be 95, 100, and now 105. So I thought God is obviously very busy and must have forgotten about me, and I don't really want to remind him.'

After living a wild life, an ageing gigolo finally found the years were catching up with him. So he went to the doctor for a medical.

'I've had a lifetime of wine, women and song,' he boasted proudly. 'And I don't think I could give it up.'

'Well, the good news,' said the doctor, 'is that you won't have to give up singing.'

A ninety-five-year-old woman at a nursing home received a visit from one of her fellow church members.

'How are you feeling, Doris?' asked the visitor.

'Oh,' said the old lady, 'I'm worried sick.'

'What are you worried about? You look like you're in good health. They are taking care of you here, aren't they?'

'Yes, they are taking very good care of me.'

'Are you in any pain?'

'No, I've never had a pain in my life.'

'Then what are you worried about?'

The old lady leaned back in her chair and explained: 'Every close friend I ever had has already died and gone to heaven. I'm afraid they're all wondering where I went!'

Old age is when your doctor doesn't give you x-rays anymore but just holds you up to the light.

An old timer was sitting on his New England porch when a young man walked up holding a pen and clipboard.

'What are you selling, son?' asked the old man.

'I'm not selling anything. I'm the census taker.'

'The what?'

'The census taker. We're trying to find out how many people there are in the United States.'

'You're wasting your time with me,' said the old man. 'I have no idea.'

A group of pensioners in the lounge of a nursing home were exchanging complaints about their ailments.

One said: 'My arms are so weak I can hardly hold this cup.'

Another said: 'My cataracts are so bad I can't even see to pour my coffee.'

Another said: 'I can't turn my head because of the arthritis in my neck.'

Another said: 'My blood pressure pills make me feel dizzy all the time.'

Another said: 'I guess that's the price we pay for getting old.'

Another said: 'But it's not all bad. We should be grateful that we can all still drive.'

An old man was running a fairground tent, which proclaimed: 'For fifty dollars I'll teach you to be a mind reader.'

Intrigued by the offer, a teenager entered the tent to try his luck.

'OK,' said the old guy, handing him a garden hose, 'I want you to hold this hose and look in the end.'

'What for?' asked the teenager.

'It's all part of teaching you to become a mind reader.'

So the teenager, somewhat reluctantly, looked in the end of the hose and saw nothing – just darkness. Then suddenly the old man turned on the tap and water came gushing out all over the young man's face.

'I knew you were going to do something like that!' yelled the drenched teenager.

The old man said: 'Then that'll be fifty dollars.'

While writing at a Post Office desk, a young man was approached by an elderly man holding a postcard.

'Excuse me, young man,' he said. 'Could you possibly address this postcard for me? My arthritis is playing up today and I can't even hold a pen.'

'Certainly,' said the young man, and he wrote down the address given to him.

'Also,' added the old man, 'would you be so kind as to write a short message on the card and sign it for me?'

'No problem,' said the young man, and he patiently wrote the message that the old man dictated to him. 'Is there anything else I can help you with?'

'Yes,' said the old man. 'At the end, could you just add "PS, please excuse the sloppy handwriting."'

You Know You're Old When:

1. You and your teeth don't sleep together.
2. You try to straighten out the wrinkles in your tights and discover you aren't wearing any.
3. At the breakfast table you hear snap, crackle and pop . . . and you're not eating cereal.
4. Your back goes out but you don't.
5. Happy hour is a nap.
6. You wake up looking like the picture on your driver's licence.
7. It takes two attempts to get up from the couch.
8. Your idea of a night out is sitting on the patio.
9. You step off a kerb and look down one more time to check that the street is still there.
10. Your idea of weightlifting is standing up.
11. You're on vacation and your energy runs out before your money does.
12. You say something to your kids that your mother always used to say to you (and you always hated it).
13. All you want for your birthday is not to be reminded of your age.
14. Well-wishers can't get near your birthday cake to count the candles because they're driven back by the heat.
15. It takes longer to rest than it did to get tired.
16. Your memory is shorter and your complaining lasts longer.
17. Most of the names in your address book start with Dr.
18. You sit in a rocking chair and can't get it going.
19. The pharmacist has become your new best friend.
20. Getting lucky means you found your car in the parking lot.
21. The twinkle in your eye is just a reflection from the sun on your bifocals.
22. Everything hurts, and what doesn't hurt doesn't work.
23. It takes twice as long to look half as good.
24. You get two invitations to go out on the same night and you pick the one that gets you home the earliest.
25. You sink your teeth into a steak – and they stay there.

26. Your get up and go has got up and gone.
27. You seem to have more patience, but really it's just that you don't care anymore.
28. You confuse having a clear conscience with having a bad memory.
29. You finally get your head together and your body starts falling apart.
30. You wonder how you could be over the hill when you don't even remember being on top of it.

Two old men – one a retired history professor, the other a retired professor of psychology – had been persuaded by their wives to take a holiday in Portugal. As they sat around on the hotel balcony watching the sunset, the history professor said to the psychology professor: 'Have you read Marx?'

To which the professor of psychology replied: 'Yes, I think it's the wicker chairs.'

An elderly lady walked into the bar on a cruise ship and ordered a scotch with two drops of water. As the bartender poured it, she revealed that it was her eightieth birthday.

Hearing this, a fellow passenger offered to buy her a drink. 'That's very kind of you,' she said. 'I'll have another scotch with two drops of water.'

As news of the celebration spread, four more passengers offered to buy her a drink. Each time she asked for a scotch with two drops of water.

The bartender was amazed at her drinking capacity but was puzzled why she always asked for two drops of water.

'Well,' she said, 'when you're my age, you learn how to hold your liquor. But water is a different matter!'

A daughter complimented her elderly father on his improved manners. 'After all these years, I notice that you have finally started putting your hand over your mouth whenever you cough.'

'I have to,' he said. 'How else can I catch my teeth?'

With a gale force wind blowing down the street, a policeman noticed an old woman standing on a corner. She was holding on tightly to her hat as her skirt blew up around her waist.

He went over to her and said: 'Look, lady, while you're holding on to your precious hat, everybody's getting a good look at everything you have!'

'Listen, sonny,' she replied. 'What they're looking at is eighty years old. But this hat is brand new!'

An old woman was feeling suicidal following the death of her beloved husband. She was so heartbroken that she decided to spare herself further pain by using her late husband's gun to shoot herself in the heart. Not wanting to miss the vital organ and become a vegetable and a burden to someone, she called her doctor to ask precisely where the heart was on a woman.

'Just below your left breast,' said the doctor.

That evening she was admitted to hospital with a gunshot wound to the knee.

An old man of ninety-one was sitting on a park bench crying. A passing police officer came over to ask him what was the matter.

'You see,' said the old man, 'I just got married to a twenty-five-year-old girl. Every morning she makes me a wonderful breakfast and then we make love. At dinner time she makes me a wonderful supper and then we make love.'

The policeman said: 'You shouldn't be crying! You should be the happiest man in the world!'

'I know!' said the old man. 'I'm crying because I can't remember where I live!'

A man went to the doctor to complain that his right knee was hurting. 'I don't think it's anything serious, doctor, but it keeps aching.'

'You're ninety-eight!' exclaimed the doctor. 'Are you surprised your knee hurts?'

'But my other knee is ninety-eight, too,' said the old man, 'and it doesn't hurt!'

Two old age pensioners were talking about their husbands over a cup of coffee. One said: 'I do wish Fred would stop biting his nails. It's such a horrible habit.'

Her friend said: 'Albert used to do the same. But I cured him of the habit.'

'How did you do that?'

'I hid his teeth!'

One-Liners
What's more dangerous than being with a fool? – Fooling with a bee.
Which English king invented the fireplace? – Alfred the Grate.
What did the bee say to the other bee in summer? – Swarm here, isn't it?
What's smelly, round, and laughs a lot? – A tickled onion.
What bird can lift the most? – A crane.
What bone will a dog never eat? – A trombone.

What can you hold without ever touching it? – A conversation.

What happens when ducks fly upside down? – They quack up.

How do crazy people go through the forest? – They take the psycho path.

What is half of infinity? – Nity.

Why did the turkey cross the road? – To prove he wasn't chicken.

What has six legs and lives in trees? – Three anti-road protestors.

What do Alexander the Great and Winnie the Pooh have in common? – They both have 'the' as their middle name.

How do you get holy water? – You boil the hell out of it.

What do you call a pigeon with a machine gun? – A military coo.

What word is always pronounced incorrectly? – Incorrectly.

What goes red, green, red, green, red, green? – A frog in a blender.

What is cleverer than a talking cat? – A spelling bee.

What has six eyes but can't see? – Three blind mice.

What do fish say when they hit a concrete wall? – Dam!

What does a caterpillar do on New Year's Day? – Turns over a new leaf.

What kind of bee can't be understood? – A mumble bee.

How did Noah see the animals in the Ark at night? – By flood lighting.

What pet makes the loudest noise? – A trum-pet.

What is a tornado? – Mother Nature doing the twist.

What do you call a calf after it's six months old? – Seven months old.

Why did the child study in an airplane? – He wanted a higher education.

What do you call a fish on a motorcycle? – A motor pike.

What has a lot of keys but can't open any doors? – A piano.

What's green and would kill you if it fell out of a tree? – A pool table.

What's yellow and dangerous? – Shark-infested custard.

What's red, flies and wobbles? – A jelly copter.

Why did the sword swallower swallow an umbrella? – He wanted to put something away for a rainy day.

Why did the man take a pencil to bed? – To draw the curtains.

What do you call a tramp with short legs? – A low down bum.

When is a door not a door? – When it's ajar.

What do you call cheese that isn't yours? – Nacho Cheese.

Why was Cinderella thrown off the basketball team? – She ran away from the ball.

Why is perfume obedient? – Because it is scent wherever it goes.

What did the fireman's wife get for Christmas? – A ladder in her stocking.

Which two words in the English language have the most letters? – Post Office.

What do you call an unemployed jester? – Nobody's fool.

Why was the teacher cross-eyed? – She couldn't control her pupils.

What has one horn and gives milk? – A milk truck.

What happens when you throw a green stone in the Red Sea? – It gets wet.

What steps would you take if you were attacked by a bear? – Great big ones.

What country makes you shiver? – Chile.

What is the best thing to do if you find a gorilla in your bed? – Sleep somewhere else.

What's round and bad-tempered? – A vicious circle.

What did one elevator say to the other? – I think I'm coming down with something.

What is it that even the most careful person overlooks? – His nose.

Why did the burglar take a shower? – He wanted to make a clean getaway.

What kind of fish can't swim? – Dead ones.

If a crocodile makes shoes, what does a banana make? – Slippers.

What word has an E at the front and an E at the end but only one letter inside it? – Envelope.

Why did the idiot put the mail in the oven? – He wanted to have hotmail.

Why didn't the ghost jump off the bridge? – He didn't have the guts.

What happened when the wheel was invented? – It caused a revolution.

Where do fortune tellers dance? – At the crystal ball.

How do you catch a one-of-a-kind rabbit? – Unique up on him.

Why did the foal cough? – Because he was a little hoarse.

What did one magnet say to the other? – I find you very attractive.

What did the mother broom say to the baby broom? – It's time to go to sweep.

What do you call a pig that does karate? – A pork chop.

What do you call the best butter on the farm? – A goat.

How do you make a hot dog stand? – Steal its chair.

What did the rug say to the floor? – Don't move, I've got you covered.

Why did the orange stop rolling down the hill? – It ran out of juice.

What was Camelot famous for? – It's knight life.

Why did Henry VIII put skittles on his lawn? – So he could take Anne Boleyn.

What has fifty feet and sings? – A choir.

How many ears did Davy Crocket have? – Three: his left ear, his right ear and his wild front ear.

Did you hear about the Native American who drank 20 cups of tea before he went to bed? – He drowned in his tee pee that night.

What did baby Superman scream while his mom was putting him to bed? – 'No, no, not the crib tonight!'

How do you make an egg laugh? – Tell it a yolk.

How can you get four suits for a dollar? – Buy a deck of cards.

How do dinosaurs pay their bills? – With tyrannosaurus checks.

What do you call a dinosaur that wears a cowboy hat and boots? – Tyrannosaurus Tex.

What do you call people who come round to your house to demonstrate vacuum cleaners? – Jehoover's witnesses.

What's green and hairy and travels at 90 mph? – A gooseberry on a motorbike.

Why did the coach go to the bank? – To get his quarterback.

What kind of shoes does a spy wear? – Sneakers.

How do we know the Native Americans were the first people in North America? – They had reservations.

Why did the boy drop a clock from the window? – He wanted to see time fly.

Why was the tissue crying? – He said people kept using him.

Why didn't the skeleton go to school? – Because his heart wasn't in it.

What's the difference between roast beef and pea soup? – Anyone can roast beef.

Did you hear about the man who drowned in a bowl of muesli? – A strong currant pulled him in.

What's the fastest way to make anti-freeze? – Hide her nightdress.

What goes zzub, zzub? – A bee flying backwards.

What's red and bad for your teeth? – A brick.

Why did the dinosaur cross the road? – Because chickens hadn't been invented.

What did the computer do at lunchtime? – It went for a byte.

What kind of mail does a superstar vampire get? – Fang mail.

What gets smaller the more you put in it? – A hole in the ground.

In which direction do you turn the key on a Victorian desk? – Antique-lock wise.

What has wheels and flies? – A garbage truck.

Who was the biggest thief in history? – Atlas, he held up the whole world.

Pets

Two dogs were walking down the street. One said: 'Wait here a minute, I'll be right back.' He then crossed the street, sniffed the fire hydrant for a while, then walked back across the street.

'What was that all about?' said the other dog.

'I was just checking my messages.'

A talent scout walking down the street noticed an accordionist with a singing puppy. The scout immediately saw the potential of such an act and took them to his office to sign them up. 'I'll have you playing Vegas within a month,' he promised.

But just as they were about to put pen to paper, a big dog marched into the office, picked up the puppy by the scruff of its neck and ran off with it.

'My act! You've stolen my act!' yelled the talent scout. 'What can we do?'

'Nothing,' said the accordionist. 'You see, that was his mother. She doesn't want him to be an entertainer – she wants him to be a doctor.'

Why is a dog so jumpy if you lightly touch its tail yet it feels nothing when it bangs it repeatedly on the kitchen table?

Two dog owners were talking in the park. One said: 'I'm fed up with my dog – he'll chase anyone on a bike.'

'What are you going to do?' asked the other. 'Have him put down?'

'No. I think I'll just take his bike away.'

Where do you find a dog with no legs? – Right where you left him.

An avid duck hunter was in the market for a new bird dog. His search ended when he found a dog that could actually walk on water to retrieve a duck. Amazed by his discovery, he was sure none of his friends would ever believe him.

He decided to try and break the news to a friend of his, an eternal pessimist who steadfastly refused to be impressed by anything. In the hope that even he would be impressed by a dog that walked on water, he was invited to join the hunter and his dog on a trip into the country. However, the hunter refrained from mentioning the dog's special talent – he wanted his pessimistic friend to see for himself.

The two men and the dog made their way to a good hunting lake and as they waited by the shore, a flock of ducks flew overhead. The men fired, and a duck fell. The dog responded and jumped into the water, but, instead of sinking, it walked across the water to retrieve the bird, never getting more than its paws wet. This continued throughout the day. Each time a duck fell, the dog walked across the surface of the water to retrieve it.

The pessimist watched carefully, observing everything, but did not say a single word. Then on the drive home, the hunter finally asked his friend: 'Did you notice anything unusual about my new dog?'

'Sure did,' responded the pessimist. 'He can't swim.'

How come a dog hates it when you blow in its face yet hangs its head out the window when you're driving?

Entering a small country store, a stranger spotted a sign saying 'Beware of the dog'. He looked around but all he could see was a harmless old dog lying fast asleep on the floor next to the counter.

The stranger said to the store manager: 'Is that the dog folks are supposed to beware of?'

'Yep.'

'Well, he doesn't look dangerous to me. Why did you put the sign up?'

'Cos people kept tripping over him.'

A woman wanted to know whether she could take her new dog on board an airplane. The customer services assistant said it would be fine as long as she paid $50 and provided her own kennel. The kennel, he added, needed to be large enough for the dog to stand up, sit down, turn around and roll over.

The woman said: 'Oh, I'll never be able to teach him all that by tomorrow!'

Did you hear about the dog that ate nothing but onions? – His bark was much worse than his bite.

A woman watched a dog go into a butcher's shop.

'What is it today?' asked the butcher. 'Pork?'

The dog shook its head.

'Beef?' suggested the butcher.

The dog shook its head.

'Lamb chops?' tried the butcher.

The dog wagged its tail excitedly.

The butcher wrapped up two lamb chops, gave them to the dog and the dog trotted out. The same thing happened the following day and the woman was so intrigued that she decided to follow the dog out of the shop. She saw the dog walk up the steps to a house, stand on his hind legs and ring the doorbell with his nose. A man answered the door and immediately started shouting angrily at the dog.

The woman was incensed. 'You should be ashamed of yourself,' she told the man. 'That is the cleverest dog I've ever seen. He goes to the butcher's, fetches your dinner, brings it home and rings the doorbell. And you treat him like that!'

'That's as maybe,' said the man, 'but it's the fourth time this week that he's forgotten his key.'

A couple shared their apartment with a parakeet. Since the exterminator was due to come, they put the parakeet in the bedroom and hung a sign on the door: 'Please skip this room. Do not open door. Pet flies.' The exterminator came, and on his receipt he wrote: 'Finished all of apartment except room with pet flies.'

A woman was walking along the street when a parrot in a pet shop window squawked: 'Hey, lady, you're ugly.' The woman tried to ignore the insult and hurried on her way.

The following day when she passed the pet shop, she quickened her stride in the hope that the parrot wouldn't spot her, but he did and squawked loudly: 'Hey, lady, you're ugly.' The woman was extremely embarrassed.

When the same thing happened for a third and fourth day, she had reached the end of her tether. She stormed into the shop and demanded to speak to the owner. She threatened to sue him and to have the parrot put down unless the abuse stopped. The owner promised faithfully that the bird wouldn't say it again.

The next day, the woman walked past the pet shop and the parrot called out: 'Hey, lady.'

The woman turned round and glared at the bird. 'Yes?'

'You know . . .'

A woman bought a parrot with beautiful plumage but the only thing it could say was 'Who is it?' After a few days she realised that the bird's colour clashed with the rest of the living room, so she called a decorator to give the room a new coat of paint. When he arrived to do the job, she had just gone out to post a letter, leaving the parrot in charge.

The decorator knocked on the front door.

'Who is it?' squawked the parrot.

'It's the decorator.'

'Who is it?' repeated the parrot.

'It's the decorator.'

'Who is it?'

'It's the decorator!' yelled the man.

'Who is it?'

'It's the goddam decorator!'

'Who is it?'

'I said, it's the decorator!'

And with that, the man suffered a fatal heart attack and collapsed on the doorstep.

A few minutes later, the woman returned home. Seeing the body on the step, she said: 'My God! Who is it?'

The parrot replied: 'It's the decorator!'

A vicar new to the area visited a little old lady who owned a pet parrot. He noticed that the bird had a ribbon tied to each leg.

'What are the ribbons for?' he inquired.

The old lady said: 'If I pull the left ribbon, he sings "Clementine", and if I pull the right ribbon, he sings "We'll Meet Again".'

'And what happens if you pull both ribbons at the same time?' asked the vicar.

'I fall off the bloody perch!' said the parrot.

165

A game warden spotted a man leaving a lake carrying two buckets of fish. 'Excuse me,' he asked. 'Do you have a licence to catch those fish?'

The man said: 'No, but you don't understand, sir. These are my pet fish.'

'Pet fish?' replied the warden incredulously.

'Yes, sir. Every night I take these fish down to the lake and let them swim around for a while. Then I whistle and they jump back into their buckets, and I take them home.'

'I've never heard such nonsense,' said the warden. 'Fish can't do that!'

The man thought for a second before suggesting: 'If you don't believe me, I'll show you.'

'I can't wait to see this!' said the warden mockingly.

So the man poured the fish into the lake and stood and waited. After several minutes, the game warden turned to him and said: 'Well?'

'Well what?' asked the man.

'When are you going to call them back?'

'Call who back?'

'The fish!' snapped the warden.

'What fish?'

A man was passing a pet shop when he saw a talking monkey advertised for sale. He was so impressed by its vocabulary that he bought it on the spot.

That evening he took it to his local bar and bet everyone $10 that the monkey could talk. A dozen people accepted the challenge but, despite his new owner's coaxing, the monkey refused to say a word and the man had to pay up. When he got it home, the man was puzzled to hear the monkey chatting away merrily.

The next evening, the man returned to the bar and bet everyone $20 that the monkey could talk. Again there were plenty of takers but, to the man's anger, the monkey remained silent. After paying up, the man took the monkey outside.

'I'm taking you back to the shop,' he stormed. 'You're a complete waste of money!'

'Chill out,' said the monkey. 'Think of the odds we'll get tomorrow.'

A cat died and went to heaven. God said: 'You've been a good cat all your life – a devoted pet. Is there anything you wish?'

The cat replied: 'I lived on a farm and always had to sleep on a hard floor, so a soft pillow would be great. Then I could sleep peacefully in heaven.'

God provided a soft pillow for the cat.

The following day six mice died and went to heaven. God told them:

'You have been good mice all your lives. Is there anything you wish?'

'Yes,' they said. 'We always had to run everywhere, being chased by cats or people. We'd love a pair of roller skates each so that we can get around heaven without having to use our little legs as much.'

So God provided each mouse with a pair of roller skates.

A week later, God thought he'd check up on the cat who was fast asleep on his new pillow.

'Is everything OK?' asked God.

The cat stretched out. 'Perfect,' he said. 'I've never been happier. The pillow is so comfortable and those meals on wheels you've been sending over are simply the best!'

What's the difference between a cat and a comma? – One has the paws before the claws and the other has the clause before the pause.

How did a cat take first prize at the bird show? – By reaching into the cage.

A man hated his wife's cat so much that he decided to get rid of it by driving it twenty blocks from home and dumping it. But as he got back home, he saw the cat wandering up the driveway. So he drove the cat forty blocks away and dumped it. But when he arrived back home, there was the cat waiting for him at the front door. In desperation, he drove the cat fifty miles out into the country and dumped it in the middle of a wood.

Four hours later his wife got a phone call at home. 'Darling,' said her husband. 'Is the cat there?'

'Yes,' said the wife. 'Why?'

'Just put him on the line will you? I need directions.'

A woman renowned for her charitable work was granted three wishes by a fairy godmother. 'To be honest,' she said, 'I have everything I could possibly want in life. What more can I wish for?' Then she thought for a moment and said: 'Well, I suppose a new dinner table would be nice. I've had that one for over 35 years.'

Within seconds, the fairy godmother had delivered a new table. 'Now what about your second wish?'

'Hmmm,' mused the woman. 'Well, if you insist, I suppose a new car would be nice for getting me to church.'

No sooner had she spoken than a brand new car appeared on the drive.

'And for your third wish?' asked the fairy godmother.

'Well, I guess there's no point in having a new car without somebody to share it with. Could you possibly turn my loyal and loving cat into a handsome young man?'

At that, the cat was transformed into a handsome hunk. The young man coolly strolled over to the woman and said: 'I bet you're sorry you had me neutered now.'

While a little boy was away at school, his cat died. Worried about how he would take the news when he got home, his mother consoled him and said: 'Don't worry, darling. Tiger is in heaven with God now.'
The boy said: 'What's God gonna do with a dead cat?'

How To Give Your Cat A Pill
1. Pick up cat and cradle it in the crook of your left arm as if holding a baby. Position right forefinger and thumb on either side of cat's mouth and gently apply pressure to cheeks while holding pill in right hand. As cat opens mouth, pop pill into mouth. Allow cat to close mouth and swallow.
2. Retrieve pill from floor and cat from behind sofa. Cradle cat in left arm and repeat process.
3. Retrieve cat from bedroom, and throw soggy pill away.
4. Take new pill from foil wrap, cradle cat in left arm holding paws tightly with left hand. Force jaws open and push pill to back of mouth with right forefinger. Hold mouth shut for a count of ten.
5. Retrieve pill from goldfish bowl and cat from top of wardrobe. Call spouse from garden.
6. Kneel on floor with cat wedged firmly between knees, hold front and rear paws. Ignore low growls emitted by cat. Get spouse to hold head firmly with one hand while forcing wooden ruler into mouth. Drop pill down ruler and rub cat's throat vigorously.
7. Retrieve cat from curtain rail, get another pill from foil wrap. Make note to buy new ruler and repair curtains. Carefully sweep shattered Doulton figures from hearth and set to one side for gluing later.
8. Wrap cat in large towel and get spouse to lie on cat with head just visible from below armpit. Put pill in end of drinking straw, force mouth open with pencil and blow down drinking straw.
9. Check label to make sure pill not harmful to humans, drink glass of water to take taste away. Apply band-aid to spouse's forearm and remove blood from carpet with cold water and soap.
10. Retrieve cat from neighbour's shed. Get another pill. Place cat in cupboard and close door onto neck to leave head showing. Force mouth open with dessert spoon. Flick pill down throat with elastic band.
11. Fetch screwdriver from garage and put door back on hinges. Apply cold compress to cheek and check records for date of last tetanus shot. Throw ripped T-shirt away and fetch new one from bedroom.
12. Call fire department to retrieve cat from tree across the road.

Apologise to neighbour who crashed into fence while swerving to avoid cat. Take last pill from foil-wrap.

13. Tie cat's front paws to rear paws with garden twine and bind tightly to leg of dining table. Find heavy duty pruning gloves from shed. Force cat's mouth open with small wrench. Push pill into mouth followed by large piece of fillet steak. Hold head vertically and pour half a pint of water down throat to wish pill down.

14. Get spouse to drive you to casualty department, sit quietly while doctor stitches fingers and forearm, and removes pill remnants from right eye. Stop at furniture shop on way home to order new table.

15. Arrange for RSPCA to collect cat, and call local pet shop to see if they have any hamsters.

A tomcat and a female tabby were courting on the back fence one night. He leaned over to her and purred seductively: 'I'd die for you.'

She looked up coyly and said: 'How many times?'

Police

A rookie cop was teamed up in a patrol car with a veteran of thirty-five years' service. On his first day out on the road, the eager youngster spotted a crowd gathered on a street corner and prepared to spring into action.

'I'm going to disperse that crowd,' he announced to his partner. 'Watch this!'

Before his colleague could answer, the rookie had jumped out of the car and was marching over towards the assembled throng.

'Come along,' he said. 'Whatever the show was, it's over now, so it's time to move on.'

The people shuffled awkwardly but appeared reluctant to move.

Producing his baton, the rookie snapped: 'Listen, I don't want to have to get rough. Move along now, folks! I'm sure none of you want a night in the cells.'

Intimidated by his threats, the crowd slowly dispersed.

Proud of his work, the rookie jumped back into the car and asked his partner: 'Well, how did I do?'

'Pretty good,' said the veteran, 'especially since this is a bus stop!'

A workman was killed at a construction site and the police began questioning a number of the other workers. Based on their previous records, many of these workers were considered prime suspects.

The electrician was suspected of wiretapping once but was never charged.

The carpenter was once arrested for getting hammered, but was never nailed.

169

The cement mixer was a hard case but there was nothing concrete to link him with the crime.

The window glazier went to great panes to conceal his past.

The painter had a brush with the law several years ago.

The mason got stoned regularly but his alibi was rock solid and they couldn't pin anything on him.

So who did it?

The window glazier. But he claimed he was framed.

A traffic cop stopped a drunk driver just after midnight in New York. 'Excuse me, sir,' said the officer, peering into the car window. 'Have you been drinking?'

'I certainly have,' replied the driver. 'I had five pints of Guinness with my buddies at lunchtime and then I spent the afternoon in O'Brien's Bar, drinking Guinness with whisky chasers. During Happy Hour I sank six double brandies and then I had a couple of drinks with old friends, just to be sociable. And then I drove one of my buddies home and had a few cans of beer at his house, because it would have been rude to refuse.'

'I see,' said the officer. 'I'm afraid I'm going to have to ask you to step out of the car and take a breathalyser test.'

'Why?' said the drunk. 'Don't you believe me?'

Man: Officer, there's a bomb in my garden!
Police officer: Don't worry, sir. If no one claims it within three days, you can keep it.

Two teenagers arrested for breaking into a school were taken to the local police station. The desk sergeant advised them that they were entitled to one phone call.

Half an hour later, a man entered the station.

'I assume you're the kids' lawyer?' said the sergeant.

'No way,' said the man. 'I'm here to deliver a pizza.'

Policeman: I'm afraid that I'm going to have to lock you up for the night.
Man: What's the charge?
Policeman: Oh, there's no charge. It's all part of the service.

Alerted by a noise in the garden, a man looked out of his bedroom window late one night and saw a gang of thieves breaking into his shed. He immediately phoned the police who informed him that no officers were available at present.

'OK,' he said, and put the phone down.

A couple of minutes later, he called the police again. 'Don't worry about sending anyone round to Woodbridge Avenue to arrest the burglars,' he said. 'I've just shot them.'

Within five minutes half a dozen police cars came screeching down the street and, naturally enough, caught the burglars.

The officer in charge was furious. He said to the houseowner: 'I thought you said you'd shot them!'

The man replied: 'I thought you said there was nobody available . . .'

A woman was driving down the highway at 75 m.p.h. when she noticed that she was being followed by a motorcycle police officer. Instead of slowing down, however, she picked up speed. When she looked back again, there were two police bikes. So she put her foot right down, doing over 100 m.p.h., and the next time she looked around, there were three police bikes. Then suddenly up ahead, she spotted a gas station, screeched to a halt and ran into the ladies' toilet. When she emerged from the toilet a few minutes later, the three officers were standing there waiting for her. She said coyly: 'I bet none of you thought I'd make it . . .'

Did you hear about the cannibal policeman who was arrested? – He was caught grilling his suspects.

A highly agitated young woman phoned the local police and said: 'I have a sex maniac in my apartment.'

'OK, ma'am, we'll be right over.'

'Oh,' she said. 'Can you wait until morning?'

A police recruit was asked during his exam: 'What would you do if you had to arrest your own mother?'

He answered: 'Call for backup!'

A farmer was stopped by a police officer for going five miles an hour over the speed limit on a straight country road. The officer's attitude was heavy-handed as he began to lecture the farmer about his speed and generally belittle him. When the officer finally got around to writing out the ticket, he had to swat some flies that were buzzing around his head.

'Having some problems with them circle flies are you?' inquired the farmer.

'Well, yeah,' said the officer, 'if that's what they're called. But I've never heard of circle flies.'

The farmer explained: 'Circle flies are common on farms. They're called circle flies because they're almost always found circling around the back end of a horse.'

'Oh,' said the officer as he continued writing out the ticket. Then it dawned on him what the farmer was implying. 'Wait a minute, are you trying to call me a horse's rear end?'

'Oh, no, officer,' said the farmer. 'I have too much respect for law enforcement to consider calling you such a thing.'

'That's all right, then.'

After a pause, the farmer added: 'Hard to fool them flies though.'

A police officer stopped a drunk wandering through the streets at six o'clock in the morning.

The policeman said: 'Can you explain why you're out at this hour?'

The drunk replied: 'If I could, I'd be home by now!'

Genuine Quotes By Traffic Cops:
- 'If you run, you'll only go to jail tired.'
- 'The handcuffs are tight because they're new. They'll stretch out after you wear them a while.'
- 'So you don't know how fast you were going? I guess that means I can write anything I want on the ticket, huh?'
- 'No, sir, we don't have quotas anymore. We used to have quotas, but now we're allowed to write as many tickets as we want.'
- 'Life's tough; it's tougher if you're stupid.'
- 'In God we trust, all others are suspects.'

A police officer came upon a terrible car smash in which the driver and passenger had both been badly injured. As he studied the wreckage, a dog came out of the bushes and hopped around the crashed car. The officer looked down at the dog and said: 'I wish you could talk.'

The dog looked up at the officer and shook his head up and down.

'You can understand what I'm saying?' asked the officer incredulously.

Again, the dog shook his head up and down.

'Well, did you see this accident?'

'Yes,' motioned the dog.

'What happened?'

The dog pretended to have a can in his hand and raised it to his mouth.

'They were drinking?' asked the officer.

'Yes,' nodded the dog.

'What else?'

The dog pinched his fingers together, held them to his mouth and adopted a dreamy expression.

'They were smoking marijuana?'

'Yes,' motioned the dog.

'Now wait,' continued the officer. 'You're saying your owners were drinking and smoking before they had the accident?

'Yes,' nodded the dog.

'And what were you doing during all this?'

'Driving,' motioned the dog.

A hole has appeared in the ladies' changing rooms at a local sports club. Police are looking into it.

A tourist asked a man in uniform: 'Are you a policeman?'

'No, I'm an undercover detective.'

'So why are you in uniform?'

'Today is my day off.'

A man was speeding down the highway, feeling secure in a gaggle of cars all travelling at the same speed. However, as they passed a speed trap, he was nailed by a speed detector and was pulled over.

As the officer took his details, the man complained: 'Officer, I know I was speeding, but I don't think it's fair. There were plenty of other cars around me going just as fast, so why did I get the ticket?'

'Ever go fishing?' asked the officer.

'Uh . . . yeah. So?'

The officer grinned and added: 'Ever catch all the fish?'

Although scheduled for all-night duty at the station, a police officer was relieved of duty early and arrived home at 2a.m. – four hours earlier than expected. Not wanting to wake his wife, he undressed in the dark, crept into the bedroom and began to climb into bed.

But just as he pulled back the covers, his wife sat up sleepily and said: 'Tom, would you go down to the all-night drug store on the next block and fetch me some aspirin? I've got a splitting headache.'

'Certainly, honey,' he said, and feeling his way across the room, he got dressed and walked to the drug store.

As he entered, the pharmacist looked up in surprise. 'Hey,' said the druggist, 'aren't you Officer Renton of the 8th District?'

'Yes, I am,' said the officer.

'Then why are you wearing the fire chief's uniform?'

Police are investigating an accident in which two trucks loaded with copies of *Roget's Thesaurus* collided as they left a London publishing house. Witnesses were stunned, startled, aghast, taken aback, shocked, stupefied . . .

A murder suspect was holed up in his house, surrounded by armed police officers. With no end to the siege in sight, the officer in charge yelled: 'Come on out, or I'll come in there myself and drag you out!'

The suspect shouted back: 'I'm warning you. If you don't wipe your feet when you come in, my wife will kill us both.'

Questions

Why does your nose run and your feet smell?

How can a person be 'pretty ugly'?

Why do they mark containers 'This end up'? If you can read the marking, isn't that end already up?

Why is it that no amount of planning will ever replace luck?

Who decided Hotpoint would be a good name for a company that sells refrigerators?

How is it possible to get clothes whiter than white?

Why do you have to work like a slave to get a Master's degree?

Is it possible for someone to write an unauthorised autobiography?

If a mute swears, does his mother wash his hands with soap?

If a parsley farmer is sued, can they garnish his wages?

If money doesn't grow on trees, why do banks have branches?

Who edits fishing shows? How do they decide what's too boring?

Why does a round pizza come in a square box?

Do illiterates get the full effect of alphabet soup?

If a stealth bomber crashes in a forest, will it make a sound?

Why is it that only adults have difficulties with childproof bottles?

If a turtle doesn't have a shell, is he homeless or naked?

If the funeral procession is at night, do folks drive with their headlights off?

Is it possible to be totally partial?

Does killing time damage eternity?

If you made wine out of raisins, would you have to wait for it to age?

What would happen if you put instant coffee in a microwave? Would you go back in time?

How can you have a self-help group?

If gravity exists, why is it harder to drop a girl than to pick one up?

Can you cry underwater?

Has Batman ever parked the Batmobile and come back to find the stereo nicked?

What would happen if birds were ticklish?

Why do they say 'new and improved'? How can it be new if it was improved?

If beauty is only skin deep, how can some people be described as having an inner beauty?

How can you tell when you're out of invisible ink?

If people evolved from apes, why are there still apes?

How come wrong numbers are never busy?

How does a thermos know whether a drink should be hot or cold?

If music be the food of love, why don't rabbits sing?

Why do banks charge a fee on 'insufficient funds' when they know there isn't enough in the bank?

If it's really evaporated milk, why is it still in the can when you open it?

When the Queen is asked for ID, does she just take out a coin?

If you worked at a fire hydrant plant, where would you park?

If I save time, when do I get it back?

If a cow laughed, would milk come out of her nose?

There are 32 points to the compass, meaning that there are 32 directions in which a spoon can squirt grapefruit. Then why does the juice invariably fly straight into the human eye?

If nothing sticks to Teflon, how does it stay on the pan?

If a candle factory burns down, does everyone just stand around and sing 'Happy Birthday'?

If olive oil comes from olives, where does baby oil come from?

Why do you press harder on a remote control when you know the battery is dead?

If one synchronised swimmer drowns, do the rest have to drown too?

If a duck only had one leg, would it swim in a circle?

How come the dove gets to be the peace symbol? What about the pillow? It has more feathers than the dove, and it doesn't have that dangerous beak.

Why do you get round from eating square meals?

Why does the National Association for Mental Telepathy have a doorbell?

If vegetarians eat vegetables, what do humanitarians eat?

What is it about cats that makes them have to do their business the minute you've cleaned their litter box?

If Polish people are called Poles, why aren't people from Holland called Holes?

Is it possible to buy something specific in a general store?

Why do they put expiry dates on preservatives?

How come Superman could stop bullets with his chest but always ducked when someone threw a gun at him?

Why do we wait until a pig is dead to cure it?

Why are people overwhelmed but never just whelmed?

If the number two pencil is the most popular, why is it still number two?

Do fish get thirsty?

If voting could really change things, wouldn't it be illegal?

Why is there only one company making the game Monopoly?

Why is a carrot more orange than an orange?

If thigh-reducing cream is so effective, why doesn't it shrink women's hands when they apply it?

Can picket fences go on strike?

Why is it called Alcoholics Anonymous when the first thing you do at a meeting is announce your name?

If you choke a Smurf, what colour does it turn?

Why doesn't glue stick to the inside of the bottle?

Why do people run over a thread a dozen times with their vacuum cleaner, reach down, pick the thread up, examine it, then put it down again to give their vacuum one more chance?

Why don't they make the rest of the airplane out of the same material as the black box?

Why is it called tourist season if we can't shoot at them?

If you're born again, do you have two bellybuttons?

Why is it that if you want to get something done, you can either do it yourself, hire someone to do it, or forbid your kids to do it?

When companies ship Styrofoam, what do they pack it in?

Why does the television news bother reporting power failures?

What do you call a male ladybird?

What hair colour do they put on the driving licences of bald men?

If you turn on the light quickly enough, can you see what the dark looks like?

If a vampire can't see himself in a mirror, why is his hair always so neat?

Why do we leave expensive cars on the drive and fill our garage with junk?

Why is it called lipstick if you can still move your lips?

Just before someone gets nervous, do they have cocoons in their stomach?

When sign makers go on strike, is anything written on their placards?

Why do we use answering machines to screen calls and then have call waiting so we won't miss a call from someone we didn't want to talk to in the first place?

Where do forest rangers go to 'get away from it all'?

If you admit to yourself that you're in denial, are you cured?

Why is paper always strongest at the perforations?

Why does mineral water that 'has trickled through mountains for centuries' have a sell-by date?

Why is it that once children grow up they stop asking you where they came from and refuse to tell you where they're going?

Do royal princes have bouncy council houses at parties?

What happens if you get scared half to death twice?

What would happen if you put a humidifier and a de-humidifier in the same room?

Why did kamikaze pilots wear helmets?

Why do they sterilise needles for lethal injections?

Why are there disabled parking places in front of a skating rink?

Why does a knife that is too blunt to cut anything else always cut your finger?

Why is the leak in the roof never in the same location as the drip?

Why do people who know the least know it the loudest?

Why do we buy hot dogs in packs of ten and buns in packs of eight?

Why do they lock gas station bathrooms? Are they afraid someone will clean them?

Why are socks angled at 120 degrees when the human foot is angled at 90 degrees?

Why does something called goose down, fluff up?

Why are there interstate highways in Hawaii?

How do they get the 'Do not walk on grass' signs in the middle of the grass?

What was the Dead Sea like before it got sick?

Religion

One day a Catholic, a Baptist and a Methodist were going fishing. No sooner had they set up their rods and nets in the middle of the lake than the Catholic remembered that he had left the food provisions on the shore. So he got out of the boat, walked on the water, picked up his supplies, walked back on the water and climbed into the boat.

Then the Baptist realised that they did not have enough bait. So he got out of the boat, walked on the water, bought a packet of bait, walked back on the water and climbed into the boat.

Then the Methodist realised that his watch wasn't working and wanted to buy a new one. So he took it off, got out of the boat . . . but sunk all the way down to the bottom of the lake.

The Catholic turned to the Baptist and said: 'I guess we should have told him where the rocks are!'

A Christian fundamentalist couple felt it important to own a pet with similar leanings, so they visited a kennels that specialised in Christian fundamentalist dogs. One particular dog caught their eye. When they asked the dog to fetch the Bible, he did it immediately. When they instructed him to look up Psalm 23, he used his paws with great dexterity to locate the exact page.

They were so impressed that they bought the dog and took him home. That night they had friends over and took the opportunity to show off their new fundamentalist dog. The friends were equally impressed and asked whether the dog could perform any of the usual doggie tricks as well. This momentarily stumped the couple who had not given any thought to ordinary dog tricks.

'We don't really know,' they said. 'We've only seen him perform religious tricks. I suppose there's only one way to find out. Let's give it a try.'

So they called the dog and clearly pronounced the command, 'Heel!'

The dog immediately jumped up, put his paw on the man's forehead, closed his eyes in concentration, and bowed his head.

A bartender was tending the bar one Tuesday when two nuns walked in. 'Sisters,' he said, 'I'm surprised to see you here.'

'Why is that?' asked one of the nuns.

The bartender said: 'Well, to be honest, we don't get many nuns in here.'

The nun said: 'We minister to fallen souls, and thought that this would be a good place to find them.'

'Fair enough,' said the bartender, and he fetched them two iced waters.

The next day, the bartender was going about his duties when two rabbis walked in. 'Well,' he said, 'I'm really surprised to see you two here.'

'Why is that?' asked one of the rabbis.

'Because, to tell the truth, we don't get a lot of rabbis in this bar.'

'The synagogue is closed for repairs,' explained the rabbi, 'and we needed somewhere quiet to debate rabbinical law.'

'Fair enough,' said the bartender, and he set them up with two orange juices.

The next day, the bartender was tending the bar when two Irish priests walked in. He said: 'Fathers, I must say I'm really surprised to see you two in here.'

One priest replied: 'And why is that, my son?'

The bartender said: 'Because you usually don't come in until the weekend.'

A four-year-old boy was asked to return thanks before Christmas dinner. He began his prayer by thanking his family – his mother, his father, his sister, his uncle, his aunt, his grandpa and his grandma, even his dog – and then he thanked God for the food. He thanked God for the turkey, the sausage, the potatoes, the cranberry sauce, the fruit salad, the pies and the cakes. Then he paused. Everyone waited. Eventually he looked up at his mother and said: 'If I thank God for the broccoli, won't he know I'm lying?'

Having left the area some years ago, a teenage girl went to confession in the church she had attended as a child. The priest recognised her and asked her what she had been doing with her life.

178

'I'm an acrobatic dancer, Father,' she replied.

'And what does that entail?'

'I can show you if you like, Father.'

'Please do.'

With that, the girl performed an impressive series of cartwheels, somersaults, handstands and backflips across the church.

Waiting their turn near the confessional were two middle-aged women. One said to the other: 'Will you just look at the penance Father O'Reilly is giving out tonight, and me with no bloomers on!'

When a priest was pulled over for speeding, the police officer noticed an empty wine bottle in his car and could smell alcohol on his breath.

'Father, have you been drinking?' asked the officer.

'Only water, my son,' replied the priest.

'Then why can I smell wine?'

The priest looked at the wine bottle and exclaimed: 'Oh my Lord! He's gone and done it again!'

Ducking into confession with a turkey in his arms, Brendan said: 'Forgive me, Father, for I have sinned. I stole this turkey to feed my family. Would you take it and ease my guilt?'

'Certainly not,' said the priest. 'As penance, you must return it to the one from whom you stole it.'

'I tried,' sobbed Brendan, 'but he refused. Oh, Father, what should I do?'

'If what you say is true, then it is all right for you to keep it for your family.'

Thanking the priest, Brendan hurried off.

When confession was over, the priest returned to his house. Walking into the kitchen, he saw that someone had stolen his turkey.

At a gathering to celebrate the church centenary, several former vicars and the bishop were in attendance. Prior to the formalities, the vicar gathered the children at the altar to talk about the importance of the day. He began by asking: 'Does anyone know what the bishop does?'

There was a moment's silence until one small boy said: 'He's the one you can move diagonally.'

Three women were talking about the declining numbers in church attendance.

One said: 'The congregation at my church is down to around forty.'

The second said: 'You're lucky. Most Sundays we consider ourselves fortunate if there are more than twenty people in the congregation at our church.'

The third said: 'That's nothing. It is so bad in our church that when the minister says "dearly beloved", I blush!'

An atheist was spending a quiet day fishing in Scotland when suddenly his boat was attacked by the Loch Ness Monster. In one easy flip, the beast tossed him and his boat high into the air. Then it opened its mouth to swallow both.

As the man flew head over heels, he yelled out: 'Oh, my God! Help me!'

Immediately this terrifying scenario was frozen in time, and as the atheist hung in mid-air, a booming voice came down from the clouds: 'I thought you didn't believe in me!'

'Come on, God, give me a break!' pleaded the man. 'Two minutes ago I didn't believe in the Loch Ness Monster either!'

A Sunday School teacher asked her class why Joseph and Mary took Jesus with them to Jerusalem. A little girl answered: 'Because they couldn't get a babysitter.'

It was the height of summer and a fearful drought threatened the crops throughout the land. One hot, dry Sunday, the village clergyman told his congregation: 'The only thing that will save us is to pray for rain. Go home, pray, believe, and come back next Sunday ready to thank God for the rain he will send.'

The people did as they were told and returned to church the following Sunday. But as soon as the clergyman saw them, he was furious.

'We can't worship,' he raged. 'You do not yet believe that God will send us rain, perhaps this very day.'

They protested: 'We prayed and we do believe.'

'Believe?' he responded. 'Then where are your umbrellas?'

A priest was speeding along on a motorbike when he was stopped by a cop. The officer said: 'I can't help noticing you've got L plates, Father. For someone who has yet to pass his test, you were going dangerously fast.'

'Don't worry, my son,' said the priest. 'Jesus is with me.'

'In that case,' said the officer, 'I'm going to have to book you. You're not allowed a pillion passenger.'

Two nuns who worked in a hospital were out driving in the country when they ran out of petrol. As they stood beside their car on the hard shoulder, a truck approached them. Noticing the nuns in distress, the truck driver stopped and offered to help. When the nuns explained that they had run out of petrol, he said he would be more than happy to drain some from his tank, but he didn't have a bucket or a can.

Hearing this, one of the nuns produced a clean bedpan from the boot of their car and asked the truck driver if it would do. He said it would and proceeded to drain a couple of quarts of petrol into the pan. He then handed the pan to the sisters, got back into his truck and waved goodbye.

While the nuns were carefully pouring the precious fuel into their petrol tank, a police officer happened to be passing by. He stopped and watched them tipping in the contents of the bedpan before remarking: 'Sisters, somehow I don't think that's going to work, but I admire your faith!'

Exiting church one Sunday, a middle-aged woman said to her husband: 'Do you think that Nicholson girl is tinting her hair?'

'I didn't even see her,' admitted the husband.

'And that skirt Mrs Rogers was wearing,' continued the woman. 'Don't tell me you thought that was suitable attire for a mother of two?'

'I'm afraid I didn't notice that either,' said the husband.

'Huh,' said the woman. 'A lot of good it does you going to church!'

A clergyman was walking down the street when he came upon a group of young boys who were crowded around a dog. Concerned that the boys might be mistreating the animal, he went over and asked them what they were doing.

One of the boys replied: 'The dog is an old neighbourhood stray. We take him home with us sometimes, but since only one of us can take him home, we're having a contest: whichever one of us tells the biggest lie can take him home today.'

The clergyman was horrified. 'You boys shouldn't be having a contest about telling lies! Don't you know it's a sin to lie?' He then launched into a ten-minute sermon against lying, concluding with the words: 'Why, when I was your age, I never told a lie.'

Stunned into silence, the boys lowered their heads. Just as the clergyman thought he had got through to them, the smallest boy gave a deep sigh and handed him the leash: 'All right, reverend,' he said. 'You win. You can take him home.'

A nun, Sister Josephine, went to heaven, only to be informed by St. Peter that there was a waiting list.

'Go home and relax,' advised St. Peter. 'Give me a call in a week and I'll let you know whether your accommodation is ready.'

The following week she phoned up and said: 'Peter, this is Josephine. I have a confession to make: I had my first-ever cigarette yesterday. Will it affect my chances of getting into heaven?'

'I'm sure it won't,' replied St. Peter. 'But your room still isn't ready yet. Call me in a week.'

A week later, she called again. 'Peter, this is Josephine. I have a confession to make: I had my first-ever alcoholic drink yesterday. Will it affect my chances of getting into heaven?'

'I shouldn't think so,' answered St. Peter reassuringly. 'But your room still isn't ready. Call me in three days.'

Three days later, she phoned again. 'Peter, this is Josephine. I have a confession to make: last night I kissed a man for the first time. Do you think it will ruin my chances of getting into heaven?'

'I very much doubt it,' said St. Peter. 'But give me a call tomorrow. By then I'll have checked it out with the boss man and I'll know about your accommodation.'

The next day, she phoned again. 'Pete, this is Jo. Forget about the room.'

A deeply religious man lived in a house by the river, but one day the banks burst and the house was flooded. As the water level rose alarmingly, the man climbed on to the roof of the house. A boat came by.

'Climb aboard,' called the captain.

'No, I shall stay here,' said the man. 'God will take care of me.'

Twenty minutes later, with the waters still rising, the man climbed on to the chimney. Another boat came past.

'Jump aboard,' said the captain.

'No, I shall stay here,' said the man. 'God will take care of me.'

With the water now up to the man's waist, a helicopter suddenly swooped down.

'Quick!' shouted the pilot. 'Climb aboard!'

'No, I shall stay here,' insisted the man. 'God will take care of me.'

The water level continued to rise and soon the man was swept from the chimney and drowned. Up in heaven, he sought out God. 'I thought you said you would take care of me,' he complained.

God said: 'I sent you two boats and a helicopter. What more do you want?'

Did you hear about the man who used to pick fluff out of his belly button but gave it up for lint?

A priest and a rabbi were based in a church and a synagogue on opposite sides of the street. Since their schedules often clashed, they decided to join forces and buy a car together. After the purchase, they drove it home and parked it on the street between them.

A few minutes later, the rabbi looked out and saw the priest splashing water on their new car. Since it didn't need a wash, he rushed out and asked the priest what he was doing.

'I'm blessing it,' replied the priest.

182

The rabbi thought about this for a moment, then went back inside the synagogue. He reappeared shortly afterwards with a hacksaw, walked over to the back of the car, and cut two inches off the exhaust.

The vicar shocked the congregation when he announced that he was resigning from the church and moving to Spain.

After the service, a distraught lady came up to him and wailed: 'Oh, vicar, we are going to miss you. We really don't want you to leave.'

The vicar patted her hand reassuringly and said: 'It's very kind of you to say that but you never know, the next vicar might be even better than me.'

'Yes,' she sighed, her voice tinged with disappointment. 'That's what they said the last time too . . .'

Jesus came upon a woman being stoned by a mob. Running over to protect her, he yelled: 'Let he who is without sin cast the next stone!'

There was silence for a few moments until a rock was thrown, hitting Jesus on the side of the head. Clutching his head, Jesus shouted: 'Damn it, Mother, I wish you'd just stay out of this!'

A woman was getting a homemade apple pie ready to put into the oven when the phone rang. It was the school nurse. The woman's son had come down with a high fever and needed collecting from school. The mother calculated how long it would take to drive to school and back, and how long the pie should bake for, and reckoned she would be back before the pie needed lifting out of the oven. So she popped the pie into the oven and left for school. However, when she arrived, her son's fever was worse and the nurse urged her to take him to the doctor.

She drove to the clinic as fast as she dared, her nerves beginning to fray. After examining the boy, the doctor told her to get him to bed immediately and gave her a prescription for some medicine. By the time she got her son home and in bed and headed out again for the shopping mall, she was not only frayed, but frazzled and frantic as well. And she had forgotten all about the pie in the oven.

At the shopping mall she found a pharmacy, collected the prescription, and rushed back to the car, only to find it locked. In her haste, she had forgotten to remove her keys from the ignition switch. And now they were locked inside the car.

She began searching the mall for a wire coat hanger so that she could break into the car, but all of the shops seemed to stock wooden or plastic hangers. Eventually, at the fifteenth store she tried, she found a wire hanger. It was only when she hurried out of the mall towards the parking lot that it dawned on her that she had no idea how to pick the lock with the hanger. Then she remembered the pie in the oven. All of the frustrations of the past hour suddenly came flooding over her and she sank to her knees, bursting into tears. Looking up to the heavens, she prayed: 'Dear Lord, my boy is sick and he needs the medicine, and my pie is in the oven, and the keys are locked in the car, and I don't know what to do with this coat hanger! Dear Lord, send somebody who knows what to do with it, and I really need that person NOW.'

As she wiped away her tears, she saw a young man climb out of a beaten-up old banger. Seizing the moment, she ran over to him, held out the wire coat hanger and gabbled: 'Do you know how to get into a locked car with one of these?'

He gawped at her for a moment, took the hanger from her hand and asked: 'Where's the car?'

Within a matter of seconds he had used the hanger to force his way into her car. All it took was a couple of twists. She was so grateful that she threw her arms around him and said: 'The Lord sent you! You're such a good boy.'

He stepped back and said: 'Actually no, ma'am, I'm not a good boy. I just got out of prison yesterday.'

With this, the woman hugged him even tighter. 'Bless the Lord!' she cried. 'He sent me a professional!'

A drunk staggered in to a Catholic church, sat down in the confession box and said nothing. The bewildered priest coughed to attract his attention, but still the drunk remained silent. The priest then knocked on the wall three times in a final attempt to get the man to speak.

The drunk said: 'No use knocking, mate. There's no paper in this one either.'

Three wise men arrived to visit the child lying in the manger. One of the wise men was exceptionally tall and bumped his head on the low doorway as he entered the stable. 'Jesus Christ!' he exclaimed.

Joseph said: 'Write that down, Mary. It's better than Wayne.'

Two youngsters were walking home from Sunday School, each deep in his own thoughts. Finally one said: 'What do you think about all this devil business we studied today?'

The other boy replied thoughtfully: 'Well, you know how Santa Claus turned out. This is probably just your Dad, too.'

How do you know when you're living in a really bad neighbourhood? – The church has a bouncer.

Just before the start of a Sunday service, the townspeople were chatting away happily to each other when Satan suddenly appeared at the front of the church. There was a mass stampede for the exit as the parishioners almost trampled each other underfoot in a frantic effort to get away from evil incarnate. Soon the church was deserted except for one old man who sat calmly in his pew without moving, seemingly oblivious to the fact that God's ultimate enemy was in his presence.

Irked by this affront to his reputation, Satan walked up to the old man and said: 'Don't you know who I am?'

'Sure do,' replied the old man.

'Aren't you afraid of me?' demanded Satan.

'Nope, sure ain't.'

'Don't you realise I could kill you with a word?'

'Don't doubt it for a minute,' returned the old man, still displaying marked indifference.

'Did you know,' persisted Satan, 'that I could cause you profound, horrifying, physical agony for all eternity?'

'Yup, I guess you could.'

'And you're still not afraid?'

'Nope.'

By now, Satan was worried that he was losing his powers of intimidation. 'Well, why aren't you afraid of me?' he roared.

The old man said: 'Been married to your sister for forty-four years!'

One afternoon a new pastor in town was doing the rounds of meeting his parishioners. All went well until he came to a cottage on the outskirts. Someone was obviously home, but, even though the pastor knocked on the door several times, nobody answered. Finally he took out his card and wrote on the back: 'Revelation 3:20.'

The next day as he was counting the collection, the pastor noticed that his card had been left in the plate. Below his message was written: 'Genesis 3:10.'

Revelation 3:20 reads: 'Behold, I stand at the door and knock. If any man hears my voice, and opens the door, I will come in to his house and eat with him, and he will eat with me.' Genesis 3:10 reads: 'And he answered, I heard you in the garden; I was afraid and hid from you because I was naked.'

A new pastor visited a children's Sunday School. After standing quietly at the back for a few minutes, he asked the youngsters: 'Who tore down the walls of Jericho?'

'It wasn't me,' shouted young Timmy.

The pastor was unfazed, and repeated: 'Come along now, who tore down the walls of Jericho?'

The teacher took the pastor to one side. 'Look, Pastor, Timmy's a good boy. If he said he didn't do it, I believe him.'

The pastor was dumbstruck by the teacher's reply and later that day related the story to the director of the Sunday School. The director frowned and said: 'I know we've had problems with Timmy in the past. I'll have a word with him.'

By now totally bewildered, the pastor left and caught up with the deacon. Once again, he told him the whole story, including the responses of the teacher and the director. The deacon listened patiently and smiled: 'Yes, Pastor, I see your problem. But I suggest we take the money from the general fund to pay for the walls and leave it at that.'

A man called on the vicar's wife, a woman well known for her charitable deeds. 'Madam,' he said, close to tears, 'I feel I must draw your attention to the awful plight of an impoverished family in this district. The father is dead, the mother is too ill to work, and the nine children are starving. They are about to be turned out onto the cold, empty streets unless someone pays their rent, which amounts to $500.'

'How terrible!' exclaimed the vicar's wife. 'May I ask who you are?'

The sympathetic visitor dabbed his handkerchief to his eyes. 'I'm the landlord.'

Three vicars were discussing their problems with cockroaches in their respective churches.

The first vicar said: 'I've tried putting down poison, but nothing seems to get rid of them.'

The second vicar said: 'I called in the council exterminator, but even he couldn't destroy them.'

The third vicar said: 'I managed to get rid of all mine. I simply baptised them all and I haven't seen them since.'

Jesus and Satan were having an ongoing argument about who was better on the computer. They had been niggling away at each other for days until God became tired of all the bickering. Finally God said: 'Enough. I am going to set up a two-hour test, with me as judge, to determine who is better on the computer.'

So Jesus and Satan sat at their respective keyboards and typed away. They did spreadsheets, they wrote reports, they sent faxes, they sent e-mail, they sent out e-mail with attachments, they downloaded, they did genealogy reports, they made cards. In fact, they did just about every known job.

But ten minutes before their time was up, lightning suddenly flashed across the sky, thunder rolled, and the electricity went off. Satan stared at his blank screen and screamed every curse word known to the under-world.

Jesus simply sighed. The electricity finally flickered back on, and both restarted their computers. Satan began searching frantically for his work. 'It's gone! It's gone!' he screamed. 'I lost everything when the power went off!'

Meanwhile Jesus quietly started printing out all of his files from the past two hours. Seeing this, Satan became furious.

'He must have cheated!' raged Satan. 'How did he do it?'

God shrugged and said: 'Jesus saves.'

Before performing a baptism, the priest approached the young father and said solemnly: 'Baptism is a serious step. Are you prepared for it?'

'I think so,' replied the man. 'My wife has been baking cakes all week, and her mother is going to lay on a nice spread – you know, sandwiches and the like.'

'I don't mean that,' said the priest. 'I mean, are you prepared spiritually?'

'Oh that! Silly me! Yes, don't worry. I also got a keg of beer and a case of whiskey.'

A devout Catholic had fifteen children by her first husband and nine by her second husband. Not surprisingly, she died relatively young.

At her funeral, the priest gazed tenderly at the coffin, looked up to the heavens and said: 'At last, they're finally together.'

A man standing next to him asked: 'Excuse me, Father, do you mean her and her first husband, or her and her second husband?'

'No,' the priest replied, 'I mean her legs!'

Arriving at church one Monday morning, a preacher discovered a dead donkey in the churchyard. He called the police, but since there was no indication of foul play, the police referred him to the public health department. They said that as there was no obvious health threat, he should call the sanitation department. The manager there said he could not collect the dead donkey without authorisation from the mayor. The preacher was reluctant to call the mayor, who had a reputation for being impatient and bad tempered, but he realised that in this instance he had little choice.

The mayor was every bit as cantankerous as the preacher had feared. 'What are you calling me for?' he raged. 'I've got better things to do with my time than worry about donkeys. Anyway I thought it was your job to bury the dead.'

Unable to resist the temptation to retaliate, the preacher replied calmly: 'Yes, mayor, it is my job to bury the dead, but I always like to notify the next of kin first!'

A priest and pastor from the local parishes were standing by the side of the road holding up a sign that read: 'The End Is Near! Turn Yourself Around Now Before It's Too Late!' They planned to hold up the sign to each passing car.

'Leave us alone, you religious nuts!' yelled the first driver as he sped by. From around the corner they then heard screeching tyres and a big splash.

'Do you think,' said the priest to the pastor, 'that maybe we should change the wording on our sign to "Bridge Out"?'

A wealthy American had one remaining wish in life – to meet the Pope in person – and to achieve his goal, he was prepared to wait in Rome for as long as it took. Week after week, he joined the crowds in St Peter's Square but never got any nearer than glimpsing the Pope on the balcony. He was bemoaning his lack of success to an English tourist who offered to sell him his ticket for a garden party that the Pope was giving in the Vatican the next day. The American willingly paid £100 for the ticket but noticed that the invitation stipulated full morning dress. So he hurried off to an exclusive Italian tailor and hired some morning clothes.

The next day, the American went to the Vatican dressed in his top hat and morning suit, and stood in a line of guests waiting for the Pope to appear. The guests were standing in two lines facing each other so that the Pope could walk down one line, turn, and then go back along the other line. When the Pope finally appeared, there was polite applause. The American waited hopefully as the Pope proceeded down the first line but, to widespread dismay, he spoke to nobody. Instead he merely waved vaguely as he passed the American and made his way to the end of the line.

The last position in the line was occupied by a tramp, looking woefully out of place in his ragged clothes. But, to everyone's amazement, the Pope stopped when he reached the tramp, put his hands on the poor man's shoulders and whispered something in his ear.

The American thought quickly. It was clear that the Pope would talk only to some hobo, someone who was in need of words of comfort, so the American grabbed hold of the tramp and offered a hefty financial inducement to persuade him to swap clothes. Dressed in tatty rags and a battered hat, the American then dashed to the end of the second line, along which the Pope was now making his way. Once again, the Pope spoke to nobody until he reached the tramp-like figure at the end of the line. The American could hardly contain his excitement as the Pope stopped and looked at him. Then the Pope put his hands on the American's shoulders and whispered in his ear: 'I thought I told you a moment ago to get lost!'

Moses was praying to God to free his people when the voice of God was heard from the heavens.

'Moses,' he said, 'I have good news and bad news.'

'What's the good news?' asked Moses.

God said: 'If Pharaoh will not let my people go, I will send down a rain of frogs, a plague of locusts and a plague of flies, and I will turn rivers to blood. And if Pharaoh pursues you, I shall open a path for you in the Red Sea but close it again to drown his army.'

'That would be so helpful,' enthused Moses. 'But tell me, what's the bad news?'

God said: 'Before I can do all this, you have to prepare an environmental impact statement.'

The minister was concerned about how to raise the $2,000 still needed to repair the church roof. Before Sunday service, he asked the organist to play some inspirational music to get the congregation into a giving mood.

'But I'm afraid I haven't any bright ideas as to what precisely you could play,' said the minister.

'Don't worry,' said the organist, 'I'll think of something.'

During the service, the minister made an appeal from the pulpit. 'As you know, we have so far raised $8,000 to repair the church roof. But we still need another $2,000. Many of you have already made generous donations, but if you were able to dig just a little deeper into your pockets, it would mean so much to the community. So, if any of you can pledge another $100, perhaps you would be so kind as to stand up.'

At that point the organist started playing the National Anthem.

While the preacher delivered his most robust fire and brimstone message, two little old ladies sat in their usual place in the front row, taking snuff.

'Those that fornicate are going to hell!' he bellowed.

'Amen, brother!' responded the two women in unison.

'. . . And those that drink alcohol are going to hell!'

'Amen, brother!' the pair sang out enthusiastically.

'. . . And those that take snuff . . .' he began, only to be interrupted by one of the old ladies, jumping to her feet.

'Hold it right there, brother! You're about to quit preachin' and start meddlin'!'

A passenger aircraft was being bounced around by severe turbulence in a thunderstorm. Things got so bad that a young woman turned to a minister sitting next to her and, with a nervous laugh, asked: 'Reverend, you're a man of God. Can't you do something about this storm?'

189

The minister replied: 'Madam, I'm in sales, not management.'

There were two Catholic boys, Declan Murphy and Antonio Secola, whose lives paralleled each other in a number of amazing ways. In the same year that Declan was born in Ireland, Antonio was born in Italy. Both took their vows to enter the priesthood early in college and upon graduation became priests. Both rose through the ranks to bishop, archbishop and eventually cardinal at an astounding rate and the entire Catholic world knew that when the Pope died, the choice for his successor would rest between Declan and Antonio.

However, it was generally accepted that for all Declan's virtues, Antonio was the outstanding candidate, and although it was officially a two-horse race, he was a very hot favourite to become the next pontiff. So when the Pope died, Antonio was confident of being appointed to the highest office, only to learn that the cardinals had decided to choose Declan instead.

Antonio was so upset at being overlooked that he demanded a private meeting with the cardinals so that they could explain their shock choice. They told him: 'We are terribly sorry for your disappointment. We knew that you were the better candidate but, in our heart of hearts, we could not bear the thought of the leader of the Roman Catholic Church being called Pope Secola.'

Various religious leaders attended a conference in an attempt to answer the vexing question: 'Where does life begin?'

'At conception,' said the Catholic firmly.

'No, at birth,' said the Presbyterian.

'It's in between,' stated the Baptist. 'Life begins at twelve weeks when the foetus develops a functional heartbeat.'

'I disagree with all of you,' said the rabbi. 'Life begins when your last child leaves home and takes the dog with him.'

A small boy was flicking through the pages of a dusty old edition of the Bible when something fell out. It was a leaf that had been pressed between the pages.

'Look what I've found, Mum,' he called out.

'What have you got there?' asked his mother.

The boy said: 'I think it's Adam's underwear!'

Sex

A salesman was testifying in divorce proceedings against his wife. His lawyer said: 'Please describe the incident that first caused you to suspect your wife's infidelity.'

The husband began: 'I'm on the road all week, so naturally when I'm home I'm very attentive to my wife. One Sunday morning we were in the middle of a really heavy session of lovemaking when the old lady in the apartment next door pounded on the wall and yelled: "Can't you at least stop all that racket at weekends?"'

Following a succession of complaints about her shortcomings as a cook and housekeeper, a maid was dismissed by her wealthy female employer.

Refusing to accept such criticism, the maid answered back. 'Your husband considers me a better cook and housekeeper than you, madam. He has told me himself. And furthermore, I am better in bed than you!'

'And I suppose my husband told you that, too?' said the rich woman angrily.

'No, madam. The postman.'

A man walked into the bedroom to find his wife in bed with another man.

'Who is this man?' demanded the husband.

'That's a fair question,' said the wife, turning to her lover. 'What is your name?'

According to the latest surveys, when making love, most married men fantasise that their wives aren't fantasising.

One day God and Adam were walking in the Garden of Eden. God told Adam that it was time to populate the Earth. 'Adam,' he said, 'you can start by kissing Eve.'

'What's a kiss?' asked Adam.

God explained, and then Adam took Eve behind a bush and kissed her.

Adam returned with a big smile on his face and enthused: 'That was terrific. What's next?'

'Now you must caress Eve,' said God.

'What's caress?' asked Adam.

God explained, and then Adam led Eve behind a bush and lovingly caressed her. Adam returned with a big smile and said: 'That was even better than a kiss. What's next?'

'I want you to make love to Eve,' said God.

'What is make love?' asked Adam.

God explained, and then Adam led Eve behind the bush.

A few seconds later Adam returned and asked God: 'What's a headache?'

Having announced that he was going to marry a woman of twenty-five, a ninety-year-old man was persuaded by his friends and family to undergo a medical examination to see whether he was still sexually fit.

The doctor said: 'Let me see your sex organs.'

The old man stuck out his tongue and his middle finger.

An old man complained to the doctor of feeling tired. The doctor asked him whether he had done anything unusual lately.

'Well,' said the old man, 'Wednesday night I did pick up a twenty-year-old secretary and nailed her three times. Then Thursday night I got off with a nineteen-year-old waitress, and we ended up in bed at her place. On Friday night I pulled an eighteen-year-old nurse and we finished up in the back of her car out at lovers' lane. Then Saturday night I was lured to a motel room by seventeen-year-old twins.'

The doctor was impressed by such stamina at his age but warned: 'I hope you took precautions.'

'Of course I did,' said the old man. 'I gave them all phoney names.'

A young couple on their first date had sex that was over in a matter of seconds. Feeling rather proud of himself, the boy said: 'If I'd known you were a virgin, I'd have taken more time.'

The girl replied: 'If I'd known you were going to take more time, I'd have taken off my tights.'

A businessman packing for a trip glanced in his briefcase and called to his wife: 'Honey.'

'Yes, darling?' she answered.

'Honey,' he said mildly exasperated, 'why do you persist in putting a condom in my briefcase every time I go on a trip? You know I only have eyes for you. I'd never be unfaithful.'

'I know, darling,' she said, 'and I trust you implicitly. It's just that, well, you know, with all those terrible diseases out there, it would make me feel better to know that if anything did happen, you'd be protected. So please, darling, take it with you, won't you? For my sake?'

'Oh, all right, if you put it like that,' he relented. 'I'll do it for you. But for heaven's sake, give me more than one!'

A nervous young man was pacing up and down the waiting room at a maternity hospital. Meanwhile a middle-aged man was relaxing reading a magazine. Sensing that the older man obviously had considerable experience of these matters, the young man asked him tentatively: 'How long after the baby is born can you have sex with the mother?'

The man raised his head from his magazine and replied: 'It depends if she's in a public ward or a private ward.'

One weekend a couple attended an agricultural show where they watched the auction of some prize bulls. The auctioneer announced that the first bull had reproduced 84 times last year.

'How about that?' said the wife, nudging her husband. 'That's seven times a month. Pity you can't match that!'

When the next bull came up for auction, the auctioneer revealed that it had reproduced 144 times in the last year.

The wife prodded her husband again. 'Did you hear that? Twelve times a month! You're not in the same league as him!'

Then a third bull was led around. The auctioneer proudly stated that the animal had reproduced 365 times over the past year.

The wife elbowed her husband hard in the ribs. 'Three hundred and sixty-five times!' she exclaimed. 'Wow! That's every day of the year. That really puts you to shame.'

By now, the husband was thoroughly irritated by the jibes. 'Sure. Great,' he said icily. 'But I bet it wasn't all with the same cow.'

A father asked his ten-year-old son if he knew about the birds and the bees.

'I don't want to know!' shouted the child, bursting into tears and fleeing the room.

Confused, the father went looking for the boy. He finally found him in the garden, still crying. 'What's wrong, son?' he asked.

'Oh, Dad,' he sobbed. 'When I was six, I got the "there's no Santa" speech. At seven, I got the "there's no Easter bunny" speech. Then at eight, you hit me with the "there's no tooth fairy" speech. If you're going to tell me now that grown-ups don't really have sex, I've got nothing left to live for!'

A woman went to consult a psychiatrist over problems she was having with her sex life. The psychiatrist asked her a series of questions but did not appear to be getting a clearer picture of her problems. Finally he asked: 'Do you ever look at your husband's face while you are having sex?'

'Well, yes,' she said. 'I did once.'

'And how did he look?'

'Really angry.'

'Now this is very interesting. We must delve deeper into this. Tell me, you say that you have only seen your husband's face once during sex; that seems somewhat unusual. How did it occur that you saw his face that one time?'

'He was looking through the window at us.'

A circus owner advertised for a new lion tamer and two young people showed up for an audition. One was a good-looking lad; the other was a beautiful blonde girl.

The circus owner told them: 'I'm going to give it to you straight. This is one ferocious lion. He ate my last tamer, so you guys had better be good or you're history. Here's your equipment: a chair, a whip and a gun. Who wants to try out first?'

The girl said: 'I'll go first.' She walked past the chair, the whip and the gun and walked straight into the lion's cage. The lion began to snarl and pant and began to charge her. But about halfway there, she threw open her coat to reveal her gorgeous naked body. The lion stopped dead in his tracks, sheepishly crawled up to her and started licking her ankles. Then he started licking her calves and kissing them tenderly before resting his head at her feet.

The circus owner was stunned. 'I've never seen a display like that in my life.' Then he turned to the young man and asked: 'Can you top that?'

The young man replied: 'No problem. But first, get that lion out of the way.'

The headmistress of a girls' school asked a male friend who was an author to give a talk to the pupils about sex. After much persuasion, the man agreed but was too embarrassed to tell his wife. So he told her instead that he was giving a school talk about sailing and wrote an appropriate entry in his diary for that day.

The day after the talk, the headmistress bumped into the wife in the shopping mall. 'Your husband was wonderful yesterday, so illuminating. I know my girls learned a lot from him.'

'I can't think how,' said the wife. 'He's only tried it twice. The first time he was sick and the second time he lost his hat.'

George went on a golfing holiday with his pal Bill, but after driving for a couple of hours they got caught up in a terrible storm. With the road ahead flooded, they realised that there was no chance of reaching their hotel and so they pulled into a nearby farmhouse and asked the attractive lady of the house whether they could possibly stay the night.

'I'm recently widowed,' she explained, 'and I'm afraid the neighbours will talk if I let you stay in my house.'

'That's no problem,' said George. 'We'll sleep in the barn.'

Ten months later, George received a letter from the widow's lawyer. George immediately phoned Bill and said: 'Bill, do you remember that good looking widow at the farm where we stayed over last March?'

'Yes, I do.'

'Did you happen to get up in the middle of the night, go up to the house and have sex with her?'

'Yes, I have to confess that I did.'

'And did you happen to use my name instead of telling her yours?'

Bill said sheepishly: 'Yes, I'm afraid I did.'

'Well, thanks pal,' said George. 'She just died and left me her farm!'

Arriving home from school, a boy asked his mother: 'What is sex?'

Dreading the day that she would have to explain all this, she spent the next hour telling him about the birds and the bees and where babies come from.

When she had finished, her son smiled, pulled a school questionnaire from his pocket and pointed to the word 'sex'. 'That's cool, mom, but how am I supposed to get it all in this little box next to the F and the M?'

According to popular belief, when God was creating the world, he called Man aside and bestowed upon him twenty years of normal sex life. Man was horrified and demanded more, but God refused to reconsider.

Then God called the monkey aside and awarded him twenty years of sex life.

'But I don't need twenty years,' said the monkey. 'All I need is ten.'

Hearing this, Man spoke up and said: 'Can't I have the other ten?' The monkey agreed to let Man have the other ten years.

Then God called the lion aside and gave him twenty years of sex life. The lion said that ten would be sufficient, whereupon Man asked for the other ten and the lion agreed.

Then God called the donkey aside and awarded him twenty years.

'I don't need twenty years,' said the donkey. 'Ten is plenty.' Once again Man asked for the other ten years and was duly given them.

All of this explains why Man has twenty years of normal sex life, ten years of monkeying around, ten years of lion about it, and ten years of making an ass of himself.

Shopping

A customer walked into a small hardware store and asked the manager: 'Do you have any brackets?'

'No, sorry.'

'Well, do you have any screwdrivers?'

'No, we're out of those, too.'

'How about hammers? Have you got any hammers?'

'No.'

'Garden forks?'

'No.'

'Shears?'

'No.'

'Door handles?'

'No.'

'This is a complete waste of time!' raged the customer. 'If you haven't got anything in stock, you might as well lock up the damn shop!'

The manager shrugged his shoulders and said: 'I haven't got a key.'

Visiting a shopping mall, a couple agreed to go their separate ways and rendezvous in an hour. So while he visited the sports shop, she hit the major clothes store. When he met up with her as arranged outside the clothes store, she was carrying a dozen bags full of items.

'Have you bought all that?' he asked incredulously.

'Well, yes,' she said. Then waving towards the interior of the shop, she added: 'But look at all the stuff I'm leaving behind.'

A customer went into a hardware store and asked for some nails.

'How long do you want them?' asked the assistant.

'Oh,' said the customer, 'I was rather hoping to keep them.'

One lunchtime, with money to waste and time to kill, a man decided to investigate a recently opened magic shop.

Inside, he told the shop owner: 'I'm looking for a fun present for myself – money no object as long as it amuses me.'

The shop owner surveyed shelves of numbered boxes before reaching into one and producing a pair of glasses. 'These are not any ordinary glasses,' he said, handing them to the customer. 'They're magic glasses. They cost $1,000, but believe me, they're worth it, because whenever you wear them, you can see people naked!'

Intrigued, the customer tried them on and, sure enough, the shop owner appeared naked. And when his pretty female assistant walked through, she was naked too. But when he removed the glasses, everyone was fully clothed.

'They're amazing,' he said. 'I'll buy them.'

He left the shop, wearing the glasses, and headed back towards his office. Everyone he passed was naked – pretty girls, old women, men with beer bellies, even traffic wardens. He was absolutely delighted with his new toy. Indeed such was his excitement that he thought it would be fun to surprise his wife, so before going back to work, he dropped in at home. He was still wearing the glasses when he walked into the living room. There were his wife and his best friend sitting on the sofa completely naked.

'Hi, surprise!' he said, removing the glasses, but they were still naked.

'Look at that,' he moaned. 'A thousand dollars for a pair of magic glasses and after half an hour they're broken!'

Why is zebra meat so popular at safari park supermarkets? Because it comes with its own barcode.

A man went to the perfume counter of a big department store and said he would like a bottle of Chanel No. 5 gift wrapped for his wife's birthday.

'A little surprise, is it?' asked the sales assistant.

'Yeah. She's expecting a cruise!'

A man bought his middle-aged wife a new line of expensive cosmetics guaranteed to make her look years younger. After painstakingly applying them over a period of hours, she said: 'Darling, tell me honestly, what age would you say I am?'

He studied her carefully before replying: 'Judging from your skin, twenty; your hair, eighteen; and your figure, twenty-four.'

'Oh, you flatterer!' she gushed.

'Hey, wait a minute!' he said. 'I haven't added them up yet.'

A wife asked her husband to buy organic vegetables. He went to the supermarket but couldn't find any. So he asked an elderly male employee for some help.

'These vegetables are for my wife. Have they been sprayed with poisonous chemicals?'

'No,' said the old man. 'You'll have to do that yourself.'

Why is a store that's open 24 hours a day called 7–11?

A store manager overheard a sales assistant saying to a customer: 'No, madam, we haven't had any for some weeks now, and it doesn't look as if we'll be getting any soon.'

Alarmed, the manager rushed over to the customer as she was walking out the door and said: 'That isn't true, madam. Of course, we'll have some soon. In fact, we placed an order for it a couple of weeks ago.'

Then the manager pulled the sales assistant to one side and growled: 'Never, ever say we don't have something. If we haven't got it, say we ordered it and we're expecting it any day. Understand? Now what was it that she wanted?'

'Rain.'

A furious customer marched in to confront a carpet shop salesman. 'I bought this rug from you yesterday and you told me it was in perfect condition. But when I got it home, I found there was a hole in the middle.'

'If you remember, sir, I said it was in mint condition.'

197

Why do supermarkets give preferential express service at the checkout tills to people named Les?

A man parked his car at a supermarket and was walking past an empty trolley when he heard a woman ask: 'Excuse me, did you want that trolley?'

'No, I'm only after one thing.'

'Huh,' she muttered. 'Typical man!'

A man stopped off at a toy store to buy a baseball bat for his son. At the cash desk, the clerk asked: 'Cash or charge?'

'Cash,' snapped the customer before apologising. 'I'm really sorry, I've just spent the whole afternoon at the car pound after my van had been clamped. It's been so frustrating.'

The clerk said: 'Shall I giftwrap the bat or are you going back there?'

A scruffy couple were looking at a new kitchen. After a while, the man said to the salesman: 'Yeah, we really like it, but I don't think we can afford it.'

The salesman said: 'You just make a small down payment, then you don't make another payment for twelve months.'

The woman growled: 'Who told you about us?'

A woman was examining an expensive jumper in a department store. She wanted to buy it but was put off by the price tag.

Sensing that she could be persuaded into a purchase, the assistant wandered over ready to deliver her sales patter.

'Can I help you, madam?' she inquired.

'Yes, this jumper's a bit overpriced, isn't it? I've seen similar garments in other shops for around $60, yet this one's priced at $190.'

'Well, you see,' began the assistant, 'there's a reason for that. This jumper is of vastly superior quality. Feel the texture. The wool actually comes from a rare breed of albino sheep confined to a tiny mountainous area in Mongolia. It's a beautiful yarn.'

'Yes,' replied the woman. 'And you tell it so well!'

Arriving home from the supermarket, a mother handed her son the box of animal crackers that he had been eagerly waiting for. He then tipped them out all over the work surface.

'Why have you done that?' she asked.

'Because the box says you can't eat them if the seal is broken. So I'm looking for the seal.'

A new mother took her baby daughter to the supermarket for the first time, with the little girl dressed in pink from head to toe. At the grocery store, the mother placed the baby's seat in the shopping trolley and placed her purchases around the seat.

When she reached the checkout, there was a small boy and his mother ahead of her in the line. The little boy was crying and begging his mum for a special treat. The new mum listened, thinking the little boy probably wanted some candy or gum, and that his mum was refusing.

Suddenly the boy's mother turned and looked at the baby in the shopping trolley. 'No, Billy,' she said, looking at the new mother and grinning. 'You may not have a baby sister today. That lady got the last one!'

Two tigers were walking down the aisle of a supermarket. One turned to the other and said: 'Quiet in here today, isn't it?'

Signs
Clever signs:
- In a dry cleaner's window: 'Drop your pants here.'
- On a septic tank truck: 'Yesterday's meals on wheels.'
- On a plumber's truck: 'We repair what your husband fixed.'
- At the electric company: 'We'd be delighted if you send in your bill. However, if you don't, you will be.'
- Over a gynaecologist's office: 'Dr. Jones, at your cervix.'
- At a funeral home: 'Drive carefully – we can wait.'
- At an optometrist's office: 'If you don't see what you're looking for, you've come to the right place.'
- On a maternity room door: 'Push, Push, Push.'
- In a music library: 'Bach in a minuet.'
- At a proctologist's door: 'To expedite your visit, please back in.'
- In a taxidermist's window: 'We really know our stuff.'
- At a car dealership: 'The best way to get back on your feet – miss a car payment.'
- In a chiropodist's window: 'Time wounds all heels.'
- On a reception desk: 'We shoot every third salesman, and the second one just left.'
- At a towing company: 'We don't charge an arm and a leg. We want tows.'
- On a plumber's truck: 'Don't sleep with a drip, call your plumber.'
- On the side of an electrician's truck: 'Let us remove your shorts.'
- In a field: 'The farmer allows walkers to cross the field for free, but the bull charges.'
- In a non-smoking area: 'If we see smoke, we will assume you are on fire and take appropriate action.'

- At motorway garage: 'Please do not smoke near our petrol pumps. Your life may not be worth much but our petrol is.'
- Outside a radiator repair shop: 'Best place in town to take a leak.'
- Outside Patel's Builders: 'You've had the cowboys, now try the Indians.'
- At a pizza shop: 'Seven days without pizza makes one weak.'
- Outside a photographer's studio: 'Out to lunch. If not back by five, out for dinner also.'
- At a tyre shop: 'Invite us to your next blowout.'
- At a propane filling station: 'Thank heaven for little grills.'
- In a veterinarian's waiting room: 'Back in five minutes. Sit! Stay!'

Unfortunate signs:
- In a restaurant window: 'Don't stand there and be hungry. Come on in and get fed up.'
- In a laundromat: 'Automatic washing machines: please remove all your clothes when the lights go out.'
- In a department store: 'Bargain basement upstairs.'
- In an office: 'Would the person who took the step ladder yesterday please bring it back or further steps will be taken.'
- Outside a farm: 'Horse manure 50p per pre-packed bag; 20p do-it-yourself.'
- In a baker's window: 'Try our homemade pies – they're a real threat.'
- In an office: 'After tea break staff should empty the teapot and stand upside down on the draining board.'
- On a leaflet: 'If you cannot read, this leaflet will tell you how to get lessons.'
- On a repair shop door: 'We can repair anything. (Please knock hard on the door – the bell doesn't work.')
- In health food shop window: 'Closed due to illness.'
- On a beach: 'Quicksand. Any person passing this point will be drowned. By order of the District Council.'
- In a dry cleaner's window: 'Anyone leaving their garments here for more than 30 days will be disposed of.'
- In a safari park: 'Elephants, please stay in your car.'
- In a toilet in an office block: 'Toilet out of order. Please use floor below.'
- Outside a disco: 'The most exclusive disco in town. Everyone welcome.'
- Outside a second hand shop: 'We exchange anything – bicycles, washing machines etc. Why not bring your wife along and get a wonderful bargain?'
- On a church door: 'This is the Gate of Heaven. Enter ye all by this door. This door is kept locked because of the draught (please use side door).'

- At a conference: 'For anyone who has children and doesn't know it, there is a day care on the first floor.'

Sport

Pat was appearing on the television quiz show *Who Wants to be a Millionaire*. He had already reached the £125,000 mark but he only had one lifeline left, which was to phone a friend.

'You've done really well to get this far,' said questionmaster Chris Tarrant. 'Now the next question is worth £250,000 if you decide to play. But remember if you get it wrong, you will lose £93,000. Are you ready?'

'Sure,' Pat nodded.

'On screen is a photograph of a famous American sportsman of the 1990s as a small baby,' continued Tarrant. 'The question is, Pat, and don't forget this is for £250,000, which sportsman is it?'

Pat studied the picture intently for a couple of minutes, muttering to himself: 'I'm pretty sure it's Pete Sampras.' Then he stated more positively: 'Yes, I'm sure it's Pete Sampras. But because this is for so much money, and I really don't want to lose £93,000, can I phone a friend just to check?'

'OK,' said Tarrant. 'Who are you going to phone?'

'My mate Mick.'

Soon the phone rang and Mick's voice was heard at the other end. Chris Tarrant explained the situation to Mick and asked him to look at the TV screen. Pat then asked him the same question.

Without any hesitation, Mick replied: 'That's definitely Andre Agassi as a baby. I'd stake my life on it.'

Pat looked worried: 'Are you sure, Mick? I'm convinced that it's Pete Sampras.'

'No, it's definitely Agassi. I'm certain of it.'

'Well, Pat,' said Chris Tarrant, 'you've used your final lifeline. Now I need your answer.'

'OK,' said Pat, looking decidedly nervous. 'I know Mick reckons it's Andre Agassi, but I still think it's Pete Sampras. So I'm going with Sampras.'

'You don't have to play, you know,' advised Tarrant. 'You can go home with the £125,000.'

'No, no,' insisted Pat. 'I want to play and it's Pete Sampras as a baby. That's my final answer. Pete Sampras.'

There was a tense silence until Chris Tarrant put his hand to his chin and sighed: 'I'm so sorry, Pat. Pete Sampras is the wrong answer. You've just lost £93,000! But here's your cheque for £32,000 and thanks for being a great contestant.'

As the audience started to applaud, Pat asked: 'What was the correct answer? It's killing me.'

'Michael Johnson.'

Did you hear who won the Bangkok marathon? – I heard it was a Thai.

God and the Devil arranged a football match between Heaven and Hell. God had a small wager on the outcome, but the Devil was supremely confident and bet $500 on a win for Hell.

'You're crazy,' said God. 'I've got all the best players in the history of the game in my team.'

'I know,' said the Devil. 'But I've got all the referees.'

A soccer fan had a lousy seat at the stadium, right behind a pillar. But he spotted an empty seat with a much better view a few rows along, and so he made his way there. When he got there, he asked the man sitting in the next seat whether the empty seat was taken.

'This is my wife's seat,' he replied solemnly. 'She passed away. She was a big United fan.'

'I'm terribly sorry to hear of your sad loss. May I ask why you didn't give the ticket to a friend or a relative?'

'They're all at the funeral.'

Reading through a magazine, a woman suddenly started laughing. She turned to her husband and said: 'There's a classified ad here where a guy is offering to swap his wife for season tickets. You wouldn't swap me for season tickets, would you?'

'Of course not, honey,' he replied.

'Ah, that's sweet.'

'The season's half over.'

Why did the chicken run on to the football pitch? – Because the referee blew for a fowl.

Julius Caesar was addressing the crowd in the Coliseum. 'Friends, Romans, countrymen, I have just returned from my campaign in France where I killed 60,000 Gauls!'

As the crowd let out an almighty cheer, Brutus suddenly jumped up and yelled: 'Caesar lies! I know for a fact that he only killed 30,000 Gauls!'

'That is true,' responded Caesar, 'but remember, away Gauls count double in Europe.'

A wife was having an affair with the TV repairman. She complained: 'My husband never pays the slightest attention to me – all he's ever bothered about is watching the football game on TV. That's why we've got the biggest set in the neighbourhood – so he can watch the game.'

Just then, she heard a key in the front door. Her husband had arrived home unexpectedly. She said to her lover: 'Quick, hide in the back of the TV!'

So the lover hid in the TV while the husband sat down to watch the football game. After ten minutes, it became so hot and uncomfortable in the back of the TV set that the lover climbed out, walked straight past the husband and out of the front door.

The husband turned to his long-suffering wife and said: 'Hey, honey, I didn't see the referee send that guy off, did you?'

Bill challenged Tom to a game of darts.
   Tom said: 'OK.'
   Bill said: 'Nearest to a bull starts.'
   Tom said: 'Baaaa.'
   Bill said: 'Moooo.'
   Tom said: 'You're closest.'

Riding in the Grand National, a jockey was leading at Becher's Brook the second time around when he was suddenly hit on the head by a chicken drumstick and a pork pie. Although he lost several places, he managed to keep control of his horse and by the Canal Turn, had fought his way back to the front, only to be hit by a smoked salmon sandwich and a half bottle of champagne. Again, he lost valuable ground but, showing commendable bravery and agility, battled back into the lead over the final fence. With victory in sight, he was struck on the head yet again, this time by a tin of caviar and half a dozen Scotch eggs. As a result, he lost control of his mount for a few vital strides, enabling another horse to pass and win the race. Highly aggrieved at finishing only second, the jockey marched straight into the stewards' room to complain that he had been hampered.

At a race meeting, a punter saw a priest blessing a horse before the first race and, thinking it was a good omen, decided to bet on that particular horse. To the punter's delight, it won. He then watched the priest do the same for the next four races and continued to win. The first five horses that the priest had blessed had come in first, earning the punter a small fortune.

Certain that he had come up with an infallible formula, he decided to bet all his winnings on the priest's chosen horse in the last race. Once again he watched as the priest went through his familiar pre-race ritual, after which the punter put every last dime on that horse. But this time the horse dropped dead two furlongs before the finish.

The furious punter sought out the priest and demanded an explanation. The priest smiled: 'That's one of the problems with you Protestants: you don't know the difference between a blessing and the last rites.'

Two country boys went away for a long weekend's fishing. They spent a fortune on renting all the equipment – reels, rods, wading suits, rowboat, car, even a cabin in the woods – but figured that it would be worth it. They found the best spot on the lake but on the first day they caught absolutely nothing. It was the same story on the second day. Not a single bite. Finally on the third day they struck lucky, but even then it was just one small fish.

As they were driving home, the brighter of the pair said: 'Do you realise that this one lousy fish we caught cost us 1500 bucks?'

'Wow!' said his friend. 'Then it's a good thing we didn't catch any more!'

Two friends were recounting their dreams.

'I dreamed I was on holiday,' said one man fondly. 'It was just me and my fishing rod and this big beautiful lake. What a dream.'

'I had a great dream too,' recalled the other. 'I dreamed I was on a date with two gorgeous women and having the time of my life.'

'Hey!' cried his friend, hurt. 'You dreamed you were with two women, and you didn't call me?'

'I did,' said the other. 'But your wife said you'd gone fishing.'

A small boy was looking after his baby sister while his parents went shopping in town. He decided to go fishing, so he took her with him.

'I'm never taking her fishing again!' he told his mother that evening. 'I didn't catch a thing.'

'Oh,' said his mother, 'next time I'm sure she'll be quiet and not scare the fish away.'

'It wasn't that,' said the boy. 'She ate all the bait!'

Two young men were out fishing in their favourite secluded location when a Game Warden suddenly emerged from the bushes. One of them immediately ran for it. The Game Warden gave chase. Hotly pursued every yard of the way, the fisherman dashed through thickets, over hillocks and across streams until, after three quarters of a mile, he finally pulled up exhausted, enabling the Game Warden to collar him.

'Right,' said the warden. 'Let's see your fishing licence.'

The young man reached into the pocket of his jacket and produced a perfectly valid fishing licence.

The warden said: 'You must be real dumb! You don't have to run from me if you have a valid licence.'

'I know,' said the fisherman. 'But the thing is, my friend back there, he ain't got a valid licence.'

The owner of a racing pigeon was worried sick when his bird was six weeks late returning to the coop after a 300-mile race. Then at last the missing pigeon arrived home without a feather out of place.
'Where have you been?' demanded the owner.
'Oh,' replied the pigeon casually, 'it was such a nice day I decided to walk.'

Two sardines were big tennis fans. 'Let's go to Wimbledon this year,' said one.
'How would we get there?' asked the other.
'On the London Underground, of course.'
'What, and get packed in like commuters?'

While performing a routine physical, a doctor noticed that his patient's shins were covered in hideous bruises.
'Tell me,' said the doctor, 'do you play soccer or rugby?'
'No,' said the man. 'But my wife and I play bridge.'

Two men were engaged in an animated conversation about the best way to ski down a particular hill. To solve the dispute, they asked the advice of a man pulling his sledge.
'Sorry,' he said. 'There's not much point asking me. I'm a tobogganist.'
'Oh,' said one of the skiers, 'in that case can I have twenty Benson and Hedges?'

A business executive injured his leg skiing one weekend. By the time he got home on the Saturday night, the leg was badly swollen and he was experiencing difficulty walking, so he called his doctor at home. The doctor advised soaking it in hot water but this caused the leg to swell up even more.
Seeing him limping in agony, the businessman's maid said: 'It's probably not my place, because I'm only a maid, but I always thought it was better to use cold water, not hot, for swelling.' So he took her advice, switched to cold water, and the swelling rapidly subsided.
The following afternoon he called his doctor again to complain. 'What kind of doctor are you? You told me to soak my leg in hot water, and it got worse. My maid told me to use cold water, and it got better!'
'Really?' said the doctor. 'I don't understand it; my maid said hot water.'

While scuba diving in the sea at a depth of twenty feet, a man noticed another guy at the same depth, but without any diving gear whatsoever. The diver plunged twenty feet deeper, but the other guy joined him minutes later. The diver went down another twenty feet, but within a few minutes, the same guy was beside him again.

Confused, the diver took out a waterproof chalk and board set, and wrote: 'How are you able to stay under this deep without equipment?'

The guy grabbed the board and chalk, erased what the diver had written, and wrote: 'I'M DROWNING, YOU IDIOT!!!'

Fred and George were playing golf when Fred sliced his ball into a deep wooded gully. Taking his eight-iron, he clambered down the embankment in search of his ball. After spending ten minutes hacking at the undergrowth, he suddenly spotted something glistening among the leaves. As he got closer, he could see that it was an eight-iron in the hands of a skeleton.

Fred immediately called up to George: 'Hey, George, I've made a shocking discovery!'

'What's up?' shouted George.

'Bring me my wedge,' yelled Fred. 'You can't get out of here with an eight-iron.'

Having been given a set of clubs as a retirement present, a guy in his sixties decided to take up golf. Explaining that he knew nothing whatsoever about the game, he asked the local professional for lessons. The pro showed him the proper stance and swing, then said: 'Just hit the ball towards the flag on the first green.'

The novice teed up and smacked the ball straight down the middle of the fairway and onto the green where it stopped inches from the hole. 'Now what?' he asked.

The pro was rendered almost speechless. 'Well, er, you're supposed to hit the ball into the cup.'

'Oh great!' exclaimed the newcomer. 'Now you tell me!'

One day, struggling golfer Terry Bradley decided to try out a new golf course where no one knew him, just to see if it would bring him a change of fortune.

He hired a caddie to guide him around the course, but after another day of slices, hooks, shanks, duff shots, misread putts and bad temper, he was visibly upset. He turned to the caddie and said: 'You know, I must be the worst golfer in the world.'

The caddie replied: 'I don't think so, sir. I have heard there is a guy named Terry Bradley from across town who is the worst player ever!'

An elderly golfer harboured a lifelong ambition to play one hole at a seaside course the same way as the professionals. They drive the ball out over the sea and onto a tiny green situated on a spit of land that juts out off the coast. It was a shot that he had tried hundreds of times without success, his ball always falling short and ending up in the sea. As a result whenever he played that hole, he always used an old ball – one with a cut or a nick.

Last year he visited the course in another attempt to fulfil his dream. At his age, who knows how many more chances he would have? When he reached the fateful hole, he teed up an old cut ball and said a silent prayer.

As he prepared to address the ball, a powerful voice from above suddenly boomed out: 'Wait. Replace that old ball with a brand new ball.'

Interpreting this vocal intervention as a sign that God was finally going to let him achieve his ambition, he duly placed a new ball on the tee. But as he stepped up in readiness for the crucial drive, the voice came down again: 'Wait. Step back. Take a practice swing.' So the golfer stepped back and took a practice swing.

The voice boomed out again: 'Take another practice swing.' Obeying God's every instruction, the old man took another practice swing.

Then there was a moment of silence before the voice spoke out again. 'Put back the old ball.'

Golf Wisdom:
- Never try to keep more than 200 separate thoughts in your mind during your swing.
- When your shot has to carry over a water hazard, you can either hit one more club or two more balls.
- If you're afraid a full shot might reach the green while the foursome ahead of you is still putting out, you have two options: you can immediately shank a lay-up or you can wait until the green is clear and top a ball halfway there.
- The less skilled the player, the more likely he (or she) is to share ideas about the golf swing.
- A ball you can see in the rough from 50 yards away is not yours. If there is a ball in the fringe and a ball in the bunker, your ball is in the bunker. If both balls are in the bunker, yours is in the footprint.
- No matter how badly you are playing, it is always possible to play worse.
- The inevitable result of any golf lesson is the instant elimination of the one critical, unconscious motion that allowed you to compensate for all of your many other errors.
- If it ain't broke, try changing your grip.

- A golf match is a test of your skill against your opponent's luck.
- It's surprisingly easy to hole a 40ft-putt . . . for an eight.
- Everyone replaces his divot after a perfect approach shot.
- There are two types of golfers – those who admit to cheating and those who lie.
- Relying on your opponent to inform you when he breaks a rule is like expecting him to make fun of his own haircut.
- Nonchalant putts count the same as chalant putts.
- When you look up, causing a terrible shot, you will always look down again at exactly the moment when you should start watching the ball if you ever want to see it again.
- Whenever a rabbit golfer makes a birdie, he must subsequently make two triple bogeys to restore the natural order of things.
- If you want to hit a 7-iron as far as Tiger Woods does, simply try to lay up just short of a water hazard or a ladies' foursome.
- The shortest distance between any two points on a golf course is a straight line that passes directly through the centre of a very large tree.
- There are two kinds of bounces – unfair bounces, and bounces just the way you meant to play it.
- Don't buy a putter until you've had a chance to throw it.
- You can hit a two-acre fairway ten per cent of the time and a two-inch branch 90 per cent of the time.
- The game of golf is 90 per cent mental and ten per cent mental.
- If you really want to get better at golf, go back and take it up at a much earlier age.

Two guys were playing golf on a Saturday, just as they had every week for the past nine years. Just as the first man was about to tee off, a woman in a wedding dress ran over to him, screaming: 'You bum! You lousy bum! You promised!'

The golfer replied calmly: 'Honey, I said only if it rains today . . .'

Watched by the club professional, a golfer enjoyed a torrid start to his first-ever game. His tee shot flew into the woods, his second ball landed in a lake and his third buried itself in a bunker. And with each passing shot, his swing grew wilder, so that by the time he had attempted to extricate himself from the bunker for the fifth time, he was brutally hacking away at the ball. With the ball still deep in the sand, he belatedly sought the advice of the professional.

'What club should I use on this shot?' he asked.

'I don't know,' replied the pro. 'What game are you playing?'

A golfer stumbled into the clubhouse and ordered a double scotch.

'What's up with you?' said the steward behind the bar. 'You look as if you've been to hell and back!'

'You'll never believe this,' he said. 'I've just lost a game to Donaldson.'

'What? Donaldson's the worst player in the club. How on earth could you lose to him?'

'He tricked me. On the first tee, he asked for a handicap and, since I've been playing pretty well lately, I told him he could have ten, twenty, thirty strokes – any handicap he wanted. He said, "Just give me two gotchas."'

'What's a gotcha?' asked the steward.

'That's what I wanted to know. But Donaldson just said, "You'll see." Then, as I was teeing off, and just at the top of my backswing, he screamed out "Gotcha!" Well, inevitably I missed the ball completely.'

'Understandably,' said the steward sympathetically. 'But still, that's only one swing. How hid he manage to win the game?'

'You try swinging at a golf ball all afternoon while waiting for that second "Gotcha!"'

A man and a woman were standing at the altar about to be married when the bride-to-be spotted that the prospective groom had a set of golf clubs with him.

'What on earth are you doing with those golf clubs in church?' she snarled.

'Well,' he said, 'this isn't going to take all afternoon, is it?'

After hitting six balls into a lake, a frustrated golfer hurled his clubs into the water and began to walk off the course. Then suddenly he turned around and jumped in the lake. His playing partners thought he must have had a change of heart about dumping such valuable golfing equipment but he emerged moments later without the clubs and headed off the course once more.

'Why did you jump into the lake?' they asked.

He replied: 'I left my car keys in the bag.'

Standing on the first tee, a golfer said to his playing partner: 'Why don't you try this ball – you can't lose it?'

'How do you mean, you can't lose it?'

'It's a special ball. If you hit it into the trees, it beeps. If you hit it in water, it sends up bubbles. If it lands in deep rough, it emits a plume of smoke.'

'Wow! That's fantastic. Where did you get it?'

'I found it.'

A golfer was in a close match with a friend, who was leading by a couple of strokes. The golfer said to himself: 'I'd give anything to sink this next putt.'

At that moment, a complete stranger walked up to him and whispered: 'Would you give up a quarter of your sex life to sink this putt?'

The golfer immediately thought the man was crazy, and that whatever he answered would be irrelevant But then, sensing that perhaps it was a good omen and that it might put him in the right frame of mind to sink the difficult putt, he replied: 'OK, I would give up a quarter of my sex life in return for sinking this putt.' And he promptly sank the putt.

Two holes later, he mumbled to himself: 'Boy, if I could only get this bunker shot in the hole.'

The same stranger appeared at his side and said: 'Would it be worth another quarter of your sex life?'

'Sure,' shrugged the golfer, and he duly holed the bunker shot.

It was all down to the final hole. The golfer needed to sink a sixty-foot putt to win – an almost impossible task. Although he said nothing, the stranger appeared at his side and said: 'Would you be willing to give up the rest of your sex life to win this match?'

'Certainly,' said the golfer, and he sank the putt.

As the golfer walked to the clubhouse, the stranger appeared along-side and said: 'You know, I've not really been fair with you because you don't know who I am. I'm the devil, and from now on you will have no sex life.'

The golfer just smiled and said: 'And I haven't been fair to you. You see, my name is Brother Benedict.'

Two golfers were talking. 'Guess what!' said one. 'I got a set of golf clubs for my wife.'

The other nodded: 'Great swap!'

After a long evening drinking in the golf club bar, a man set off for home but half a mile down the road his car was pulled over by a police officer.

The officer did not need a breathalyser to see what the problem was. 'You're too drunk to drive,' he said.

'Too drunk to drive?' repeated the golfer. 'I'm too drunk to putt!'

A hack golfer was enduring a particularly torrid round. His tee shot on the first hole sailed out of bounds, his fourth shot ended up in the woods, and his sixth in the lake. In total, he lost three brand new golf balls on that hole.

Teeing off at the second hole, he hooked his drive wildly into a plan-tation. 'Damn!' he cursed. 'There goes another new ball!'

His next shot fared no better, flying into a field. 'I don't believe it!

That's yet another new ball I've lost! This round is costing me a fortune!'

Watching his struggles, a player in the group behind advised: 'Seeing how you lose so many balls, why don't you play with an old ball?'

'Because,' said the hack golfer caustically, 'I've never had one!'

Jim and Harry headed out of their weekly round of golf. Jim suggested: 'To make it more interesting, why don't we have $5 on the lowest score for the day?'

Harry agreed, and they enjoyed a great game. With one hole to play, Harry led by a single stroke, but then on the 18th, he cut his ball into the rough.

'Help me find my ball,' he called to Jim. 'You search over there, I'll look around here.'

After five minutes of fruitless searching, Harry, knowing only too well that he was facing a disastrous penalty for a lost ball, sneakily pulled a ball from his pocket, dropped it on the ground and called out triumphantly: 'Hey, I've found my ball!'

Jim looked across at him despairingly. 'After all the years we've been friends, how could you cheat on me at golf for a measly five bucks?'

'What do you mean cheat?' protested Harry. 'I found my ball sitting right there!'

'And a liar too!' exclaimed Jim in disbelief. 'I'll have you know I've been standing on your ball for the last five minutes!'

'Why don't you play golf with Neil any more?' the wife asked her husband.

'Would you play with someone who moves his ball to a better lie when no one is looking, who deliberately coughs half-way through his opponent's backswing and who lies about his handicap?'

'Well, no,' said the wife.

'Neither will Neil.'

A man in his eighties moved to a new town and joined the local golf club. When he went there hoping to play his first round, he was told that all the tee times were booked for that day. Seeing his disappointment, the assistant professional offered to let the old man join him on his round and suggested a twelve-stroke handicap.

The old man said: 'I really don't need a handicap. The only real problem I have is getting out of bunkers.'

Both men played well and coming to the final hole, a short par-three, the scores were even. The pro landed his tee shot on the edge of the green, but the old man put his drive into a greenside bunker. Steadying himself in the sand, the octogenarian then played a superb bunker shot that ended with the ball in the hole.

The assistant pro was stunned. 'Great shot, but I thought you said you have a problem getting out of bunkers.'

'I do,' replied the old man. 'Give me a hand.'

Golfer: That can't be my ball. It looks much too old.

Caddie: Well, it's a long time since we started.

The Pope met with the College of Cardinals to discuss a proposal from Shimon Peres, the former leader of Israel.

'Your holiness,' said one of the cardinals, 'Mr Peres wants to determine whether Jews or Catholics are superior by challenging you to a golf match.'

The Pope was greatly disturbed, as he had never held a golf club in his life. 'Don't worry,' said the cardinal. 'We'll call America and talk to Jack Nicklaus. We'll make him a cardinal. He can play Shimon Peres. We can't lose!'

Everyone agreed it was a good idea. The call was made, and Jack Nicklaus was honoured to play.

The day after the match, Nicklaus reported to the Vatican to inform the Pope of the result. 'I came second, your Holiness,' he said.

'Second?' exclaimed the Pope, surprised. 'You came second to Shimon Peres?'

'No,' said Nicklaus, 'second to Rabbi Woods.'

'How was your golf game, honey?' asked Tom's wife.

'Well, I was hitting pretty well, but my eyesight's now so bad that I couldn't see where the ball went. I ended up losing four balls!'

'But you're seventy-five years old, Tom!' admonished his wife. 'Next time you play, why don't you take my brother Ken along?'

'But he's eighty-eight and doesn't even play golf anymore,' protested Tom.

'I know he hasn't got all his faculties, but he has got perfect eyesight. He could watch your ball.'

So Tom took his wife's advice and the next day he teed off with Ken looking on. Tom swung and the ball disappeared down the middle of the fairway.

'Did you see it?' asked Tom.

'Yup,' said Ken.

As they set off down the fairway, Tom peered ahead: 'Well, where is it?' he yelled.

Ken said: 'I forget.'

A guy was lining up his drive when a voice from the clubhouse called out: 'Will the gentleman on the ladies' tee please move back to the men's tee!'

The golfer ignored the request and continued with his practice swings. The voice called out again: 'Sir, will you please move back to the men's tee now!'

The golfer carried on regardless and was just addressing the ball when the voice called out for a third time: 'You are violating club rules! Move back to the men's tee immediately or I will have you thrown off the course!'

The golfer turned angrily in the direction of the clubhouse and shouted back: 'Do you mind shutting up while I play my second shot!'

T-Shirts

The following slogans and messages have been seen on T-shirts:

- Due to budget cuts, the light at the end of the tunnel has been turned off.
- I can only please one person per day. Today is not your day. Tomorrow is not looking good either.
- I refuse to have a battle of wits with an unarmed person.
- Tell me what you need, and I'll tell you how to get along without it.
- THE FOUR STAGES OF LIFE: 1. You believe in Santa Claus 2. You don't believe in Santa Claus 3. You become Santa Claus 4. You start to look like Santa Claus.
- Cleverly Disguised As A Responsible Adult.
- I don't have an attitude problem. You have a perception problem.
- The money is always greener in the other guy's wallet.
- My reality check bounced.
- If We Quit Voting, Will They Go Away?
- When money talks, no one criticises its accent.
- Too many freaks. Not enough circuses.
- Chaos. Panic. Disorder. My work is done here.
- I thought I wanted a career. It turns out I just wanted a pay check.
- I love my cat. My cat does not care.
- If At First You Don't Succeed . . . Blame Someone Else And Seek Counselling.
- My bank account needs month-to-month resuscitation.
- Everyone needs to believe in something. I believe in chocolate.
- I don't suffer from stress. I am a carrier.
- Work Harder. People On Welfare Depend On You.
- You're Just Jealous Because The Voices Are Talking To me.
- If I throw a stick, will you leave?

- Errors have been made. Others will be blamed.
- I'm out of bed and dressed. What more do you want?
- Do not meddle in the affairs of dragons because you are crunchy and taste good with ketchup.
- Growing old is mandatory. Growing up is optional.
- Never argue with an idiot. They drag you down to their level then beat you with experience.
- Where there's a will, I want to be in it.
- It's lonely at the top but you eat better.
- The 11th Commandment: Thou Shalt Not Whine.
- Lottery: a tax on people who are bad at math.
- Princess, having sufficient experience with princes, seeks frog.
- Failure is not an option! It comes bundled with the software.
- What if the Hokey Cokey is really what it's all about?
- Sarcasm is just one more service we offer.
- God put me on earth to accomplish a certain number of things. Right now, I am so far behind I will live forever.
- If the left side of the brain controls the right hand, then only left-handed people are in their right mind.
- Born Free. Taxed To Death.
- All Men Are Animals. Some Just Make Better Pets.
- Eat one live toad first thing in the morning. Nothing worse will happen to you for the rest of the day.
- If you want breakfast in bed, sleep in the kitchen.
- It's hard to make a comeback when you haven't been anywhere.
- Raising teenagers is like nailing blancmange to a tree.
- Pride is what I have. Vanity is what others have.
- Think nobody knows you're alive? Try missing a payment.
- I started out with nothing and I still have most of it left.
- Ignore the dog. Watch out for the owner.
- Who are these kids and why are they calling me Mom?
- I used to have a handle on life but it broke.
- I have plenty of talent and vision. I just don't care.
- Just hand over the chocolate and no one will get hurt.
- On the keyboard of life, always keep one finger on the escape key.
- If life is like a bowl of cherries, then I'm living in the pits.
- I don't suffer from insanity – I enjoy every minute of it.
- Don't treat me any differently than you would the Queen.
- Friends are the chocolate chips in the cookies of life.
- The only substitute for good manners is fast reflexes.
- When you're finally holding all the cards, why does everyone else decide to play chess?
- No one pays attention until you make a mistake.
- Jesus loves you, but I think you're a jerk.

- Learn from the mistakes of others. You can't live long enough to make them all yourself.
- Education is expensive but ignorance is more so.
- Give me ambiguity or give me something else.
- Seen it all. Done it all. Can't remember most of it.
- Change is inevitable, except from a vending machine.
- The trouble with life is there's no background music.
- Out of my mind. Back in five minutes.
- The gene pool could use a little chlorine.
- Germs attack people where they are weakest. This explains the number of head colds.
- It's not just the ups and downs that make life difficult. It's the jerks.
- Coffee. Chocolate. Men. Some things are better rich.
- I don't know what I want, but I do know I don't have it.
- Enthusiasm is contagious. Start an epidemic!
- Once you've climbed the ladder of success, you're over the hill.
- There will always be death and taxes. But death doesn't get worse every year.
- Brain cells come and brain cells go, but fat cells live forever.
- Two wrongs do not make a right . . . but three lefts do.
- I don't know what your problem is, but I bet it's hard to pronounce.
- I'll try being nicer if you try being smarter.
- Today's mighty oak is just yesterday's acorn that held its ground.
- I'm really easy to get along with once people learn to worship me.
- Thousands of years ago cats were worshipped as gods. Cats have never forgotten this.
- I don't work here. I'm a consultant.
- The screw up fairy has visited us again.
- Don't be old until you have lived!
- Who do you want to talk to: 1. The man in charge or 2. The woman who really knows what's going on?
- What am I? Flypaper for freaks?
- If they don't have chocolates in heaven, I'm not going.
- I'm not rude. You're just insignificant.
- Eating prunes gives you a good run for your money.

Travel

A man was walking down the street when he stopped to look in a travel agent's window. Seeing a cheap cruise advertised for $80, he went into the agency and handed over the money. The travel agent then whacked him over the head with a baseball bat and threw him into the river.

A few minutes later another man was walking down the street when he noticed the same advert. He went into the agency and paid his $80.

The travel agent then whacked him in the ribs with the baseball bat and hurled him into the river.

Soon afterwards the two men were floating down the river together.

The first man said: 'Do you think they'll serve any food on this cruise?'

'I don't think so,' said the second man. 'They didn't last year.'

A drunk boarded a bus late one night and lurched along the centre gangway. Suddenly he stopped and shouted that everyone in the seats to his right was an idiot and that everyone in the seats to his left was an asshole.

An angry passenger stood up and said: 'How dare you! I'm not an idiot!'

The drunk yelled back: 'So move to the other side then.'

Three men hired a small plane to hunt moose in Canada, but the pilot warned them: 'This is a very small plane, so you can only bring back one moose.'

Inevitably the men got carried away and ended up killing three moose. When they brought their trophies back to the plane, the pilot was appalled.

'I said one moose only!'

'That's what you said last year,' replied one of the hunters, 'but for an additional $100 you then allowed us to take the three moose on the plane. So, here, take the $100 now.'

The pilot relented and allowed the three moose on board, but shortly after take-off the plane crashed. Pulling himself from the wreckage, one hunter looked around semi-conscious and asked: 'Where are we?'

One of his colleagues muttered: 'About 100 yards from where we crashed last year.'

At a plane crash site, the lone survivor sat with his back against a tree, chewing on a bone. As he tossed the bone onto a huge pile of bones, he noticed the rescue team. 'Thank heavens!' he cried out in relief. 'I am saved!'

Seeing the pile of human bones beside the lone survivor, the rescue team were too stunned to speak. He had obviously eaten his comrades. The survivor detected the look of horror on their faces and hung his head in shame.

'You can't judge me for this,' he pleaded. 'I had to survive. Is it so wrong to want to live?'

The leader of the rescue team stepped forward, shaking his head in disbelief. 'I won't judge you for doing what was necessary to survive,' he said, 'but for goodness sake, your plane only went down yesterday!'

216

Airline Pilots' Rulebook:
1. Every takeoff is optional. Every landing is mandatory.
2. If you push the stick forward, the houses get bigger. If you pull the stick back, they get smaller. That is, unless you keep pulling the stick all the way back, in which case they get bigger again.
3. Flying isn't dangerous. Crashing is what's dangerous.
4. The only time you have too much fuel is when you're on fire.
5. The propeller is just a big fan in front of the plane used to keep the pilot cool. When it stops, you can actually see the pilot start sweating.
6. When in doubt, maintain your altitude. No one has ever collided with the sky.
7. A 'good' landing is one from which you can walk away. A 'great' landing is one after which they can use the plane again.
8. There are three simple rules for making a smooth landing. Unfortunately no one knows what they are.
9. If all you can see out of the window is ground that's going round and round and all you can hear is screaming from the passenger compartment, things are not as they should be.
10. In the ongoing battle between objects made of aluminium going hundreds of miles per hour and the ground going zero miles per hour, the ground has yet to lose.
11. It's always a good idea to keep the pointy end going forward as much as possible.
12. Remember, gravity is not just a good idea. It's the law. And it's not subject to repeal.
13. The four most useless things to a pilot are the altitude above you, runway behind you, gas back at the airport, and a tenth of a second ago.
14. There are old pilots and there are bold pilots. But there are no old, bold pilots.
15. Always try to keep the number of landings you make equal to the number of takeoffs you've made.

A man on holiday in Spain thought he would e-mail his sister back in England to tell her what a great time he was having. Unfortunately instead of sending it to Joan Foster, he made a mistake with the address, as a result of which it went to Jean Foster, a recently widowed vicar's wife. When she looked at the e-mail, she promptly fainted. It read: 'Arrived safely, but it sure is hot down here.'

An airplane was already virtually full and in danger of exceeding its baggage allowance when a last-minute passenger asked for the one remaining ticket.

The clerk was unsure whether to give him the ticket. 'Do you mind me asking how much you weigh?'

'With or without clothes?' queried the passenger.

'Well,' said the clerk, 'how do you intend to travel?'

A tourist was being led through the swamps of Florida. 'Is it true,' he asked the guide, 'that an alligator won't attack you if you carry a flash-light?'

'That depends,' replied the guide, 'on how fast you carry the flash-light!'

When a taxi passenger tapped the driver on the shoulder to ask a question, the driver screamed, lost control of the vehicle, nearly hit a bus, mounted the pavement and stopped just short of a shop window.

As he came to his senses, the driver shouted at the passenger: 'Don't ever do that again! You scared the living daylights out of me!'

The passenger apologised and said that he hadn't realised a little tap would scare him so much.

'No, I'm sorry,' said the driver, calming down. 'It's not really your fault. Today is my first day as a cab driver – I've been driving hearses for the last twenty-five years!'

A coach load of tourists arrived at Runnymede. They gathered around the guide who said: 'This is the spot where the barons forced King John to sign Magna Carta.'

An American tourist asked: 'When did that happen?'

'1215,' said the guide.

'Damn!' said the American, looking at his watch. 'Missed it by half an hour.'

A photographer wanted to take some aerial shots of the countryside and so he booked a flight with the local aerodrome. On arrival, he was directed to the runway and told that the plane was waiting for him. Seeing a light aircraft with its engine running, he climbed in and told the pilot: 'Let's go.'

Shortly after take-off, the photographer said: 'Now, if you can come in low over that lake, I'll be able to take some nice pictures.'

'Why do you want to do that?' asked the pilot.

'It's my job. I'm a photographer.'

'Oh,' said the pilot, ashen-faced. 'So you're not the flight instructor?'

Two anthropologists flew to a pair of adjacent South Sea Islands to study the natives. A few months later one of them paddled a canoe over to the other island to see how his colleague was doing. On arrival, he found the other anthropologist surrounded by a group of natives.

'How's it going?' said the visiting anthropologist.

'Amazingly well,' enthused the other. 'I have discovered an important fact about the local language. Just watch this.'

And he pointed at a palm tree and asked the natives: 'What is that?'

In unison they answered: 'Umpeta.'

Then he pointed at a rock and asked them: 'What is that?'

Together the natives replied: 'Umpeta.'

'You see!' said the anthropologist excitedly, they use the same word for palm tree and rock!'

'That's incredible!' said the visitor. 'On the other island, the same word means "index finger".'

The flight attendant listened patiently to the man's tirade. 'You bring me cold coffee, you feed me lousy food. I can't see the movie, not that it matters anyway because you didn't bring me any headphones, and my window doesn't have a shade so that I can close it and go to sleep.'

When he had finally finished, she said: 'Just shut up and land the plane!'

Jack said to his friend Bob: 'I reckon I'm about ready for a holiday. But this year I'm going to do it a little different. The last few years, I've taken your advice about where to go. Three years ago you told me to go to Majorca. I went to Majorca and Susan got pregnant. Then two years ago, you told me to go to the Bahamas, and Susan got pregnant again. Last year you suggested Greece, and, blow me, Susan got pregnant again!'

Bob asked: 'So what are you going to do this year that's different?'

Jack said: 'This year I'm taking Susan with me.'

A tourist was admiring a necklace worn by a local Indian. 'What is it made of?' she asked.

'Alligator's teeth,' replied the Indian.

'I suppose,' said the tourist patronisingly, 'that they mean as much to you as pearls do to us?'

'No,' said the Indian. 'Anybody can open an oyster.'

A little old lady was on a National Express coach travelling north out of London. After just a few minutes of the journey, she asked the driver: 'Are we at Sheffield yet?'

'No,' said the driver. 'I'll let you know when we are.'

Ten minutes later, she asked him again: 'Are we at Sheffield yet?'

'No,' he answered, struggling to keep his patience. 'Like I say, I'll let you know when we are.'

She kept this up for the next four hours. Every ten minutes or so, she would ask the driver whether they were at Sheffield yet and each time he would tell her no. Finally, with his nerves almost in shreds, Sheffield coach station came into view and the relieved driver announced: 'Right, madam, this is Sheffield. Off you get.'

'Oh, no, driver,' she said. 'I'm going all the way to Edinburgh. It's just that my daughter told me that when I got to Sheffield I should take my blood pressure tablet.'

A woman boarded the bus with her young son and tried to get away with paying only one fare. The driver wasn't having any of it and insisted that she pay for the boy, too.

'But children under six ride free,' she protested.

'He doesn't look a day under thirteen,' said the driver.

The woman said: 'Can I help it if he worries a lot?'

After crawling along at a pitifully slow pace for miles, a passenger train finally came to a complete halt. Seeing the guard walking alongside the track, a passenger leaned out of the window and asked: 'What's going on?'

'There's a cow on the track,' replied the guard.

Ten minutes later, the train moved off and resumed its slow pace, but within five minutes it had stopped again.

The passenger saw the same guard walking past outside once more and inquired: 'What happened? Did we catch up with the cow again?'

A plane was delayed for nearly an hour on take-off. When it eventually took to the air, the passengers asked the flight attendant the reason for the late departure.

'Well,' she explained, 'the pilot was worried about a noise he heard coming from one of the engines and it took us a while to get a new pilot.'

Following a particularly bumpy landing, the plane cabin crew stood at the door while the passengers exited, thanking each person for flying with the airline. The last person to leave was an old lady who, still recovering from the jolts and jerks, said falteringly: 'Do you mind if I ask a question?'

'Sure,' replied the flight attendant.

'Did we land or were we shot down?'

As a coachload of tourists drove through Wiltshire, the guide was pointing out places of interest. When they approached Stonehenge, the guide announced: 'This is Stonehenge, a megalithic monument dating from about 2800 BC. It consisted originally of thirty upright stones, their tops linked by lintel stones to form a continuous circle about 100 ft across. The uprights were built from local sandstone and each stone weighs around twenty-six tons.'

At the back of the coach one tourist turned to his wife and said: 'Pretty impressive, huh?'

'Yes,' she agreed. 'But wouldn't you think they'd have built it further back from the main road?'

A holidaymaker phoned a seaside hotel to check on its precise location. The proprietor said: 'It's only a stone's throw from the beach.'

'But how will I recognise it?'

'It's the one with all the broken windows.'

An airline pilot with poor eyesight had always managed to pass his vision tests by memorising the eye charts beforehand. One year, however, the doctor used a new chart that the pilot had never seen before and the game was up. The pilot proved to be as blind as a bat.

The doctor was curious as to how he had managed to fly a plane for so many years without incident. 'For example, how do you taxi the plane out to the runway?'

'Well,' said the pilot, 'it's really not that difficult. All you have to do is follow the instructions of the ground controller over the radio. Besides, all the landmarks have become quite familiar to me over the years.'

'I can understand that,' said the doctor. 'But what about take-off?'

'Again, a simple procedure. I just aim the plane down the runway, go to full throttle, pull back on the stick, and off we go!'

'And once you're aloft?'

'Oh, everything's fully automated these days. The flight computer knows our destination, and all I have to do is hit the autopilot and the plane pretty much flies itself.'

'But I still don't see how you land!'

'Oh, that's the easiest part of all,' said the pilot. 'All I do is use the airport's radio beacon to get us on the proper glide path. Then I just throttle down and when the co-pilot screams in terror, I pull the nose up, and the plane lands just fine!'

A Swiss man, looking for directions, pulled up at a bus stop where two Americans were waiting.

'Entschuldigung, koennen Sie Deutsch sprechen?' he asked. The two Americans just stared at him blankly.

'Excusez-moi, parlez-vous Français?' he tried. The two continued to stare.

'Parlare Italiano?' No response.

'Hablan ustedes Español?' Still nothing.

As the Swiss guy drove off, disgusted, one American turned to the other and said: 'Y'know, maybe we should learn a foreign language.'

'Why?' said the other. 'That guy knew four languages, and it didn't do him any good.'

Visiting his cousin in the valley, an old hillbilly was fascinated by the railroad. He had never seen a train before and so when one came whistling and steaming down the track towards him, it needed his cousin to drag him to safety at the last minute.

'You could have been killed there!' said the cousin. 'Lucky I was around!'

The cousin carried the shaken hillbilly back to his cabin to recuperate. The cousin put a kettle on the stove to make some tea and then went outside to chop some wood. He returned to find the hillbilly raining blows on the kettle with the butt of a shotgun.

'Why are you smashing my kettle?' demanded the cousin.

'These darned things are dangerous,' said the hillbilly. 'I'm killin' this one before it gets a chance to grow up!'

The navigator of the *QE2* was steering the ship through dense fog. Suddenly he turned to the captain and said: 'Sir, I think something is wrong with our compass.'

'Why do you say that?' asked the captain.

'Because we've just been overtaken by a number 36 bus!'

Making her first airplane trip, a young woman found herself a window seat in a no-smoking area and settled down. A few minutes later, a man came over and insisted that she was in his seat, but she flatly refused to move. In the end he said: 'OK, lady, if that's the way you want it, you fly this plane!'

Among a group of Americans touring Ireland, one woman was constantly complaining. The bus seats were uncomfortable; the food was terrible; the weather was too hot; the weather was too cold; the hotels were awful – to her mind, everything was wrong.

When the group arrived at the site of the famous Blarney Stone, the tour guide said: 'Good luck will be following you all your days if you kiss the Blarney Stone. But unfortunately it's being cleaned today and so no one will be able to kiss it. Perhaps we can come back tomorrow.'

'We can't be here tomorrow,' moaned the unpleasant woman. 'We have some other boring tour to go on. So I guess we can't kiss the stupid stone.'

'Well now,' said the guide, 'it is said that if you kiss someone who has kissed the stone, you'll have the same good fortune.'

'And I suppose you've kissed the stone?' sneered the woman.

'No, ma'am,' replied the guide, beginning to lose his patience with her, 'but I have sat on it!'

An airline stewardess was just finishing her standard safety briefing to passengers. 'In the event of a water landing, your seat cushion may be used as a flotation device.'

At this, a male passenger called out: 'Hey! If the plane can't fly, why should I believe the seat can float?'

During the 1960s space race, NASA decided that it needed a special ballpoint pen capable of writing in the zero gravity confines of its space capsules. After years of research and development, the Astronaut Pen was produced at a cost of $1 million. The Soviet Union, faced with the same problem, used a pencil.

A husband and wife were travelling on holiday in Scotland. As they approached Kirkcudbright, they started arguing about the pronunciation of the town. The argument raged until they stopped for lunch. As they stood in the restaurant, the husband asked the girl behind the counter: 'Before we order, could you please settle an argument for us? Would you please pronounce where we are, very slowly?'

The girl leaned over the counter and said: 'Burrrr . . . gerrrrrr . . . Kiiiing.'

It was mealtime on a small budget airline. 'Would you like dinner?' asked the flight attendant.

The passenger said: 'What are my choices?'

The flight attendant replied: 'Yes or no.'

A New York taxi driver and a priest went to heaven on the same day. St. Peter was waiting to greet them.

'You must be Lennie Roberts, the New York taxi driver,' said St. Peter. 'Come through and try on your silk robe with your golden sceptre.'

While the taxi driver was being fitted out, St. Peter returned to attend to the priest. 'And you must be Father Murphy, the priest of St. John's. Come through and try on your cloth robe with your wooden sceptre.'

'Excuse me,' said the priest, irked. 'But how is it that I, a man of the cloth, only get a cloth robe and a wooden sceptre while that New York taxi driver gets a silk robe and a golden sceptre?'

'Well,' explained St. Peter, 'we work on a performance scale. You see, while you preached, everybody slept; but when he drove a taxi, everybody prayed!'

A husband and wife were relaxing on the beach on holiday when the wife suddenly exclaimed: 'Oh my God! I've just remembered I left the oven on!'

'Don't worry about it,' said her husband reassuringly. 'The house won't burn down. I've just remembered I left the bath running!'

With an hour to wait before his flight to Los Angeles, a man was propping up the bar, downing a succession of whiskeys. He was sweating profusely and his hands were shaking. Seeing his obvious distress, a priest came over to try and calm him down.

'Are you nervous about flying?' asked the priest.

'N-n-nervous? I'm t-t-terrified. I j-just kn-know the p-plane is g-going to c-crash and we're all g-going to d-d-die!'

'Is this your first time flying?'

'No, I fly c-cross-c-country all the time. It's my j-j-job.'

'Why don't you ask your boss if you can drive cross-country instead?'

'He'd n-never let me d-do that.'

'Why not?'

'Because I'm the p-p-pilot.'

A travel writer was checking out of his Canadian hotel when he spotted an Indian chief sitting in the lobby.

'Who's that?' the writer asked the hotel manager.

'Oh, that's Big Chief Forget Me Not. He's ninety-five and has a fantastic memory – he can remember every single detail of his life.'

Intrigued, the writer went over to the chief and tried to engage him in conversation.

'Hi there,' said the writer.

Preoccupied with carving a wooden tool, the chief mumbled a scarcely audible reply.

'Can you tell me what you had for breakfast on your twenty-first birthday?' persisted the writer.

'Eggs,' said the chief, and he carried on with his carving.

The travel writer recounted this story to a number of people and was advised that the correct way to address an Indian chief was not 'Hi there' but 'How?' Six months later he was staying at the same Canadian hotel and, to his amazement, Big Chief Forget Me Not was still sitting in the lobby.

The writer went over to him and said: 'How?'

'Scrambled,' said the chief.

Truths

No one has ever complained of a parachute not opening.

Love is photogenic. It needs darkness to develop.

A good discussion is like a mini skirt – short enough to be interesting and long enough to cover the subject.

Never entrust your life to a surgeon with more than three Band Aids on his fingers.

Generally speaking, you're not learning much when your mouth is moving.

Never give yourself a haircut after three margaritas.

When you make a mistake, make amends immediately: it's easier to eat humble pie while it's still warm.

Talk is cheap because supply exceeds demand.

You can't respect a man who carries a dog.

No one knows the origins of their metal coat hangers.

Driving through a tunnel makes you feel excited.

The severity of the itch is inversely proportional to the ability to reach it.

You never ever run out of salt.

Everywhere is within walking distance if you have the time.

Too many people find fault as if there is a reward for it.

Never pass up an opportunity to pee.

Drive carefully – it's not only cars that can be recalled by their maker.

Everyone seems normal until you get to know them.

In every plate of fries there is a bad fry.

If you woke up breathing, congratulations! You have another chance!

Whatever hits the fan will not be evenly distributed.

Everybody always remembers the day a dog ran into your school.

A thing not worth doing isn't worth doing well.

Despite constant warning, you have never met anybody who has had their arm broken by a swan.

Be really nice to your friends and family: you never know when you are going to need them to empty your bedpan.

Birds of a feather flock together and then poop on your car.

The sooner you fall behind, the more time you have to catch up.

The most embarrassing thing you can do at school is to call your teacher Mum or Dad.

If you can't be kind, at least have the decency to be vague.

Opportunities always look bigger going than coming.

You always feel a bit scared when stroking a horse.

It is easier to get forgiveness than permission.

The older you get, the tougher it is to lose weight, because by then your body and your fat are really good friends.

The most painful household incident is stepping on an upturned plug while wearing socks.

He who hesitates is probably right.

If you think there is good in everybody, you haven't met everybody.

When it's you against the world, I'd bet on the world.

People who can't drive slam car doors too hard.

A closed mouth gathers no foot.

There is no substitute for genuine lack of preparation.

The smaller the monkey, the more it looks like it would kill you at the first given opportunity.

Never miss a good chance to stop talking.

Timing has an awful lot to do with the outcome of a rain dance.

The mind is like a parachute – it works much better when it's open.

Show me a man who always has both feet on the ground, and I'll show you a man who can't put on his trousers.

It's always darkest before dawn, so if you're going to steal your neighbour's newspaper that's the time to do it.

Never test the depth of the water with both feet.

It may be that your sole purpose in life is simply to serve as a bad example.

You've turned into your Dad the day you put aside a thin piece of wood specifically for stirring paint.

Every man has at some stage while taking a pee, flushed halfway through and then raced against the flush.

We are born naked, wet and hungry. Then things get worse.

If you tell the truth, you don't have to remember anything.

The sole purpose of a child's middle name is so he can tell when he's really in trouble.

The journey of a thousand miles begins with a broken fan belt and a puncture.

You're never quite sure whether it's OK to eat green potato crisps.

Some days you are the bug, some days you are the windshield.

The shortest measurable period of time is the time between the moment one puts a little extra aside for a sudden emergency and the arrival of that emergency.

You're never quite as stupid as when you think you know everything.

Information does not constitute knowledge any more than loose ingredients constitute a cake.

It only seems kinky the first time.

One of the most awkward things that can happen in a pub is when your pint-to-toilet cycle gets synchronised with a complete stranger.

If it really were the thought that counted, more women would be pregnant.

The bigger they are, the harder they hit.

The quickest way to double your money is to fold it in half and put it in your pocket.

226

It's impossible to look cool while picking up a Frisbee.

Those who can't laugh at themselves leave the job to others.

Good news is just life's way of keeping you off balance.

When you're arguing with an idiot, try to make sure he isn't doing the same.

Needing someone is like needing a parachute. If they aren't there the first time you need them, chances are you won't be needing them again.

At the end of every party, there is always a girl crying.

Most of us know a good thing as soon as someone else sees it.

One good turn gets most of the blanket.

Old women with mobile phones look wrong.

Always speak well of your enemies – after all, you made them.

Where there's a will, there are plenty of relatives.

Sharpening a pencil with a knife makes you feel macho.

If you want to forget all your troubles, buy a pair of tight shoes.

Triangular sandwiches taste better than square ones.

If a thing's worth doing, it would have been done already.

Never get in a bank queue behind someone wearing a ski mask.

No man is really successful until his mother-in-law admits it.

It's a small world – so you need to use your elbows a lot.

Don't hate yourself in the morning – sleep till noon.

You never know where to look while eating a banana.

Don't kick a man when he's down unless you can be absolutely certain that he won't get up.

If flattery gets you nowhere, try bribery.

Intelligence has much less practical application than you think.

It's impossible to describe the smell of a wet cat.

All things are possible, except skiing through a revolving door.

Rummaging in an overgrown garden will always turn up a bouncy ball.

Always keep your words soft and sweet – in case you have to eat them.

As you journey through life, take a moment every now and then to think about others – they could be plotting something.

Knowledge is knowing a tomato is a fruit; wisdom is not putting it in a fruit salad.

Women

Two elderly widows, Rhoda and Norma, were curious about the latest arrival in their apartment block. He was a quiet, distinguished gentleman who seemed to believe in keeping himself to himself.

One day Rhoda said: 'Norma, you know how shy I am and you're so much more confident in these matters. Why don't you ambush him at the pool and find out a little more about him? He looks so lonely.'

So Norma went over to talk to the man as he sat by the pool. 'My friend and I were wondering why you look so lonely,' she said.

'Of course I'm lonely,' he snapped. 'I've spent the last 30 years in prison.'

'Oh, why?'

'I strangled my third wife.'

'Oh. What happened to your second wife?'

'I shot her.'

'And what about your first wife?'

'We had a fight and she fell off a high building.'

'Oh my!' Then Norma turned to her friend on the other side of the pool and called out: 'Yoo hoo, Rhoda! It's OK. He's single!'

Things You'll Never Hear a Woman Say To Another Woman:
1. His new girlfriend is thinner and prettier than me, and I'm happy for them both.
2. He earned more than I do, so I broke up with him.
3. Oh look, that woman is wearing the same dress as me! I think I'll go and introduce myself.
4. That swimsuit really flatters your figure. Would you mind keeping my husband company while I go for a swim?
5. If he doesn't let me hold the remote, I get all moody.
6. I'm sick of dating doctors and lawyers. Give me a good old-fashioned waiter with a heart of gold any day.
7. We're redecorating the bedroom, and he keeps bugging me to help him with the colour scheme.
8. I just realised: my butt doesn't look fat in this – my butt is fat!
9. He talks our relationship to death! It's driving me crazy!
10. Why can't I find a guy who just wants a one-night stand?

A man was walking through the woods when he stumbled across a lamp. In time-honoured tradition, he picked it up, rubbed it, and out popped a genie who granted him three wishes.

'I'd like a million dollars,' said the man. And POOF! A million dollars appeared.

'And what is your second wish?' asked the genie.

'I'd like a new Ferrari,' said the man. And POOF! A gleaming new Ferrari suddenly appeared.

'And for your third wish?'

'I'd like to be irresistible to women.'

And POOF! He was turned into a box of chocolates.

What do you call a woman with a screwdriver in one hand, a knife in the other, a pair of scissors between the toes on her left foot, and a corkscrew between the toes on her right foot? – A Swiss Army wife.

Things Women Can't Do:
1. Know anything about a car except its colour.
2. Understand a movie plot.
3. Go 24 hours without sending a text message.
4. Lift.
5. Throw.
6. Park.
7. Read a map.
8. Rob a bank.
9. Resist Ikea.
10. Sit still.
11. Argue without shouting.
12. Get told off without bursting into tears.
13. Tell a joke.
14. Play pool.
15. Understand fruit machines.
16. Eat a kebab whilst walking.
17. Pee out of a train window.
18. Do magic tricks.
19. Get to the point.
20. Buy plain envelopes.
21. Take less than 20 minutes in the toilet.
22. Sit in a room for five minutes without saying 'I'm cold.'
23. Go shopping without phoning half a dozen friends.
24. Walk past a shoe shop.
25. Walk past a jeweller's.
26. Not comment on a stranger's clothes.
27. Assemble furniture.
28. Set a video recorder.
29. Not try and change you.
30. Buy a purse that fits in their pocket.
31. Make a decent bacon sandwich.
32. Understand why flirting can be dangerous.
33. Dive into a swimming pool.
34. Use small amounts of toilet paper.
35. Let you sleep with a hangover.
36. Drink a pint gracefully.
37. Go to the toilet in a nightclub by themselves.
38. Get a round of drinks in.
39. Throw a punch.
40. Get this far without having argued with at least one of the above.

God said: 'What's the matter, Adam? You look so miserable all the time.'
    Adam said: 'I'm bored having nobody to talk to.'

'Right,' said God, 'I'm going to give you a companion. She will be called a woman. This person will gather food for you, cook for you, and when you discover clothing, she'll wash it for you. She will always agree with whatever you say. She will bear your children and never ask you to get up in the middle of the night to take care of them. She will not nag you and will always be the first to admit she was wrong when you've had a disagreement. She will never have a headache and will freely give you love and passion whenever you need it.'

'She sounds great,' said Adam. 'But what will a woman like this cost?'

'An arm and a leg,' said God.

Adam thought for a moment. 'What can I get for a rib?'

The rest is history . . .

There are two theories to arguing with women. Neither one works.

Female version:

First Woman: Oh, you got a haircut! That's so cute!

Second Woman: Do you think so? I wasn't sure when she gave me the mirror. I mean, you don't think it's too fluffy-looking?

First Woman: Oh God, no! No, it's perfect. I'd love to get my hair cut like that, but I think my face is too wide. I'm pretty much stuck with it how it is, I think.

Second Woman: Are you serious? I think your face is adorable. And you could easily get one of those layer cuts – that would really suit you. I was going to do that except that I was afraid it would accentuate my long neck.

First Woman: What's wrong with your neck? I would love to have a neck like yours: anything to take attention away from my awful shoulder line.

Second Woman: Are you kidding? I know girls that would love to have your shoulders. Everything hangs so well on you. You're like a walking fashion catalogue. But look at my arms – see how short they are? If I had your shoulders, I could get clothes to fit me so much easier.

Male version:

First Man: Haircut?

Second Man: Yeah.

Two men were propped up against the bar at the end of a heavy drinking session.

'Tell me,' said one. 'Have you ever gone to bed with a really ugly woman?'

'No,' replied the other. 'But I've woken up with plenty!'

A male charity collector knocked on a woman's front door and asked her if she had any old beer bottles.

She was highly indignant. 'Do I look as if I drink beer?' she snapped.

The collector looked at her and said: 'So, have you got any vinegar bottles?'

What's the best way to get a youthful figure? – Ask a woman her age.

A man was sitting alone in his office one night when a genie popped up out of the filing cabinet and asked: 'And what will your third wish be?'

The man looked at the genie and said: 'Huh? How can I be getting a third wish when I haven't had a first or second wish yet?'

'You have had two wishes already,' maintained the genie, 'but your second wish was for me to put everything back the way it was before you made your first wish. Thus you remember nothing because everything is the way it was before you made any wishes. You now have one wish left.'

'OK,' said the man, 'I don't believe this, but what the heck! I've always wanted to understand women. I'd love to know what's going on inside their heads.'

'Funny,' said the genie as it granted his wish and disappeared forever. 'That was your first wish, too!'

Two men were admiring a famous actress. 'Still,' said one, 'if you take away her fabulous hair, her magnificent breasts, her beautiful eyes, her perfect features, and her stunning figure, what are you left with?'

The other replied: 'My wife.'

A Man's Guide to Womanspeak
She says: 'I can't believe how skinny Liz Hurley has become.'
She means: 'I've put on weight.'

She says: 'You know, a lot of men like girls with fuller figures.'
She means: 'I've put on weight.'

She says: 'You can't trust the dress sizes in shops these days.'
She means: 'I've put on weight.'

She says: 'I like to see you enjoying your food.'
She means: 'Because then you'll be as fat as me.'

She says: 'Go on, it's your birthday – enjoy yourself.'
She means: 'Take me out to dinner.'

She says: 'No pudding for me, but you carry on.'
She means: 'I'll be having half of it.'

She says: 'Thanks for washing the dishes.'
She means: 'I wonder if he's having an affair?'

She says: 'You don't think this outfit's too young for me, do you?'
She means: 'Think very carefully before answering. Your life could depend on it.'

She says: 'It's your decision, dear.'
She means: 'Provided I agree with it.'

She says: 'He wasn't a real boyfriend – I didn't like him that much anyway.'
She means: 'He dumped me.'

She says: 'I'm just not ready for a relationship.'
She means: 'Not with you.'

She says: 'You're more like a brother to me.'
She means: 'I find you physically repellent.'

She says: 'I haven't got any secrets from you.'
She means: 'Apart from the ones you haven't found out about yet.'

She says: 'I'll be ready in two minutes.'
She means: 'Give or take an hour.'

After examining a female patient, a doctor took the woman's husband to one side.

'I'll have to be honest with you,' said the doctor ominously, 'but I don't like the look of your wife.'

'Me neither,' said the husband. 'But she's a smashing cook and great with the kids!'

Two women in their sixties – fierce rivals in high society – met at a posh party.

'My dear,' said the first patronisingly, 'are those real pearls?'

'They are.'

'Of course,' continued the first, smiling, 'the only way I could tell would be for me to bite them.'

'Yes,' countered the second, 'but for that, you would need real teeth.'

Work

The managing director was scheduled to speak at an important convention, so he asked Jenkins, one of his employees, to write him a punchy, twenty-minute speech. When the MD returned from the big event, he was livid.

'What's the idea of writing me an hour-long speech?' he raged at Jenkins. 'Half the audience walked out before I was finished.'

Jenkins was baffled. 'I wrote you a twenty-minute speech,' he said. 'I also gave you the two extra copies you asked for.'

Trying to surprise her husband, an executive's wife stopped by his office. She found him with a secretary sitting on his lap.

Without hesitating, he dictated: '. . . and in conclusion, gentlemen, shortage or no shortage, I cannot continue to operate this office with just one chair.'

The boss of a small firm reluctantly told four of his employees: 'I'm going to have to let one of you go.'

The black employee said: 'I'm a protected minority.'

The female employee said: 'And I'm a woman.'

The oldest employee said: 'Fire me, pal, and I'll hit you with an age discrimination suit so fast it'll make your head spin!'

They all turned to look at the young, white, male employee who thought for a moment before saying: 'I think I might be gay . . .'

It was a baking hot day in the office. The temperature was nudging 100 outside and a really foul smell was wafting around the room. As the odour grew more intense, the fourteen-strong workforce began to suffer.

Eventually one man said pointedly: 'Clearly someone's deodorant isn't working.'

A guy in the corner called out: 'Well it can't be me because I'm not wearing any.'

Why is it that the less important you are in a company, the more your absence is noticed?

Having finally run out of patience, the boss called a young employee into his office. 'It has not escaped my attention that every time there's a home game at the stadium, you have to take your aunt to the doctor.'

The employee looked thoughtful and said: 'You know, you're right, sir. I didn't realise. You don't suppose she's faking it, do you?'

Manager: Sorry, I can't give you a job. I don't need much help.

Applicant: That's OK. In fact I'm just the right man for you. You see, I won't be of much help anyway!

On his first day in the office, a young trainee picked up the phone and said: 'Get me a coffee!'

The voice on the other end boomed: 'You idiot, you've dialled the wrong extension! Do you know who you're talking to, you fool?'

'No,' said the trainee.

'This is the managing director!'

'And do you know who you're talking to, you fool?' responded the trainee.

'No.'

'Good.' And the trainee put down the phone.

A clean desk is a sign of a cluttered desk drawer.

A boss collared one of his employees and said: 'I know you were skiving yesterday. You were out playing golf!'

The employee retaliated: 'That's a damn lie, and I have the fish to prove it!'

Signs That You're A Corporate Geek:
- You ask the waiter what the restaurant's core competencies are.
- You decide to rearrange your family into a 'team-based organ-isation'.
- You refer to dating as 'test marketing'.
- You can spell 'paradigm'.
- You actually know what a paradigm is.
- You understand your airline's fare structure.
- You write executive summaries on your love letters.
- You celebrate your wedding anniversary by conducting a perform-ance review.
- You believe you never have any problems in your life, just issues and improvement opportunities.
- You end every argument by saying, 'Let's talk about this offline.'
- You can explain the difference between downsizing, rightsizing, restructuring, and firing people.
- You insist on conducting further market research before you and your spouse produce another child.
- You use the term 'value-added' without laughing.
- You talk to the waiter about process flow when your meal arrives late.
- Your refer to your partner as 'my co-CEO'.
- You start to feel sorry for Dilbert's boss.
- You give constructive feedback to your dog.

- You believe the best tables and graphs take at least an hour to comprehend.
- Your Valentine's Day cards have bullet points.

Boss: Do you think you can handle a variety of work?
Applicant: I ought to be able to. I've had eight different jobs in the past three months.

Three weeks after a young man had been hired by a top hotel, he was called into the personnel manager's office.

The manager said: 'You told us you had two years' experience at the Dorchester, followed by three years at the Ritz, and that you had organised royal banquets. Now we find that your only previous job was serving in McDonald's!'

'Well,' said the young man. 'In your advert you did say you wanted someone with imagination!'

Why is it that when bosses talk about improving productivity, they never mean themselves?

A female worker told her boss she was going home early because she didn't feel well. Since the boss was just recovering from illness himself, he wished her well and said he hoped it wasn't something that he'd given her.

'So do I,' she said. 'I've got morning sickness!'

Doing a job right the first time gets the job done. Doing the job wrong eleven times gives you job security.

A trade union leader was reading his grandson a bedtime story: 'Once upon a time and a half . . .'

Teamwork means never having to take all the blame.

A businessman arrived home exhausted one evening and slumped on the sofa.

'You poor darling, ' said his wife tenderly. 'You must have had a terrible day.'

'You're not kidding,' he replied. 'The computer system crashed and we all had to think for ourselves.'

If work is so terrific, how come they have to pay you to do it?

Negotiations between union members and their employer were at an impasse, the union denying that their workers were flagrantly abusing the sick leave provisions set out by their contract.

Then one morning at the bargaining table, the company's chief negotiator held up a newspaper. 'This man,' he said, 'called in sick yesterday.' There on the sports page was a photo of a supposedly ill employee who had just won a local golf tournament with an excellent score.

Everyone present waited for a response from the union negotiator. After a moment or two he broke the silence by saying: 'Just think of the score he could have made if he hadn't been sick.'

Office advice:

Don't be irreplaceable. If you can't be replaced, you can't be promoted.

If everything's going much better than you expected, it can only mean one thing – you've overlooked something.

Never put off until tomorrow what you can avoid altogether.

There is always one more idiot than you counted on.

You have to get right behind your boss – it's the only way to stab him in the back.

Never be afraid to try something new. Remember, amateurs built the Ark, professionals built the *Titanic*.

Never do today that which will become someone else's responsibility tomorrow.

An employee went to his boss and said: 'Is there any chance I could have tomorrow off? My wife wants me to help clear out the attic and the garage, and then to fix the guttering?'

'I'm sorry,' said the boss. 'You know we're short-staffed. I can't let you have the day off.'

'Thanks, boss,' said the employee. 'I knew I could count on you!'

Two men – Tarquin and Kev – were waiting for a job interview. Tarquin spoke with an educated accent and was immaculately dressed in a smart blazer and an Oxford University tie; Kev had an old jacket, frayed cuffs and greasy hair.

After a few minutes, Tarquin noticed Kev's tie. 'Oh,' he said, 'I see you're wearing an Oxford tie, too.'

'Yeah,' replied Kev.

'I hope you don't take this the wrong way,' continued Tarquin, 'but you don't look like the sort of chap who'd have gone to Oxford.'

'Nah,' said Kev.

'So,' said Tarquin, 'when you were at Oxford? What did you do there?'

'Bought a tie,' said Kev.

Advice for Project Managers:

- It takes one woman nine months to have a baby. It cannot be done in one month by impregnating nine women.
- Nothing is impossible for the person who doesn't have to do it.
- You can fool someone into agreeing to an impossible deadline, but you cannot fool him into meeting it.
- Managing IT people is like herding cats.
- A two-year project will take three years; a three-year project will never finish.
- If you don't know how to do a task, start it, then ten people who know less than you will tell you how to do it.
- The person who says it will take the longest and cost the most is the only one with any idea how to do the job.
- Warning: dates in a calendar are closer than they appear to be.
- What you don't know hurts you.
- A little risk management saves a lot of fan cleaning.
- Anything that can be changed will be changed until there is no time left to change anything.
- If at first you don't succeed, remove all evidence you ever tried.
- Good project management is not so much knowing what to do and when, as knowing what excuses to give and when.
- The good thing about not planning is that failure comes as a complete surprise rather than being preceded by a period of worry and depression.
- If you're six months late on a milestone due next week but really believe you can make it, you're a project manager.

Reviewing a potential employee's application form, the manager of a large retail store noted that the candidate had never previously worked in that field.

'I must say that for a man with no experience, you're certainly asking for a high wage.'

'Well,' replied the applicant, 'the work is so much harder when you don't know what you're doing.'

If a train station is where a train stops and a bus station is where a bus stops, what's a workstation?

After sixteen years with the company, a man was so excited about his promotion to vice president that he bragged about to his wife for weeks on end. She became so fed up with his posturing and preening that she eventually felt obliged to take him down a peg or two.

'Your new title means nothing,' she said. 'It's just for show. These days virtually every organisation has a string of vice presidents. Why, even the grocery store on the corner has a vice president of peas!'

'I don't believe you,' he said. 'You're just jealous. You're making it up.'

'OK then. Go ahead. Phone the store.'

So he rang the corner store and said in mocking tones: 'Can I speak to the vice president of peas?'

'Certainly,' said the operator. 'Dried, tinned or frozen?'

Two men were talking about their jobs. One said: 'The company where I work is installing a computer system and it's going to be putting a lot of people out of work. Have they started that at your place?'

'Oh, we've had computers for three years,' said the other. 'But they can't replace me because nobody has been able to figure out exactly what I do!'

A registered nurse had become disenchanted with her place of work, and so she handed in her notice. Since there was a shortage of nurses in the area, she didn't anticipate any problems in finding another job. She e-mailed cover letters to dozens of potential employers, attaching her CV to each letter. Three weeks later, she was disappointed and bewildered that she had not received even one request for a job interview.

Finally she received a message from a prospective employer that explained why she had not heard from anyone else. It read: 'Your CV was not attached as stated. I do, however, thank you for the vegetable lasagne recipe.'

The boss called one of his employees into the office. 'Michael,' he said, 'you've been with the company for twelve months. You started off in the mailing room. Just one week later you were promoted to a sales position, and one month after that you were promoted to district sales manager. Just four months later, you were promoted to vice president. Now it's time for me to retire, and, despite the fact that you haven't been with us for long, I want you to take over the running of the company. So what do you say to that?

'Thanks,' said the employee.

'Thanks?' replied the boss. 'Is that all you can say?'

'Oh, I'm sorry. Thanks, Dad.'

Why do they call them 'briefings' when they take so long?

A secretary arrived at work late for the third day in a row. The boss summoned her to his office.

'Now look, Samantha. I know we had a fling for a while, but that's over. I expect you to behave like any other employee. Who told you that you could come and go as you please around here?'

238

The secretary replied coolly: 'My lawyer.'

A new young salesman was asked to report to the manager's office. The manager explained: 'We have a critical shortage of typists, and I'd like you to help out. I'll give you a little test. Here, type this.' And with that, the manager handed him a pamphlet to copy and a sheet of paper, and pointed to a desk across the room. On the desk were a typewriter and an adding machine.

Reluctant to become any sort of typist, even a temporary one, the salesman deliberately typed slowly and inaccurately, making as many mistakes as he could. He then handed the sheet of paper back to the manager who gave it little more than a cursory glance before commenting: 'That's fine. Report for work in the typing pool tomorrow.'

'But aren't you going to check the test?' asked the worried salesman.

The manager said: 'You passed the test the moment you sat down at the typewriter instead of the adding machine!'

Genuine comments by candidates at job interviews:
'I know this is off the subject but will you marry me?'
'I am fascinated by fire.'
'Will the company move my rock collection from California to Maryland?'
'People are always watching me.'
'Would it be a problem if I'm angry most of the time?'
'I feel uneasy indoors.'
'What is it that you people do at this company?'
'I get excited very easily.'
'Does your company have a policy regarding concealed weapons?'
'I know who is responsible for most of my troubles.'
'Will the company pay to relocate my horse?'
'Sometimes I feel like smashing things.'
'What is the company motto?'
'Women should not be allowed to drink in cocktail bars.'
'Do you think the company would be willing to lower my pay?'
'Why aren't you in a more interesting business?'
'I have no difficulty in starting or holding my bowel movement.'
'Does your health insurance cover pets?'
'I would have been more successful if nobody had snitched on me.'
'What are the zodiac signs of all the board members?'
'Why do you want references?'
'At times I have the strong urge to do something harmful or shocking.'
'Do I have to dress for the next interview?'
'Why am I here?'
'I think I'm going to throw up.'

A salesman called into an office to see a business customer, but found there was nobody about except for a large dog emptying the waste paper baskets. The salesman stared at the animal, wondering if his mind was playing tricks on him.

Eventually the dog looked up and said: 'Don't be surprised. This is part of my job.'

'This is incredible!' exclaimed the salesman. 'Does your boss know what a gem he has with you? A dog that can talk!'

'Please don't tell him I can talk,' said the dog. 'He'll have me answering the phones as well!'

At a job interview, an office manager asked a female applicant whether she had any unusual talents. She said that she had won several prizes in crossword puzzle and slogan-writing competitions.

'That's very good,' said the manager, 'but we want somebody who can be smart during office hours.'

'Oh,' said the applicant. 'That was during office hours.'

Why is Christmas like a day at the office? – You do all the work and a fat guy in a suit gets all the credit.

A man walked into the human resources department of a large company and handed in his job application. As the executive scanned the CV, he noticed that the applicant had been fired from every post he had ever held.

'I have to say,' remarked the executive, 'your work history is terrible. You've been fired from every job.'

'Yes,' agreed the man.

'Well, I'm afraid it's not very impressive. Can you name one positive aspect to such a dismal employment record?'

'Yes. At least it shows I'm not a quitter!'

Why is that your boss calls all your ideas lousy until his boss has the same idea?

A company security guard was told by his bosses to find some method of preventing employees using the side door of the factory. So he put up a sign saying 'Please do not use this door' but everyone ignored it. Then he erected a sign that read 'Using this door will activate an alarm' but still everybody ignored it and carried on using that door. Next he put up a sign saying 'Anyone using this door will be subject to a $50 fine' but still the workforce ignored it. In desperation he hired an artist to draw a picture of a vicious-looking Alsatian and pinned up a 'Beware of the dog sign' above the door but still employees walked in and out of the door as they pleased.

Just when he was about to admit defeat, he had a brainwave and put up a new sign on the door. From the moment the notice appeared, not one worker used that side door again. The sign read simply 'Wet paint'.

Comments from actual job resumes:
- 'Here are my qualifications for you to overlook.'
- 'I'm married with nine children. I don't require prescription drugs.'
- 'I am extremely loyal to my present firm, so please don't let them know of my immediate availability.'
- 'I am a man filled with passion and integrity, and I can act on short notice. I'm a class act and do not come cheap.'
- 'I intentionally omitted my salary history. I've made money and lost money. I've been rich and I've been poor. I prefer being rich.'
- 'Please don't misconstrue my 14 jobs as "job-hopping". I have never quit a job.'
- 'Number of dependents: 40.'
- 'Marital Status: Often. Children: Various.'
- 'I have minor allergies to house cats and Mongolian sheep.'
- 'I was proud to win the Gregg Typting Award.'
- 'Work Experience: Dealing with customers' conflicts that arouse.'
- 'Develop and recommend an annual operating expense fudget.'
- 'I'm a rabid typist.'
- 'Instrumental in ruining entire operation for a Midwest chain operation.'

Reasons for leaving last job:
- 'Responsibility makes me nervous.'
- 'Was met with a string of broken promises and lies, as well as cockroaches.'
- 'I was working for my mom until she decided to move.'
- 'They insisted that all employees get to work by 8.45 every morning. Couldn't work under those conditions.'
- 'The company made me a scapegoat – just like my three previous employers.'

A situations vacant ad called for an experienced lumberjack and at the job interview the applicant was asked to describe his experience.

'I've worked in the Sahara Forest,' he said.

The personnel manager looked puzzled. 'You mean the Sahara Desert?'

'Sure, that's what they call it now!'

A boss was laying down the law to one of his employees for being late yet again.

'Do you know when we start work in this office?' he said.

'No,' replied the employee. 'They're usually hard at it by the time I get here.'

A shop steward stood up before the gathering of the workforce to announce the results of protracted negotiations with the employers. 'From next week,' he told his members triumphantly, 'your wages will increase by sixty per cent, you will each get a company house and car, and you will only have to work on Wednesdays.'

'What!' came a cry from the back of the hall. 'Every bloody Wednesday?'

At a job interview, the employer was weighing up the applicant's potential.

'You see,' said the employer, 'in this job we need someone who is responsible.'

'Then I'm your man,' replied the applicant eagerly. 'At my last job, whenever anything went wrong, they said I was responsible.'

Company executives recount genuine occurrences during job interviews:
- A job applicant challenged the interviewer to arm wrestling.
- Interviewee wore a Walkman, explaining that she could listen to the interviewer and music at the same time.
- Candidate said he never finished high school because he was kidnapped and kept in a closet in Mexico.
- Balding candidate excused himself and returned to the office a few minutes later wearing a hairpiece.
- Applicant interrupted interview to phone her therapist for advice on how to answer specific interview questions.
- Candidate brought large dog to interview.
- Applicant said if he were hired he would demonstrate his loyalty by having the corporate logo tattooed on his forearm.
- Candidate fell and broke arm during interview.
- Candidate announced she hadn't had lunch and proceeded to eat a burger and fries in the interviewer's office.
- Applicant refused to sit down and insisted on being interviewed standing up.
- Candidate explained that her long-term goal was to replace the interviewer.
- Candidate fell asleep during interview.

A

Accident
Did you hear about the millionaire who had a bad accident? He fell off his wallet.

Actor
Why was the actor pleased to be on the gallows? Because at last he was in the noose.

What's the definition of a good actor? Somebody who tries hard to be everybody but himself.

Neighbor: 'Haven't I seen you on TV?' Actor: 'Well, I do appear, on and off, you know. How do you like me?' Neighbor: 'Off.'

Advice
Take my advice, I don't use it anyway.

Age
Teacher: 'That's an excellent essay for someone your age.' Girl: 'How about for someone my Mom's age?'

Age is a very high price to pay for maturity.

Alarm clock
Alarm clock: a small, mechanical device to wake up people without children.

Algebra
What do you mean, my spelling isn't much good – that's my algebra.

Aliens
How did the aliens hurt the farmer? They trod on his corn.

American
Why are American schoolchildren extremely healthy? Because they have a good constitution.

Angel
An angel in heaven was welcoming a new arrival. 'How did you get here?' he asked. And the new angel replied, 'Flu'.

Animal

I think animal testing is a bad idea. They get nervous and give the wrong answers.

Ant

Why did the ant elope? Nobody gnu.

What's worse than ants in your pants? A bat in your bra.

If ants are such busy insects, how come they find the time to turn up to picnics?

How many ants are needed to fill an apartment? Tenants.

Two ants were watching a useless golfer swing wildly. One said to the other, 'Come on, lets get on the ball before he hits us.'

Apartment

'The walls in my apartment are very thin,' a young girl complained to her friend. 'You mean you can hear everything that's going on next door?' 'Not just that, when they peel onions I start to cry!'

Appearance

Beautician: 'Did that mud pack I gave you for your wife improve her appearance?' Man: 'It did for a while – then it fell off.'

Father: 'Jennifer, I've had a letter from your teacher. It seems you've been neglecting your appearance.' Jennifer: 'Dad?' Father: 'He says you haven't appeared in school all week.'

Appetite

'Don't eat the biscuits so fast – they'll keep.' 'I know, but I want to eat as many as I can before I lose my appetite.'

Apple

Why didn't the two worms go into Noah's ark in an apple? Because all the animals had to go in pears.

'Waiter, why is my apple pie all mashed up?' 'You did ask me to step on it, sir.'

Armor

If a long dress is evening wear, is a suit of armor silverware?

244

Army

Mom: 'Jimmy, where are you off to now?' Jimmy: 'I'm going to join the army.' Mom: 'But legally you're only an infant.' Jimmy: 'That's all right. I'm going to join the infantry.'

Why did the python go to the army? He was coiled up.

Art

Why are art galleries like retirement homes for teachers? Because they're both full of old masters.

'I asked you to draw a pony and trap,' said the art teacher, 'You've only drawn the pony. Why?' 'Well, I thought the pony would draw the trap.'

The old teacher was taking a class round an art gallery. She stopped in front of one exhibit and sneered at the guide, 'I suppose that's some kind of modern art?' 'No, madam,' replied the guide, 'I'm afraid it's a mirror.'

Model: 'That painting you did of me doesn't do me justice.' Artist: 'It's not justice you want, it's mercy!'

Art teacher: 'What color would you paint the sun and the wind?' Nicholas: 'The sun rose, and the wind blue.'

Astronaut

What did the astronaut say to the author? I took your book into orbit and I couldn't put it down.

Atheism

Atheism is a non-prophet organization.

Aunt

A stern aunt had been staying with Chelsey's parents, and one day she said to the little girl, 'Well, Chelsey, I'm going tomorrow. Are you sorry?' 'Oh yes Auntie,' replied Chelsey, 'I thought you were going today.'

Australian

Did you hear about the stupid Australian who received a new boomerang for his birthday? He spent two days trying to throw the old one away.

B

Baby

'Dad, can I have another glass of water please?' 'But that's the tenth one I've given you tonight!' 'Yes, but the baby's room is still on fire'.

Do you like my new baby sister? The stork brought her. 'Hmm, it looks as if the stork dropped her on her head.'

Baby-sitter

A baby-sitter is a teenager acting like an adult while the adults are out acting like teenagers.

Bald

'Doctor, can you give me something for my baldness?' 'How about a few pounds of pig manure?' 'Will that cure my baldness?' 'No, but with that on your head no one will come near enough to notice that you're bald.'

Ballet

'Ann', said the dance instructor, 'There are two things stopping you becoming the world's greatest ballerina?' What are they?' asked Ann. 'Your feet.'

Banana

Time flies like an arrow, but fruit flies like a banana.

'Here's a banana if you can spell it.' 'I can spell banana. I just don't know when to stop.

If a crocodile makes shoes, what does a banana make? Slippers.

Bar

What did the termite say in the saloon? 'Is the bar tender here?'

Father: 'There are 54 bars in this town and I'm proud to say that I've never been in one of them.' Mother: 'Which one is that?'

A man with a newt on his shoulder walked into a bar. 'What do you call him?' asked the bartender. 'Tiny', said the man. 'Why do you call him Tiny?' 'Because he's my newt!'

A man walked into a bar holding a cow pat in his hand. 'Look, everyone!' he cried. 'See what I almost stood on!'

246

Two peanuts walk into a bar. One was a salted.

Two guys walked into a bar. The third one ducked.

Barbie
If Barbie is so popular, why do you have to buy her friends?

Bargain
A bargain is something you don't need at a price you can't resist.

Bark
Teacher: 'Mason, what is the outer part of a tree called?' Mason: 'I don't know.' Teacher: 'Bark, boy, bark!' Mason: 'Woof, woof!'

Bat
'Doctor, I keep dreaming of bats, creepy-crawlies, demons, ghosts, monsters, vampires, werewolves, and yetis.' Doctor: 'How interesting. Do you always dream in alphabetical order?'

What do you get if a huge hairy monster steps on Batman and Robin? Flatman and Ribbon.

Bath
What's the difference between a Peeping Tom and someone who's just got out of the bath? One is rude and nosey, the other is nude and rosey.

'What's the matter?' one man asked another. 'My wife left me when I was in the bath last night,' sobbed the second man. 'She must have been waiting for years for the chance,' replied the first.

Hotel guest: 'Can you give me a room and a bath, please?' Receptionist: 'I can give you a room, but you'll have to bath yourself.'

'But she's so young to get married,' sobbed Diana's mother. 'Only seventeen!' 'Try not to cry about it,' said her husband soothingly. 'Think of it not as losing a daughter but as gaining a bathroom.'

'You have to be a good singer in our house.' 'Why's that?' 'There's no lock on the bathroom door.'

Bear
A man in a movie theater notices what looks like a bear sitting next to him. 'Are you a bear?' 'Yes.' 'What are you doing at the movies?' 'Well, I liked the book.'

Grandfather to grandson's teacher: 'Have you ever hunted bear?'
Teacher: 'No, but I've been fishing in shorts.'

Beauty
First woman: 'I went to the beauty parlor yesterday. I was there for three hours.' Second woman: 'Oh, what did you have done?' First woman: 'Nothing, I was just going in for an estimate.'

Chloe: 'I've just come back from the beauty parlour.' Kayla: 'Pity it was closed!'

Emma: 'Joshua told me last night that he'd met the most beautiful girl in the world.' Hannah: 'Oh, dear, I'm so sorry. I thought he was going to marry you.'

Bed
The hotel we stayed in for our holiday offered bed and board, but it was impossible to say which was the bed and which was the board.

Why was the mother kangaroo cross with her children? Because they ate cookies in bed.

Bee
Why did the bee start spouting poetry? He was waxing lyrical.

Boy scout: 'I'm in agony. I've been stung by a bee.' Scout leader: 'Well, we'll put some cream on it.' Boy scout: 'You'll be lucky, it must be miles away by now.'

Beef
Girl: 'We had Auntie Audrey for lunch last Sunday.' Boy: 'Really? We had roast beef.'

Bell
The teacher was furious when Kyle knocked him down with his new bicycle in the playground. 'Don't you know how to ride that yet?' he roared. 'Oh yes!' shouted Kyle over his shoulder. 'It's the bell I can't work yet.'

First mouse: 'I've trained that crazy science teacher at last.' Second mouse: 'How have you done that?' First mouse: 'I don't know how, but every time I run through that maze and ring the bell, he gives me a piece of cheese.'

Bicycle

'My dog is a nuisance. He chases everyone on a bicycle. What can I do?'
'Take his bike away.'

A bicycle can't stand on its own because it's two-tired.

Bikini

Brooke's mother said no young man in his right mind would take her to the prom in her bikini, so she decided to go with her friend's stupid brother.

Bird

The early bird gets the worm, but the second mouse gets the cheese.

What's the difference between a fly and a bird? A bird can fly but a fly can't bird.

Biology Teacher: 'What kinds of birds do we get in captivity?' Natalie: 'Jailbirds!'

Which bird is always out of breath? A puffin.

Did you hear about the village idiot who bought some birdseed? He said he wanted to grow some birds.

Teacher: 'Why do we put a hyphen in bird-cage?' Taylor: 'For a parrot to perch on.'

Birthday

Flash Harry gave his girlfriend a mink stole for his birthday. Well, it may not have been mink, but it's fairly certain it was stole.

A man who forgets his wife's birthday is certain to get something to remember her by.

'Come here, you greedy boy! I'll teach you to eat all your sister's birthday candy.' 'It's okay, Dad, I know how.'

Diplomatic husband to his wife, 'How do you expect me to remember your birthday when you never look any older?'

Bison

Teacher: 'What's the difference between a buffalo and a bison?' Tyler: 'You can't wash your hands in a buffalo.'

249

Bitch
You say I'm a bitch like it's a bad thing.

Black cat
When is it unlucky to see a black cat? When you're a mouse.

Black eye
Dylan: 'How did you manage to get a black eye?' Cody: 'You see that tree over there?' Dylan: 'Yes.' Cody: 'Well, I didn't.'

Father: 'Justin! You mustn't fight! You must learn to give and take!' Justin: 'But I did! I gave him a black eye and took his baseball!'

Blonde
Why are blonde jokes so short? So men can remember them.

Boar
What do you get if you cross a snake with a pig? A boar constrictor.

'We had roast boar for dinner last night.' 'Was it a wild boar?' 'Well, it wasn't very pleased.'

Boat
What happened to the boat that sank in the sea full of piranha fish? It came back with a skeleton crew.

Two fishermen were out in their boat one day when a hand appeared in the ocean. 'What's that?' asked the first fisherman, 'It looks as if someone's drowning!' 'Nonsense!' said the second, 'It was just a little wave.'

Body
Why didn't the skeleton go to the party? He had no body to go with.

Hunter: 'Your body's quite well organised.' Travis: 'How do you mean?' Hunter: 'The weakest part – your brain – is protected by the strongest – your thick skull!'

Bone
'Doctor, I swallowed a bone.' 'Are you choking?' 'No, I'm serious.'

Book
Our librarian is so stupid she thinks that an autobiography is a book about the life story of a car.

Boot

Why don't centipedes play football? Because by the time they've got their boots on it's time to go home.

Why did the cowboy die with his boots on? Because he didn't want to stub his toes when he kicked the bucket.

Bore

You might find my sister a bit dull until you get to know her. When you do you'll discover she's a real bore!

Boxer

What's the difference between a nail and a boxer? One gets knocked in, the other gets knocked out.

Boyfriend

Your sister's boyfriend certainly has staying power. In fact, he never leaves.

My boyfriend has only two faults – everything he says and everything he does!

Brain

'Doctor, how long can one live without a brain?' Doctor: 'That depends. How old are you?'

'Doctor, I'm nervous, this is the first brain operation I've had.' 'Don't worry, it's the first I've performed.'

Brother

'My brother's just opened a shop.' 'Really? How's he doing?' 'Six months. He opened it with a crowbar.'

'So you're distantly related to the family next door, are you?' 'Yes – their dog is our dog's brother.'

Jared: 'My brother wants to work badly.' Alexis: 'As I remember, he usually does.'

My dad once stopped a man ill-treating a donkey. It was a case of brotherly love.

My brother's looking for a wife. Trouble is, he can't find a woman who loves him as much as he loves himself.

Olivia: 'What position does your brother play in the school football team?' Brandon: 'I think he's one of the drawbacks.'

Bucket

How do you keep flies out of the kitchen? Put a bucket of manure in the lounge.

Budget

A budget is just a means of worrying both before and after you spend money.

Bus

A very fat lady got on a crowded bus. 'Is no one going to give me a seat?' she boomed. A very small man stood up and said, 'I'll make a small contribution.'

Business

What happens when business is slow at a medicine factory? You can hear a cough drop.

Why did the donut maker retire? He was fed up with the hole business.

'Why did you leave your last job?' 'Something the boss said.' 'Was he abusive?' 'Not exactly.' 'What did he say, then?' 'You're fired!'

Mom and dad are in the iron and steel business. She does the ironing and he does the stealing.

Butcher

'Mr Butcher, have you got a sheep's head?' 'No, madam, it's just the way I part my hair.'

Butter

Why did the butterfly? Because it saw the milk-float.

'Leah! What did I say I'd do if I found you with your fingers in the butter again?' 'That's funny, Mom.' 'I can't remember either.'

C

Cake

Madison: 'Did you like that cake, Mrs Jones?' Mrs Jones: 'Yes, very much.' Madison: 'That's funny. My mum said you didn't have any taste.'

Mom: 'Sydney, there were two chocolate cakes in the larder yesterday, and now there's only one. Why?' Sydney: 'I don't know. It must have been so dark I didn't see the other one.'

Camel
He's so stupid he thinks Camelot is where Arabs park their camels.

Candy
Strangers have the best candy.

Capitalism
Capitalism can exist in one of two states: welfare and warfare.

Car
What should a teacher take if he's run down? The number of the car that hit him.

What do you call a country where everyone has to drive a red car? A red carnation.

I couldn't repair your brakes so I made your horn louder.

If you lined up all the cars in the world, someone would be stupid enough to try to pass them.

Does a man who runs behind a car get exhausted?

Never lend your car to anyone to whom you have given birth.

Care
Just because I don't care, doesn't mean that I don't understand.

Career
Teacher: 'Who can tell me what an archaeologist is?' Kaylee: 'It's someone whose career is in ruins.'

Cargo
How is it that ships transport 'cargo' and UPS sends 'shipments' by road?

Cartoon
My sister is so dim she thinks that a cartoon is a song you sing in a car.

Cat
Wife: 'Have you put the cat out?' Husband: 'Was he burning again?'

What kind of cat likes to go bowling? An alley cat.

Anything not nailed down is a cat toy.

Do radioactive cats have 18 half-lives?

Celebrity
A celebrity is someone who works hard all his life to become known and then wears dark glasses to avoid being recognized.

Change
Change is inevitable, except from a vending machine.

Cheese
What cheese is made backwards? Edam.

Chemistry
What's the most important thing to remember in Chemistry? Never lick the spoon.

Cheerios
Are Cheerios donut seeds?

Cheese
Poets have been curiously silent on the subject of cheese.

Chicago
What were the Chicago gangster's last words? 'Who put that violin in my violin case?'

Chicken
On which side does a chicken have the most feathers? On the outside.

What do you get if you cross a chicken with a cow? Roost beef.

Christmas
Father: 'Would you like a pocket calculator for Christmas, son?'
Son: 'No thanks, Dad. I know how many pockets I've got.'

Cigarette

A cigarette is a pinch of tobacco, wrapped in paper, with fire at one end, and a fool at the other.

City

A city is a large community where people are lonesome together.

Cold

How do you prevent a Summer cold? Catch it in the Winter.

Coffee

'Doctor, every time I drink a cup of coffee I get a sharp pain in by nose.'
' Have you tried taking the spoon out of the cup?'

Woman: 'If you were my husband I'd poison your coffee.' Man: 'And if you were my wife, I'd drink it.'

Comedian

Did you hear about the comedian who entertained at a werewolves' party? He had them howling in the aisles.

Committee

A committee is a group of people who can do nothing individually, but as a group decide that nothing can be done.

Common sense

Common sense isn't.

Computer

A computer beat me at chess once, but it was no match for me at kick boxing.

A TV can insult your intelligence, but nothing rubs it in like a computer.

How do I set my laser printer on stun?

A printer consists of three main parts: the case, the jammed paper tray, and the blinking red light.

Bad Command or File Name. Good try though.

Hit any user to continue.

Conclusion

A conclusion is simply the place where you got tired of thinking.

Confidence
Confidence: the feeling you have before you understand the situation.

Conversation
I think someone has to be listening for it to be an actual conversation.

Cookie
'Jimmy, how many more times must I tell you to come away from that cookie barrel?' 'No more, mom. It's empty.'

Corn
What has 100 legs and goes in one ear and out the other? A centipede in a corn field

Cornflakes
Two flies were on a cornflakes packet. 'Why are we running so fast?' asked one. 'Because,' said the second, 'it says "tear along the dotted line"!'

Cowboy
Who is in cowboy films and is always broke? Skint Eastwood.

Coyote
What's the difference between a coyote and a flea? One howls on the prairie, and the other prowls on the hairy.

Crime
Even crime wouldn't pay if the government ran it.

The crimes we are about to depict have been specially committed for this program.

Crisis
He who smiles in a crisis has found someone to blame.

Crocodile
What is worse than a crocodile with toothache? A centipede with athlete's foot.

A teacher went into a shoe shop. 'I'd like some crocodile shoes, please,' she said. 'Certainly, Madam,' said the salesgirl. 'How big is your crocodile?'

Cyclops

Why did the Cyclops give up teaching? Because he only had one pupil.

D

Dance

What do ghosts dance to? Soul music.

Dark

What's the speed of dark?

It's always darkest just before the dawn, so if you're going to steal your neighbour's newspaper that's the time to do it.

Dead

How do you know a zombie is tired? He's dead on his feet.

If a skeleton rings your doorbell is he a dead ringer?

Did you hear about the man who left his job at the mortuary? It was a dead-end job.

Did you hear about the two men who were cremated at the same time? It was a dead heat.

Teacher: 'Why are you late, Megan?' Megan: 'I was obeying the sign that says "Children – Dead Slow".'

Teacher: 'If I had ten flies on my desk, and I swatted one, how many flies would be left?' Girl: 'One – the dead one.'

What happens if you get scared half to death twice?

Before you die your life passes before your eyes – it's called living.

Deaf

What do you call a deaf teacher? Anything you like, he can't hear you.

Boy: 'Did you know the most intelligent kid in our class is deaf?' Girl: 'That's unfortunate.' Boy: 'What did you say?'

A man sat on a train chewing gum and staring vacantly into space, when suddenly an old woman sitting opposite said, It's no good you talking to me, young man, I'm stone deaf!

Deer
What's the difference between a deer running away and a small witch? One's a hunted stag and the other's a stunted hag.

Deja fu
Deja fu: the feeling that somehow, somewhere you've been kicked in the head like this before.

Delaware
What did Delaware? Her New Jersey.

Democracy
The theory that the common people know what they want, and deserve to get it, good and hard.

Dentist
Did you hear about the dentist who became a brain surgeon? His drill slipped.

Cameron: 'You said the school dentist would be painless, but he wasn't.' Teacher: 'Did he hurt you?' Cameron: 'No, but he screamed when I bit his finger.'

Deodorant
My uncle spent a fortune on deodorants before he found out that people didn't like him anyway.

Depression
Depression is merely anger without enthusiasm.

Desk
A clean desk is a sign of a cluttered desk drawer.

Diamond
A little thing, a pretty thing, without a top or bottom. What am I? A diamond ring.

Dinosaur
What do you call a dinosaur that destroys everything in its path? Tyrannosaurus wrecks.

Diplomacy
Diplomacy is the art of saying, 'Good doggie . . .' while looking for a bigger stick.

Dirty
That boy is so dirty, the only time he washes his ears is when he eats watermelon.

Doctor
'What did the doctor say to you yesterday?' asked the teacher. 'He said I was allergic to horses.' 'I've never heard of anyone suffering from that.' 'What's the condition called?' 'Bronco-itis.'

'Doctor, I keep losing my memory.' 'When did you first notice that?' 'When did I first notice what?'

'Doctor, I'm at death's door!' 'Don't worry, Mrs Jenkins. An operation will soon pull you through.'

Never go to a doctor whose pot plants have died.

Dog
Teacher: 'Who can tell me what "dogma" means?' Dustin: 'It's a lady dog that's had puppies.'

Mother: 'Keep that dog out of the house, it's full of fleas.' Son: 'Keep out of the house, Lassie, it's full of fleas.'

Jacob: 'Our dog is just like one of the family.' Joseph: 'Which one?'

What dog smells of onions? A hot dog.

'My dog plays chess.' 'Your dog plays chess? He must be really clever!' 'Oh, I don't know. I usually beat him three times out of four.'

'Why are you crying, little boy?' 'We've just had to have our dog put down!' 'Was he mad?' asked the old lady. 'Well, he wasn't too happy about it.'

James: 'That ointment the vet gave me for the dog makes my fingers smart.' Jonathan: 'Why don't you rub some on your head then?'

A dog in the audience of a flea circus is likely to steal the show.

My goal in life is to be the kind of person my dog thinks I am.

Doll

Teacher: 'Why are you crying, Kylie?' Katelyn: 'Haley broke my new doll.' 'How did she do that?' 'I hit her on the head with it.'

Dollar

'I'll lend you a dollar if you promise not to keep it too long.' 'Oh, I won't. I'll spend it right away.'

'Why did you leave your last employment?' 'The boss accused me of stealing a five dollar bill.' 'But why didn't you make him prove it?' 'He did.'

I wish the buck stopped here. I could use one.

Door

'Mom! There's a man at the door collecting for the Old Folks' Home. Shall I give him Grandma?'

A tramp knocked at a door and asked a woman for some food. 'Didn't I give you some pie a week ago?' asked the woman. 'Yes,' said the tramp, 'but I'm all right again now.'

Caleb: 'Dad, there's a man at the door collecting for the new swimming pool.' Dad: 'Give him a glass of water!'

Dress

'Yes, I do like your dress – but isn't it a little early for Halloween?'

How do teachers dress in mid-January? Quickly.

Driver

Why did the stupid racing driver make ten pit stops during the Grand Prix? He was asking for directions.

'Take the wheel!' said the nervous learner to his driving instructor, 'There's a tree coming straight for us!'

If everything is coming your way, you're probably in the wrong lane.

Drive carefully, it's not only cars that can be recalled by their maker.

I drive way too fast to worry about cholesterol.

You only really learn to swear when you learn to drive.

Duchess
'Have you ever seen a duchess?' 'Yes, it's the same as an English "s"!'

Dyslexia
A dyslexic agnostic doesn't believe in Dog.

E

Eagle
What do you get if you cross an eagle with a skunk? A bird that stinks to high heaven.

Eagles may soar, but weasels don't get sucked into jet engines.

Earth
What did one worm say to another when he was late home? Why in earth are you late.

What did ET's mother say to him when he got home? Where on Earth have you been?

Easter
'I like your Easter tie.' 'Why do you call it my Easter tie?' 'It's got egg on it.'

Why does the Easter Bunny have a shiny nose? His powder puff is on the wrong end.

Eel
Why did the slippery eel blush? Because the sea weed.

Egg
'How can you drop an egg six feet without breaking it?' 'By dropping it seven feet – it won't break for the first six.'

What happens if you play table-tennis with a bad egg? First it goes ping, then it goes pong.

Electric
What do you get if you cross a bottle of water with an electric eel? A bit of a shock really!

Elephant
What do you get if you cross an elephant with some locusts? I'm not sure, but if they ever swarm – watch out!

What did the grape do when the elephant sat on it? It let out a little wine.

Engagement
Claire had broken off her engagement. Leah asked her what had happened. 'I thought it was love at first sight,' said Leah. 'It was, but it was the second and third sights that changed my mind.'

Evil
When choosing between two evils I always like to try the one I've never tried before.

Exam
Student: 'Excuse me, but I don' t think I deserve a mark of 0 for this exam paper.' Teacher: 'Neither do I, but it's the lowest mark I can give.'

Teacher: 'In this exam you will be allowed ten minutes for each question.' Boy: 'How long is each answer?'

Eyes
Caleb: 'That pretty girl over there just rolled her eyes at me.' Tristan: 'Well you'd better roll them back to her, she might need them.'

What has four eyes and a mouth? The Mississippi.

Why did the two cyclops' fight? They could never see eye to eye over anything.

F

Face
Jared: 'You have the face of a saint.' Tyler: 'Really? Which one?' Jared: 'A Saint Bernard.'

Ashley: 'I have the face of a 16-year-old girl.' Jessica: 'Well, you'd better give it back, you're making it all wrinkly.'

Mason: 'You've got a Roman nose.' Dalton: 'Like Julius Caesar?' Mason: 'No, it's roamin' all over your face.'

'How did your mom know you hadn't washed your face?' 'I forgot to wet the soap.'

I never forget a face, but in your case I'll make an exception.

Two old friends met, ten years after the end of the Second World War. One said, 'Is that your face or are you still wearing your gas mask?'

Patient: 'The trouble is, doctor, I keep pulling ugly faces.' Doctor: 'Don't worry, I don't expect anyone will notice.'

You can read his mind in his face. 'Yes, it's usually a complete blank.'

The last time I saw a face like yours I threw it a banana.

Faith
Faith is not faith until it's all you're holding onto.

Fall
It's not the fall that kills you, it's the sudden stop at the end.

False teeth
What did the vampire call his false teeth? A new-fangled device.

Why did the old lady cover her mouth with her hands when she sneezed? To catch her false teeth.

Knock, knock. Who's there? Dishes. Dishes who? Dishes the way I talk now I've got false teeth.

Family
Girl: 'Do you now what family the octopus belongs to?' Boy: 'No one in our street.'

Kyle: 'Our family's descended from royalty.' Lily: 'Who? King Kong?'

Jack: 'I can trace my family tree way back.' Kaylee: 'Yes, back to the time you lived in it!'

Farmer
What did the neurotic pig say to the farmer? 'You take me for grunted.'

Fat

Did you hear about the two fat men who ran in the New York Marathon? One ran in short bursts, the other in burst shorts!

What's the difference between a square peg in a round hole and a pound of lard? One's a fat lot of good and the other's a good lot of fat!

What did the speak-your-weight machine say when the fat lady stepped on? 'One at a time, please.'

New wife: 'Will you love me when I'm old and fat and ugly?' New husband: 'Of course I do!'

Father

A father is someone who carries photographs where his money used to be.

Did you hear about the very well behaved little boy? When he was good his father would give him a cent and a pat on the head. By the time he was sixteen he had $25 and a totally flat head.

'Nathaniel,' groaned his father when he saw his son's school report, 'Why are you so awful at geography?' 'It's the teacher's fault, Dad. He keeps telling us about places I've never heard of.'

One day Joshua's mother turned to Joshua's father and said, 'It's such a nice day, I think I'll take Joshua to the zoo.' 'I wouldn't bother,' said father, 'If they want him, let them come and get him.'

Justin's father called up to him: 'Justin, if you don't stop playing that trumpet I think I'll go crazy.' 'I think you are already,' replied Justin, 'I stopped playing half an hour ago.'

Logan: 'I must rush home and cut the lawn.' Teacher: 'Did your father promise you something if you cut it?' Logan: 'No, he promised me something if didn't!'

Mom: 'Marcus, go outside and play with your whistle. Your father can't read his paper.' Marcus: 'But I'm only eight, and I can read it!'

A boy had been spanked by his father one morning. When his dad came in from the office that evening, the boy called out sulkily, 'Mom! Your husband's just come home.'

Mother: 'What did your father say about your report?' Girl: 'Well, if you want me to cut out the swear words, he didn't really say anything.'

Feet
What do you get when you cross a stream and a brook? Wet feet.

'Can you stand on your head?' 'I've tried, but I can't get my feet up high enough.'

Blake: 'Do you have holes in your underpants?' Teacher: 'No, of course not.' Blake: 'Then how do you get your feet through?'

'Doctor, I can't stand being three feet tall any longer.' 'Then you'll just have to learn to be a little patient.'

'Brooke, pick up your feet when you walk.' 'What for, mom? I've only got to put them down again.'

If a dog is tied to a rope 15 feet long, how can it reach a bone 30 feet away? The rope isn't tied to anything!

Female
Is a myth a female moth?

My sister is so dumb, she thinks that a buttress is a female goat.

Fence
Did you hear that in the recent gales the fence blew down around the nudist camp? A group of builders is looking into it.

Fight
What do you do when two snails have a fight? Leave them to slug it out.

'Waiter, this lobster's only got one claw.' 'It must have been in a fight, sir.' 'Then bring me the winner.'

'Nathan, you've been fighting again, haven't you?' 'Yes, Mom.' 'You must try to control your temper. Didn't I tell you to count to ten?' 'Yes, but Jack's mom only told him to count up to five, so he hit me first!'

Remember, always pillage before you burn.

If you can't beat them, arrange to have them beaten.

Firefly

Why did the firefly keep stealing things? He was light-fingered.

What goes 'snap, crackle, pop'? A firefly with a short circuit.

A little firefly was in school one day and he put up his hand. 'Please may I be excused?' 'Yes,' replied the teacher, 'when you've got to glow, you've got to glow.'

What happened to the glowworm who was squashed? He was de-lighted.

First

Patrick: 'Who was the fastest runner in history?' Sam: Adam. 'He was first in the human race.'

The first commandment was when Eve told Adam to eat the apple.

I just want you to remember one thing, Michael, said the managing director to the new sales manager. If at first you don't succeed – you're fired!

Fish

Teacher: 'Mia, put some more water in the fish tank.' Mia: 'But they haven't drunk the water I gave them yesterday.'

What fish do dogs chase? Catfish.

What do you call a fish with no eyes? A fsh.

Fishing

A first man fishing is joined by a second. 'Have you had any bites?' asked the newcomer. 'Yes, lots,' replied the first man, 'but they were all mosquitoes.'

Passer-by to fisherman: 'Is this river any good for fish?' Fisherman: 'It must be. I can't get any of them to leave it.'

Fisherman: 'What are you fishing for?' Boy: 'I'm not fishing, I'm drowning worms.'

Just before the Ark set sail, Noah saw his two sons fishing over the side. 'Go easy on the bait,' he said, 'Remember I've only got two worms.'

Flagpole

A man was given the job of painting a flagpole but he didn't know how much paint he would need. Lay it down and measure it, suggested a friend. That's no good, said the man, I need to know the height, not the length.

Flea

First cat: 'Where do fleas go in winter?' Second cat: 'Search me!'

Two fleas were sitting on Robinson Crusoe's back. One hopped off saying, 'Bye! See you on Friday!'

Two fleas went to the cinema. When they came out, one said to the other, 'Shall we walk or take a dog?'

Flies

If there are five flies in the kitchen, which one is the football player? The one in the sugar bowl.

'Waiter, I don't like all these flies in this dining room!' 'Tell me which ones you don't like and I'll chase them out for you.'

Visitor: 'You have a lot of flies buzzing round your horses and cows. Do you ever shoo them?' Rancher: 'No we just let them go barefoot.'

Floor

Waiter, you have your thumb on my steak! I know sir, I don't want it to fall on the floor again!

Florist

Did you hear about the florist who had two children? One's a budding genius and the other's a blooming idiot.

Flower

Why did the headmaster stop wearing a flower in his buttonhole? He got tired of the pot hitting his chest.

Fly

Waiter! There's a fly in my soup! Yes, sir, he's committed insecticide.

Waiter! There's a fly in my soup. Yes, madam, it's the bad meat that attracts them.

Waiter! There's a fly in my soup. Not fussy what they eat, are they, sir?

Waiter! There's a fly in my soup! Just wait until you see the main course.

Waiter! What's this fly doing in my ice cream? Maybe he likes winter sports.

Flying
What's the best way to see flying saucers? Pinch the waitress.

Food
Waiter, this food isn't fit for a pig! All right, I'll get you some that is.

Patrick and Alan took their lunches to the local cafe to eat. 'Hey!' shouted the proprietor, 'You can't eat your own food in here!' 'Okay,' said Patrick. So he and Alan swapped their sandwiches.

Fool
Nothing is foolproof to a sufficiently talented fool.

Football
Michael: 'My girlfriend and I fell out last night. She wanted to go and watch ice-skating, but I wanted to go to the football match.' Nicholas: 'What was the ice-skating like?'

Football combines the two worst things in American life. It is violence punctuated by committee meetings.

Fork
I wonder where I got that puncture? Maybe it was at that last fork in the road.

Fortune cookie
I got a fortune cookie once that said, 'You like Chinese food'.

Fortune telling
'Five dollars for one question!' said the woman to the fortune teller, 'That's very expensive, isn't it?' 'Yes. Next!'

Music teacher: 'Do you like opera, Rachel?' Rachel: 'Apart from the singing, yes.'

Frankenstein's monster
What did one of Frankenstein's monster's ears say to the other? I didn't know we lived on the same block.

Why did Dr Frankenstein have his telephone cut off? Because he wanted to win the Nobel prize!

What did Frankenstein's monster say when he was struck by lightning? Thanks, I needed that.

Freezer
A customer in a supermarket was leaning over the freezer looking for some frozen chips when ten fish fingers crept up and pulled him in.

French
Is a guillotine a French chopping center?

Friend
My friend is so stupid that he thinks twice before saying nothing.

My friend is so stupid he thinks that an autograph is a chart showing sales figures for cars.

A friend in need is . . . someone to avoid!

I was the next door kid's imaginary friend.

Friends may come and go, but enemies accumulate.

Frog
When is a car like a frog? When it's being toad.

What kind of shoes do frogs like? Open toad sandals.

What do you call a girl with a frog on her head? Lily.

A woman walked into a pet shop and said, 'I'd like a frog for my son.' 'I'm sorry, madam,' said the shopkeeper, 'We don't do part exchange.'

Fruit
Why is history like a fruit cake? Because it's full of dates.

First boy: 'She has a beautiful pair of eyes, her skin has the glow of a peach, her cheeks are like apples and her lips like cherries – that's my girl.' Second boy: 'Sounds like a fruit salad to me.'

Fur
What's furry, has whiskers and chases outlaws? A posse cat.

Furniture
What's the longest piece of furniture in the school? The multiplication table.

G

Game
What's the very lowest game you can play? Baseball.

Jesse: 'Let's play a game of wits.' Olivia: 'No, let's play something you can play too.'

Gas
What gas do snails prefer? Shell.

General
Where does a general keep his armies? Up his sleevies.

Geography
Michelle was writing a geography essay. It began, 'The people who live in Paris are called parasites . . .'

Mother: 'Did you get a good place in the geography test?' Daughter: 'Yes, Mom, I sat next to the cleverest kid in the class.'

Chloe: 'How come you did so badly in History? I thought you had all the dates written on your sleeve?' Brianna: 'That's the trouble, I put on my geography blouse by mistake.'

Ghost
'This woman wanted to marry a ghost. I can't think what possessed her.'

Ghoul
What keeps ghouls cheerful? The knowledge that every shroud has a silver lining.

Giant
Where do you find giant snails? On the end of a giant's fingers.

Girls
What did one magician say to another? 'Who was that girl I sawed you with last night?'

Two young boys were watching TV when Cameron Diaz appeared on the screen. 'If I ever stop hating girls,' said one to the other, 'I think I'll stop hating her first.'

She's the kind of girl that boys look at twice – they can't believe it the first time.

Glasses
School doctor to parent: 'I'm afraid your daughter needs glasses.' Parent: 'How can you tell?' School doctor: 'By the way she came in through the window.'

Glove
Why do elephants have trunks? Because they don't have glove compartments.

Gossip
She's such a gossip it doesn't take her long to turn an earful into a mouthful.

Grass
Why is grass so dangerous? Because it's full of blades.

Guitar
Sign on the school noticeboard: 'Guitar for sale, cheap, no strings attached'.

H

Hair
Teacher: 'I see you don't cut your hair any longer.' Anthony: 'No, I cut it shorter.'

She's so stupid she thinks hair spray is something you use to get rid of rabbits.

Noah: 'Do you like my new hairstyle?' Luis: 'In as much as it covers most of your face, yes.'

Halloween
What do stupid kids do at Halloween? They carve a face on an apple and go bobbing for pumpkins.

Why was the boy unhappy to win the prize for the best costume at the Halloween party? Because he'd only come to pick up his little sister.

Hamburger
Why did the teacher have her hair in a bun? Because she had her nose in a hamburger.

Hat
My grandad has so many wrinkles he can screw his hat on.

'Does she have something on her mind?' 'Only if she's got a hat on.'

What did the necktie say to the hat? 'You go on ahead. I'll hang around for a while.'

Head
What did the two acrobats say when they got married? 'We're head over heels in love!'

Why does an ostrich have such a long neck? Because its head is so far from its body.

How do you cure a headache? Put your head through a window, and the pane will disappear.

Health
Health is merely the slowest possible rate at which a person can die.

Hell
Where am I going? And why am I in this handbasket?

Help
I'd like to help you out. Which way did you come in?

Hippie
Teacher: 'Who knows what a hippie is?' Zachary: 'Is it something that holds your leggy on?'

History
Samantha: 'I wish I'd been alive a few hundred years ago.' History teacher: 'Why?' Samantha: 'There'd have been a lot less history to learn.'

Hole
Why did the golfer wear an extra pair of trousers? In case he got a hole in one.

Homework
Father: 'Would you like me to help you with your homework?' Son: 'No thanks, I'd rather get it wrong by myself.'

Hospital
'Your pupils must miss you a lot,' said the woman in the next bed to the teacher in hospital. 'Not at all! Their aim's usually good. That's why I'm here.'

A doctor visited his patient in the hospital ward after the operation. 'I've got some bad news – we amputated the wrong leg. Now the good news – the man in the next bed wants to buy your slippers.'

How does a pig go to hospital? In a hambulance.

Hospitality
Hospitality: Making guests feel at home, even when you wish they were.

House
What clothes does a house wear? Address.

Hunting
Two men went duck-hunting with their dogs but without success. 'I know what we're doing wrong,' said the first one. 'What's that then?' said the second. 'We're not throwing the dogs high enough!'

Hypochondriac
What was written on the hypochondriac's tombstone? 'I told you I was ill.'

I

IRS
We've got what it takes to take what you've got.

Idiot
How does an idiot call for his dog? He puts two fingers in his mouth and then shouts, 'Lassie!'.

Did you hear about the idiot who invented the one-piece jigsaw puzzle?

Why did the idiot have his sundial floodlit? So he could tell the time at night.

Did you hear about the idiot who won the Tour de France? He did a lap of honor.

If idiots could fly this place would be an airport.

Ignorance
Nathan: 'They say ignorance is bliss.' Samantha: 'Then you should be the happiest boy in the world.'

Ink
Is an inkling a baby fountain pen?

Insult
Benjamin: 'I didn't come here to be insulted.' Alexis: 'Oh really, where do you usually go?'

Intelligent life
The surest sign that there is intelligent life elsewhere in the Universe is that it has not tried to contact us.

Interview
A teacher was being interviewed for a new job and asked the principal what the hours were. 'We try to have early hours you know. I hope that suits you.' 'Of course,' said the teacher. 'I don't mind how early I leave.'

The headmaster was interviewing a new teacher. 'You'll get $10,000 to start, and $15,000 after six months.' 'Oh!' said the teacher. I'll come back in six months then.'

Island
Why is an island like the letter T? Because the're both in the middle of water.

J

Jack
What do you call a man with a car on his head? Jack.

Journey
A journey of a thousand miles begins with a slow puncture and a broken fan belt.

Jury
Jury: twelve people who determine which client has the better lawyer.

K

Karate
People skilled in karate can, using only their hands and feet, make the worst movies in the world.

Kentucky
Kentucky: five million people, fifteen last names.

Kid
Boy: 'Where does the new kid come from?' Girl: 'Alaska.' Boy: 'Don't bother – I'll ask her myself.'

I like kids, but I don't think I could eat a whole one.

Be nice to your kids – they're the ones who choose your nursing home.

Kleptomania
My friend has kleptomania, but when it gets really bad, he takes something for it.

L

Lace
We're so poor that mum and dad can't afford to buy me shoes. I have to blacken my feet and lace my toes together.

Lady
The garbage men were just about to leave the street when a woman came running out of the house carrying some cardboard boxes. 'Am I too late for the garbage?' she called. 'No, lady,' replied one of the men, 'Jump right in!'

'I'd like a cheap parrot, please,' an old lady said to a pet shop owner. 'This one's cheap and it sings a number of sea shanties.' 'Never mind that,' said the old lady, 'Is it tender?'

Laugh

He who laughs last, thinks slowest.

Laugh and the world laughs with you. Cry and the world laughs harder.

Laws

Laws are like sausages – it's better not to see them getting made.

Cole's Law: thinly sliced cabbage.

Lawyer

What's the difference between a lawyer and a tick? A tick drops off you when you die.

Leg

My uncle must be the meanest man in the world. He recently found a crutch – then he broke his leg so he could use it.

Dad, when I get old will the calves of my legs be cows?

Lego

What do you get if you cross a snake with a Lego set? A boa constructor.

Letter

Which two letters are rotten for your teeth? D K.

Why is the letter 't' so important to a stick insect? Without it it would be a sick insect.

Library

Did you hear about the schoolgirl who was so excited about a book she found in the library called How to Hug? It turned out to be volume eight of an encyclopedia.

Life

We are born naked, poor and hungry. Then things get worse.

You can't win. You can't break even. You can't even quit the game.

Even if you're on the right track, you'll get run over if you just sit there.

Life is like a box of chocolates – too big a box with too few chocolates.

Light

Light travels faster than sound. That's why some people appear bright until they speak.

Lite: the new way to spell 'light', now with 20% fewer letters!

Little

Why was the little bird expelled from school? She was always playing practical yolks.

'Doctor, I've got a little sty.' 'Well, you'd better buy a little pig then.'

'Knock, knock. Who's there?' 'Little old lady.' 'Little old lady who?' 'I didn't know you could yodel.'

Did you hear about the little boy who was named after his father? They called him 'Dad'.

Teacher: 'I wish you'd pay a little attention.' Girl: 'I'm paying as little as possible.'

London

A man telephoned Heathrow Airport in London. 'How long does it take to get to New York?' 'Just a minute.' 'Thanks very much.'

Lonely

Poor old Cameron sent his photograph off to a Lonely Hearts Club. They sent it back saying that they weren't that lonely.

Long

'They're not going to grow bananas any longer.' 'Really? Why not?' 'Because they're long enough already.'

'How old is your Grandad?' 'I don't know, but we've had him a long time.'

'What's wrong with this fish?' 'Long time, no sea.'

Love

Amber: 'Boys whisper they love me.' Jason: 'Well, they wouldn't admit it out loud, would they?'

Lunch
'Why do you keep doing the backstroke?' 'I've just had lunch and don't want to swim on a full stomach.'

M

Magic
What do you get if you cross two snakes with a magic spell? Addercadabra and abradacobra.

A magician was driving down the road, then he turned into a driveway.

Marriage
One good turn gets most of the duvet.

A man is incomplete until he is married. Then he is finished.

Marriage isn't a word. It's a sentence.

Masks
'Why do surgeons wear masks in the operating theater?' 'So that if they make a mistake no one will know who did it.'

Math
Mother: 'Do you know a girl named Jenny Simon?' Daughter: 'Yes, she sleeps next to me in math.'

Girl: 'Mom, you know you're always worried about me failing math?' Mother: 'Yes.' Girl: 'Well, your worries are over.'

Medical
My son's just received a scholarship to medical school – but they don't want him while he's alive.

Melting pot
America is a melting pot. The people at the bottom get burned and the scum rises to the top.

Memory
Everyone has a photographic memory, just some of us have no film.

Men

Did you hear about the man with grease stains all over his jacket? He had a chip on his shoulder.

Did you hear about the man who was so stupid that when he picked his nose he tore the lining of his hat?

It is better to have loved a short man than never to have loved at all.

Coffee, chocolate, men . . . some things are just better rich.

Menu

'Waiter, are there snails on the menu?' 'Oh yes, sir, they must have escaped from the kitchen.'

Metaphor

A metaphor is like a simile.

Microsoft

Oxymoron: Microsoft Works.

Milk

Why did the butterfly? Because it saw the milk-float.

What happened at the badly organized milking contest? There was udder chaos.

Money

Money talks, but all mine ever says is goodbye.

Money can't buy you love, but it can rent a very close imitation.

If you think nobody cares about you, try missing a couple of payments.

I don't blame Congress. If I had $600 billion dollars, I'd be careless too.

Monster

A little boy came running into the kitchen. 'Dad, dad,' he said, 'there's a monster at the door with a really ugly face.' 'Tell him you've already got one,' said his father.

Moon

What kind of insects live on the moon? Lunar ticks.

Morning

My dad is rather tired this morning. Last night he dreamed he was working.

A noise woke me up this morning. What was that? The crack of dawn.

Moth

Why did the moth nibble a hole in the carpet? He wanted to see the floor show.

'Knock knock.' 'Who's there?' 'Moth.' 'Moth who?' 'Motht people know the anthwer.'

Mother

What do you call a ghost's mother and father? Transparents.

Dylan is the type of boy that his mother doesn't want him to associate with!

'My mother gets migraine.' 'Probably because her halo's too tight.'

Jacob: 'When my mother was young she had a coming-out party.' Joshua: 'When they saw her they probably sent her back in again.'

Motor

My friend is so stupid he thinks a fjord is a Norwegian motor car.

Movie

Teacher: 'You weren't at school last Friday, Ryan. I heard you were out playing baseball.' Ryan: 'That's not true, and I've got the movie theater tickets to prove it.'

Multiply

Why did some snakes disobey Noah when he told them to 'go forth and multiply'? They couldn't – they were adders.

Mushroom

Which vegetable goes best with jacket potatoes? Button mushrooms.

Music

What kind of music do witches play on the piano? Hagtime.

Why don't skeletons play music in church? They have no organs.

Writing about music is like dancing about architecture.

N

Nervous
What do you call a nervous insect? A jitterbug.

What lies at the bottom of the sea and shivers? A nervous wreck.

Northern
Which is the most dangerous animal in the Northern Hemisphere? Yak the Ripper.

Norse
How did the Vikings communicate with one another? By Norse code.

Nun
What do you get if you cross a nun and a chicken? A pecking order.

Nursery
'Welcome to school, Benjamin,' said the nursery school teacher to the new boy. 'How old are you?' 'I'm not old,' said Benjamin, 'I'm nearly new.'

Nut
The most dangerous part of a car is the nut behind the wheel.

O

Ocean
I wonder how much deeper the ocean would be without sponges.

Octopus
How did the octopus lovers walk down the road? Arm in arm in arm in arm in arm in arm in arm in arm.

What do octopuses play in their spare time? Name that tuna.

Open
Claire: 'I have an open mind.' Michelle: 'Yes, there's nothing in it.'

Opinion
When I want your opinion, I'll give it to you.

Opposite

When can't you bury people who live opposite a graveyard? When they're not dead.

Orange

What do you get if you cross an orange with a comedian? Peels of laughter.

Ox

'Dad, if an ox is a sort of male cow and equine means something to do with horses, then what is an equinox?'

P

Paper

Teacher: 'What happened to your homework?' Boy: 'I made it into a paper plane and someone hijacked it.'

Parrot

What do you get if you cross a centipede and a parrot? A walkie-talkie.

Patient

I'm extraordinarily patient, provided I get my own way in the end.

Peach

Girl: 'My teacher's a peach.' Mother: 'You mean she's sweet.' Girl: 'No, she has a heart of stone.'

Pedestrian

Why did the witch have pedestrian eyes? They looked both ways before they crossed.

Perfume

Nice perfume, but must you marinate in it?

Phone

I see you've burnt your ear. Were you doing the ironing when the phone rang?

Piano

'Do you think, Professor, that my wife should take up the piano as a career?' 'No, I think she should put down the lid as a favor.'

At my piano teacher's last performance the audience cheered and cheered. The piano was locked!

'Waiter, does the pianist play requests?' 'Yes, sir.' 'Then ask him to play tiddlywinks until I've finished my meal.'

Picture
Some people who are the picture of health are just painted that way.

Pirate
What did everyone say about the kind-hearted pirate? That his barque was worse than his bite.

Places
'Doctor, I've broken my arm in two places.' Doctor: 'Well don't go back to those places again.'

'They say he's going places.' 'The sooner the better!'

Plane
Why did the stupid pilot land his plane on a house? Because the landing lights were on.

Two wrongs don't make a right, but two Wrights make a plane.

Play
'Would you like to play with our new dog?' 'He looks very fierce. Does he bite?' 'That's what I want to find out.'

Please
I can only please one person each day. Today is not your day. Tomorrow is not looking good either.

Poison
What's the best thing about deadly snakes? They've got poisonality.

Pole
What kind of pole is short and floppy? A tadpole.

Politically correct
European Economic Community fries.

Positive
I'm going to start thinking positive, but I know it won't work.

Power
Power corrupts, but absolute power is kind of neat.

Prayer
As long as there are tests there will be prayer in public schools.

Price
Maya: 'Do you like my dress? I bought it for a very low price.'
Samantha: 'You mean for a ridiculous figure.'

Teacher: 'I'd like to go through one whole day without having to punish you.' Girl: 'You have my permission.'

Problem
I don't know what your problem is, but I bet it's hard to pronounce.

Procrastination
I always wanted to be a procrastinator, but I never got round to it.

Procrastinate later.

Puratinism
The haunting fear that someone, somewhere may be happy.

Python
'Doctor, I keep thinking I'm a python.' Doctor: 'You can't get round me like that, you know.'

Q

Question
When doing exams Lucas knows all the answers. It's the questions that get him confused.

Questions
Before they invented drawing boards, what did they go back to?

Do infants enjoy infancy as much as adults enjoy adultery?

Why do irons have a setting for permanent press?

How can you tell when sour cream goes bad?

How much sin can I get away with and still go to heaven?

How young can you die of old age?

Can you be arrested for selling illegal-sized paper?

If all the nations in the world are in debt, where did all the money go?

If you try to fail, and succeed, which have you done?

If you steal a clean slate, does it go on your record?

If you were going to shoot a mime, would you use a silencer?

What if there were no hypothetical situations?

Where would we be without rhetorical questions?

Will your answer to this question be no?

Could it be that all those trick-or-treaters wearing sheets are dressing up as mattresses?

If a man is standing in the middle of the forest speaking and there is no woman around to hear him, is he still wrong?

Is there another word for synonym?

Isn't it a bit unnerving that doctors call what they do 'practice?'

Could crop circles be the work of a cereal killer?

Why doesn't Tarzan have a beard?

Do good S&M fans go to Hell?

If swimming's such good exercise, how come whales are so fat?

How do Keep Off The Grass signs get there?

Why don't sheep shrink in the rain?

If a person told you they were a pathological liar, would you believe them?

If pro is the opposite of con, and progress is moving forward, what is Congress?

Why don't you ever see the headline 'Psychic Wins Lottery'?

Why is 'abbreviated' such a long word?

Why is it that to stop Windows 98, you have to click on 'Start'?

Why is lemon juice made with artificial flavor and dishwashing liquid made with real lemons?

Why is the man who invests all your money called a broker?

Why is the time of day with the slowest traffic called rush hour?

Why isn't there mouse-flavored cat food?

When dog food is new and improved tasting, who tests it?

Why didn't Noah swat those two mosquitoes?

Why do they sterilize the needle for lethal injections?

Why are they called apartments when they are all stuck together?

Why can't women put on mascara with their mouth closed?

Why do people with closed minds always open their mouths?

If love is blind, how can we believe in love at first sight?

Why is it that rain drops, but snow falls?

What was the best thing before sliced bread?

If a drug store is open 24 hours, why are there locks on the doors?

If you make a cow laugh, will milk come out its nose?

Why can't Mr Fork and Mr Electrical Socket be friends?

If a tree falls on a mime in the woods, and there's no one there to hear it, does the mime make a sound?

Why doesn't onomatopoeia sound like what it is?

Why is minimalism such a big word?

What would happen if the man took the Advimil and the woman took the Viagra?

Why do ballerinas stand on their toes? Can't they just get taller women?

Do fish get thirsty?

If you learn from mistakes, why aren't I a genius?

Why don't people on TV ever go to the bathroom?

If the police arrest a mime, do they tell him he has the right to remain silent?

Why do they put Braille on the drive-through bank machines?

How do they get the deer to cross at that yellow road sign?

Whose cruel idea was it for the word 'Lisp' to have an 'S' in it?

Why do banks leave both doors open, yet they chain pens to the counter-tops?

Why do people order a double cheeseburger, large fries, and a diet soda?

Who copyrighted the copyright symbol?

Doesn't expecting the unexpected make the unexpected the expected?

If a building is on fire, and you make more fire, would it be considered making the fire worse or better?

Why are there five syllables in the word 'monosyllabic'?

How is it that 'Fat Chance' and 'Slim Chance' mean the same thing?

R

Raindance
Timing has an awful lot to do with the outcome of a raindance.

Read
Jacob: 'David's gone to live in the city.' Ryan: 'Why's that?' Jacob: 'He'd read in the papers that the country was at war.'

Reason
A real person has two reasons for doing anything: a good reason, and the real reason.

Recognize
I didn't recognize you for a minute. It was one of the happiest minutes of my life.

Refined
What is black, gushes out of the ground and shouts, 'Excuse me'? Refined oil.

Refuse
'Why did you refuse to marry Jacob, Ashley?' Ashley: 'He said he would die if I didn't and I'm curious.'

Reincarnation
Did you hear about the man who believed in reincarnation? In his will he left his money to himself.

Reindeer
I don't care who you are, get those reindeer off my roof.

Report
Father: 'This report gives you a D for conduct and an A for courtesy. How on earth did you manage that?' Son: 'Easy. Whenever I punch someone, I apologize.'

Restaurant
'Waiter, could you make my pork chop lean?' 'Certainly, sir, which way?'

At our local restaurant you can eat dirt cheap – but who wants to eat dirt?

'Waiter, how long have you worked here?' 'Six months, sir.' 'Well, it can't have been you who took my order.'

Revolving door
'Why are you covered in bruises?' 'I started to walk through a revolving door and then I changed my mind.'

Rich
Two weevils came to town from the country. One worked hard and became very rich. The other became the lesser of two weevils.

Riding
When my girlfriend goes out riding, she looks like part of the horse. When she dismounts, she still looks like part of the horse.

Room
There's a large crack in the wall of Jesse's house so he goes around telling everyone that he's from a broken home.

Man: 'I'd like a room, please.' Hotel Receptionist: 'Single, Sir?' Teacher: 'Yes, but I am engaged.'

Rope
Ethan: 'Why have you given me this piece of rope?' Noah: 'They say if you give someone enough rope they'll hang themselves!'

Run over
How did the man feel when he got run over by a car? Tyred.

S

Sailor
Why did the stupid sailor grab a bar of soap when his ship sank? He thought he could wash himself ashore.

Salad
Why was the tomato red? Because it saw the salad dressing.

Sanity
Some people are on the edge. Some people are over it. I'm hang-gliding.

The voices may not be real, but they have some pretty good ideas.

Saving
The best way of saving money is to forget who you borrowed it from.

School
'And what might your name be?' the school secretary asked the new boy. 'Well, it might be Cornelius, but it's not. It's Sam.'

When I was at school I was as smart as the next boy. It's a pity the next boy was such an idiot.

Mother: 'What did you learn at school today?' Son: 'Not enough. I have to go back tomorrow.'

'What did you learn in school today, son?' 'I learned that those sums you did for me were wrong!'

Teacher: 'Who was the first woman on earth?' Stephanie: 'I don't know.' Teacher: 'Come on, Stephanie, it has something to do with an apple.' Stephanie: 'Granny Smith?'

Teacher: 'Your books are a disgrace, Zachary. I don't see how anyone can possibly make as many mistakes in one day as you do.' Zachary: 'I get here early.'

The class was set an essay on Shakespeare. Ashley wrote in her book, 'Shakespeare wrote tragedy, comedy, and errors.'

Today in English we learned absolutely nothing about killing mockingbirds.

I think I'll skip English tomorrow. There are just certain aspects of Moby I don't want to know about.

Science
Why did the science teacher marry the school cleaner? Because she swept him off his feet.

Scream
It's been lovely, but I have to scream now.

Seal
What's gray, eats fish, and lives in Washington, D.C.? The Presidential Seal.

290

Seconds
'Doctor, I've only got 50 seconds to live.' 'Just sit over there a minute.'

Secret
'What do you mean by telling everyone I'm an idiot?' 'I'm sorry, I didn't know it was supposed to be a secret.'

Self-Help
I asked the sales assistant in a book store where the self-help section was and she said if she told me it would defeat the purpose.

Selling
If it were worth buying they wouldn't be selling it door to door.

Sex
At 66 I'm bisexual – I said bye to sex.

Sex is not the answer. Sex is the question. 'Yes' is the answer.

Shamrock
Teacher: 'Can anyone tell me what a shamrock is' Brandon: 'It's a fake diamond.'

Shoe
If the shoe fits, get another just like it.

Short
Teacher: 'Hannah, what is "can't" short for?' Hannah: 'Cannot.' Teacher: 'And what is "don't" short for?' Hannah: 'Donut!'

Shovel
Just when you hit the bottom, someone tosses you a shovel.

Signs
My dog saw a sign that said: 'Wet Paint' – so he did!

Sign in shop window: 'For Sale. Pedigree bulldog. House trained. Eats anything. Very fond of children.'

Sign in a launderette: 'Those using automatic washers should remove their clothes when the lights go out.'

A man went into the local department store where he saw a sign on the escalator – Dogs must be carried on this escalator. The man then spent the next two hours looking for a dog.

Singing
Gabrielle's singing is improving. People are putting cotton wool in only one ear now.

Sledge
Alex: 'I never had a sledge when I was a kid. We were too poor.' Natalie, feeling sorry for him: 'What a shame! What did you do when it snowed.' 'Slid down the hills on my cousin.'

Sleep
What is the best advice to give a worm? Sleep late.

I'm not saying our teacher's fat, but every time he falls over he rocks himself to sleep trying to get back up.

Snoring
'Do men always snore?' 'No, only when they're asleep.'

Snowman
One snowman to another: 'Funny, I smell carrots too.'

Soccer
Soccer coach: 'Why didn't you stop the ball?' Chelsea: 'I thought that's what the net was for.'

Sons
Thought for the day: Where do fathers learn all the things they tell their sons not to do?

Specific
I always wanted to be somebody. I should have been more specific.

Statue
William: 'You remind me of a Greek statue.' Ashley: 'Do you mean you think I'm beautiful?' William: 'Yes, beautiful, but not all there.'

Store
I went to a general store. They wouldn't let me buy anything specific.

Story
Did you hear the story of the three holes? Well, well, well.

Strings
There are some strings, they're just not attached.

Stupidity
Did you hear about the stupid tap dancer? He fell in the sink.

Never assume malice for something which could be explained by stupidity.

Artificial Intelligence is no match for natural stupidity.

I refuse to have a battle of wits with an unarmed opponent.

Success
If at first you don't succeed, redefine success.

If at first you don't succeed, destroy all evidence that you tried.

If at first you do succeed, try not to look astonished.

Suffer
I need not suffer in silence when I can still moan, whimper, and complain.

Sulk
What's large and green and sits in a corner on its own all day? The Incredible Sulk.

Superstitious
'Are you superstitious?' 'No.' 'Then lend me $13.'

Sweat
Don't sweat petty things, or pet sweaty things.

T

Talking
Jacob: 'It's hard for my sister to eat.' Brianna: 'Why?' Jacob: 'She can't bear to stop talking.'

After all is said and done, more is said than done.

Target
To be sure of hitting the target, shoot first, and call whatever you hit the target.

Tax
A fine is a tax for doing wrong. A tax is a fine for doing well.

Teacher
Teacher: 'That's the stupidest boy in the whole school.' Mother: 'That's my son.' Teacher: 'Oh! I'm so sorry.' Mother: 'You're sorry?'

Anna: 'How do you spell ichael?' Teacher: 'Don't you mean Michael?' Anna: 'No, I've written the "M" already.'

Ben's teacher regards Ben as a wonder child. He wonders whether he'll ever learn anything.

It's a note from the teacher about me telling lies – but it's not true.

Teacher: 'I want you all to give me a list of the lower animals, starting with Rachel Morgan . . .'

Teacher: 'I wish you'd pay a little attention.' Girl: 'I'm paying as little as possible.'

Telekinesis
If you believe in telekinesis, raise my hand.

Television
It's true that there is a connection between television and violence. I told my teacher I had watched television instead of doing my homework, and she hit me.

Tennis
Really bad tennis beginner: 'How would you have played that last shot?' Coach: 'In disguise!'

In which Biblical story is tennis mentioned? When Moses served in Pharoah's court.

Tennessee
What did Tennessee? The same thing Arkansas.

Tense
I'm not tense, just very, very alert.

Tequila
If life hands you lemons, break out the tequila!

Therapy
I'm sorry, do I resemble your therapist?

Therapy is expensive. Popping plastic bubblewrap is cheap.

Thought
She got lost in thought, it was unfamiliar territory.

Tiger
'Have you ever seen a man-eating tiger?' 'No, but in the cafe next door I once saw a man eating chicken!'

Time
'What time is it when you sit on a pin?' 'Spring time.'

Tooth
Why did the termite eat a sofa and two chairs? It had a suite tooth.

Toys
An unbreakable toy is useful for breaking other toys.

Tree
What is a tree's favorite drink? Root beer.

Trouble
'Doctor, I'm having trouble with my breathing.' Doctor: 'I'll give you something that will soon stop that.'

She once had a million-dollar figure. Trouble is, inflation set in.

U

Under
Did you hear about the boy who sat under a cow? He got a pat on the head.

Unique
Always remember, you're unique. Just like everyone else.

V

Vacation
It was so hot when we went on vacation last year that we had to take turns sitting in each other's shadow.

The seaside resort we went to last year was so boring that one day the tide went out and never came back.

Vampire
Why are vampires artistic? They're good at drawing blood.

'Mom, mom, what's a vampire?' 'Shut up and drink your tomato juice before it clots.'

'Doctor, I think I've been bitten by a vampire.' 'Drink this glass of water.' 'Will it make me better?' 'No, but I'll be able to see if your neck leaks.'

Vanity
Megan: 'I spend hours in front of the mirror admiring my beauty. Do you think that's vanity?' Kylie: 'No, it's imagination.'

Vase
'Mom, you know that vase that's been handed down from generation to generation?' 'Yes.' 'Well, this generation's dropped it.'

Vegetable
What is a skeleton's favorite vegetable? Marrow.

Venetian
How do you make a venetian blind? Poke him in the eye.

Vinegar
What do you call a cat that drinks vinegar? A sour puss.

Viper
Why did the viper want to become a python? He got the coiling.

Voting
If we quit voting, would they all go away.

W

Waist
What did the middle-aged woman say as she tucked into her donuts? 'I'm afraid all this food is going to waist.'

War
Teamwork is essential – it gives the enemy someone else to shoot at.

The only thing more accurate than incoming enemy fire is incoming friendly fire.

Tracers work both ways.

Never forget your weapon is made by the lowest bidder.

The enemy attacks on two occasions. When he's ready and when you're not.

Watch
'I got a gold watch for my girlfriend.' 'I wish I could make a trade like that!'

'Is this a second-hand shop?' 'Yes, sir.' 'Good. Can you fit one on my watch, please?'

Water
Sign in a cafe: 'All drinking water in this establishment has been personally passed by the management.'

Weight
'He's watching his weight.' 'Yes, watching it go up!'

Werewolf
I used to be a werewolf but I'm all right nooooooooooooooooooow!

What do you get if you cross a werewolf with a hyena? I don't know but if it laughs I'll join in.

What happens if you cross a werewolf with a sheep? You have to get a new sheep.

Never moon a werewolf.

Whole
As the judge said to the dentist, 'Do you swear to pull the tooth, the whole tooth, and nothing but the tooth?'

Mother: 'I told you not to eat cake before supper.' Daughter: 'But Mom, it's part of my homework: "If you take an eighth of a cake from a whole cake, how much is left?"'

Wig
Woman: 'Officer you must help, I've just lost my wig.' Police officer: 'Certainly madam, we'll comb the area.'

Wild
How do you make a tame duck wild? Annoy it.

Will
Where there's a will, I want to be in it.

Wind
Trees are planted to stop the wind. A larch can break wind at 40 yards.

Window
'Who broke the window?' 'It was Kyle, Dad. He ducked when I threw a stone at him.'

'Don't look out of the window, Olivia, people will think it's Halloween.'

Witch
What's the best advice you can give to a witch on a broomstick? 'Don't fly off the handle!'

Women

First woman: 'Whenever I'm down in the dumps I buy myself a new hat.' Second woman: 'Oh, so that's where you get them.'

'Mom, that awful woman down the road said Dad wasn't fit to live with pigs!' 'What did you say?' 'Oh, I defended him, I said of course he was!'

Middle-aged woman: 'I've kept my schoolgirl complexion.' Friend: 'Yes, I see, covered in spots.'

Anyone who claims he can see through women is missing a lot.

Wonderful

I've had a perfectly wonderful evening. This wasn't it, though.

Woodworm

Surveyor: 'This house is a ruin. I wonder what stops it from falling down.' Owner: 'I think the woodworm are holding hands.'

Word

Crossword fan: 'I've been trying to think of a word for two weeks!' Friend: 'How about a fortnight?'

Work

He does the work of two men – Tweedledum and Tweedledee.

X

X-ray

What happened to Ray when a ten-ton truck ran over him? He became X-Ray.

Xmas

What do Scully and Mulder look into in December? The Xmas Files.

Y

Yeti

What's the difference between a very old, shaggy yeti and a dead bee? One's a seedy beast and the other's a deceased bee.

What do you get if you cross an elephant with the abominable snowman?
A jumbo yeti.

Z

Zen
That was Zen, this is Tao.

Zombies
What do you call zombies in a belfry? Dead ringers.

AND THE THICKO WHO THOUGHT
A BROTHEL WAS A BOWL OF SOUP